A MIDWIFE'S STORY

for Chuck and Michael

PENNY ARMSTRONG

Penny Armstrong has delivered over 1,000 babies and enjoyed a 25-year career in nurse-midwifery including teaching and practice in home, hospital and birth centers. She and her husband, Rich, currently live and work in their home state of Maine where she counsels people on living healthy lifestyles.

SHERYL FELDMAN

Sheryl Feldman is a writer, teacher, and not–for-profit communications manager. She also co-founded Hedgebrook, a retreat for women writers and is the initiator of its community residency project Women Writers of the Arab World. As well as *A Wise Birth* and *A Midwife's Story*, she also wrote *Bangkok Zigzag*, a documentary on motorcycle taxi drivers in Bangkok. Passionate about international travel and crossing cultures, she lives in Seattle and has two sons and two granddaughters.

Also by Penny Armstrong & Sheryl Feldman
from Pinter & Martin:

*A Wise Birth: Bringing Together the Best
of Natural Childbirth and Modern Medicine*

www.pinterandmartin.com

A MIDWIFE'S STORY

PENNY ARMSTRONG & SHERYL FELDMAN

pinter
&
martin

PINTER & MARTIN

A Midwife's Story

First published in the US by Arbor House 1986
and in the UK by Corgi Books 1987
This edition published by Pinter & Martin Ltd 2006

ISBN-10: 1-905177-04-6
ISBN-13: 978-1-905177-04-2

British Library Cataloguing-in-Publication Data
A catalogue record for this book is available from the British Library

All the names in this book are real, except for certain members
of the medical and nursing professions in the United States

Set in Sabon

Printed and bound in Great Britain by
Creative Print & Design, Ebbw Vale, Wales, UK

Pinter & Martin Ltd
6 Effra Parade
London SW2 1PS

www.pinterandmartin.com

CONTENTS

Preface

I recently attended the wedding of my Amish namesake in the Lancaster County, Pennsylvania community that we wrote about in *A Midwife's Story* 20 years ago. I once again enjoyed the feeling of being part of something timeless and right. As the women prepared for the wedding, a large gathering of family and community which includes hundreds, I rejoined the conversations I had left behind when I retired. Though Plain women are traditionally shy about pregnancy and birth, there are always side conversations swirling about as groups of women gather to prepare for such weddings, and the funerals, house-centered church, and quiltings. In content these conversations have remained unchanged for generations: the ins and outs of making family within a community deeply rooted in the earth, the desire to preserve privacy and choice in their birthing place, and the well being of mothers and babies.

It was also obvious that in the face of burgeoning technology in all quarters of life, the Plain communities continue to evaluate each new technological invention in terms of its impact on the family. The decisions that the Plain communities make about what to embrace and what to reject, is confusing to those outside the community (yes to a contraption that converts a *Mr Coffee* to a gas stove-top appliance, and no to computers). It remains confusing because most of the outside world now measures the worth of a new invention by the time it will save them and the work that is avoided. For Plain families, work is a concept that is embraced, and even the smallest child enjoys the satisfaction of doing their part. For women, the work of bringing forth children is an accepted part of their lives, and a way to avoid this work is not a subject of those swirling side conversations.

Considering the rising rate of interventions in obstetrics, and the lack of a concomitant improvement in outcome statistics, perhaps it is time to re-examine what a healthy woman actually needs to give birth. To yet again explore the value for new mothers in that powerful feeling that comes with bringing forth new life, delivering it into the hands of a trusted caregiver, and introducing the newborn to a community that respects and supports the work that goes into making family. In the hopes that the words we crafted some 20 years ago might help frame a small portion of that discussion, we welcome the republication of A *Midwife's Story* and A *Wise Birth*.

Penny Armstrong – August 2006

Acknowledgements

It was interesting for me to watch the development of this book; painful, funny and soul searching. I am a doer, not a recorder and it took me a long time to become comfortable with the publication of this book and the book that followed. But in the end, it proved to be a worthy activity as *A Midwife's Story* generated hundreds of letter from women and families who felt that we had somehow captured their desire to have a birth that was theirs. Those letters in turn inspired *A Wise Birth*.

I cannot name all of the people who have helped me hone my skills, practice my art and survive a demanding career, but I deeply appreciate your support and friendship. All that I have done I have done with the support of my parents, my brothers and their wonderful partners, and my partner in all, Rich. A special thanks to my friends who shared my work in Lancaster County and have remained friends always, Shirley Wenger, Sue Ellen Loebach, Carol Snapp, Randy Testa, Hugh Silk, Sheryl Feldman and my special Aunt Ellie.

I would also like to thank the doctors I have met along the way who either inspired me or helped to pave the way for birthing women. A great doctor infused with the spirit of a midwife, is a wonderful thing to behold and seldom applauded.

I want to acknowledge Jamie, my Little Sister, for her efforts to keep me hip and for her courage, playfulness and inspiration. I also want to acknowledge my namesake, Penny Anne. She and Jamie are the future, and the future is bright.

My love and respect for the people I served in Lancaster County is boundless. They taught me everything I know about the power of birth, how to make a safe and satisfying birth experience for families, and how to sort out the important items from the ones that only seem important, both in the birthing room and in life.

Lastly, I also would like to thank Sheila Kitzinger for her kindness and support, and Martin Wagner for making this republication possible.

Penny Armstrong

This book is an interpretation of events in Penny's life as she has told them to me and as I have understood them over the many years of our friendship. It is written in the first person, from Penny's point of view, because midwifery is an intimate business.

I have tried to write her story as accurately as possible, but to protect the privacy of her patients and the Amish community I have changed names and scrambled circumstances. The only names not changed are those of Penny's immediate family members and the names and places in the chapter *Booth*. Booth Maternity Hospital, Penny thought, deserves recognition for the quality of its program. Other minor changes in events have been made in the interest of storytelling.

I learnt about home birth by assisting at about 30 of them over a period of five years, and I learnt about the Amish while living with Penny and her husband in Lancaster County, Pennsylvania, for nearly nine months.

Among the Amish, there is a keen understanding that the work we do is part of the community's work. This book is a result of the work, generosity, insight and wisdom of many people, but I am especially grateful to Penny and Richard Armstrong, the Bradbury and Howard families, Thelma and

Murray Studley, Nancy Nordhoff, Jim Coffin, Lewis O Saum, Phyllis Hatfield, Don and Lyn Kartiganer, Sue Ellen Loebach, Sue Yates, Lise Wells, Marlene Sanker and Terry DiJoseph Sears.

Jakes and Lydia Beiler honored me with nothing more and nothing less than their friendship. I hope my appreciation of the Amish people is expressed by this book. I thank each person; knowing them has been an extraordinary privilege.

Sheryl Feldman

A MIDWIFE'S STORY

1

Their Way

Here around Honeybrook it's hillier than where Richie and I live. Small woods are more common, the banks of the streams are higher and the water runs with more snap. Fields rise quickly and disappear abruptly over low ridges. It's dark outside now, but soon the mist will start rising from the streams and will seep out to fill the hollows in the fields. The corn waits, stiff and crackling, for the farmers to get up and begin cutting. Most of the cows will still be settled on their knees before I leave this delivery and, at this time of year, it might even be eight o'clock before the ducks start dropping into the ponds.

Amos and Naomi's kitchen table, where I will fill out my paperwork, is covered with a green-and-white checked oilcloth, which has been scrubbed and left bare except for a glowing kerosene lantern. Amos is in the bedroom with Naomi, who's almost ready to have her baby. As soon as she's a little farther along, I'll go back into the bedroom and help her.

I've been delivering babies for Amish couples since 1979. I'm not Amish myself. In fact, I am, or was, about as 'English', or non-Amish, as they come. That is to say, I was aggressive and wilful. But I believe I'm becoming less so every day. I'm trying.

In the early months of my practice, I was enchanted with these people, the way I might become attached to a simple, engaging melody. It's easy for that to happen. Take this young Amishman, Amos; he's irresistible. For one thing, he is in splendid good health. Since he spends his days jumping on and off his wagon, tossing around loads of hay or corn, pulling, carrying, lifting, and driving his team through the fields, he's strong and lithe. Then, too, I think he's a joy to watch, doing all his working and playing in black, baggy pants cut off short at the shins and held up by a pair of braces. Solid, bright-colored shirts make his shiny eyes seem even brighter than they actually are. His hair is cut bluntly just below the earlobes, and when he combs it, he parts it in the center and drags the comb dead flat against the curve of his head, as if to get the furrows straight. He wears a flat-brimmed, black felt hat for dress and a straw hat for field-work, and since he's married, he's got an untrimmed Abraham Lincoln beard.

The main thing, though, is his Amishman's face and eyes. 'English' men, as the Amish call the rest of us, rarely have faces like these men. I think it's because the English always have to go to meetings where they must outmanoeuvre, out-smart and beat the other fellows to the punch, whereas an Amishman's only meetings are on Sunday mornings in some-body's kitchen when he prays. An Amishman passes his days riding a wagon slung on leather straps, making agreements with the weather and when he's done with that he has only to walk the path through the pole beans to get dinner with his family. In the silence of his farmhouse, before and after each meal, he drops his head and prays silently.

An Amishman usually looks like something special is hap-pening to him. He has the face of a boy who has been teach-ing ducks to swim in a metal tub and now he's come in to tell his mother about it and while he talks, jumping around, she's taking cookies out of the oven.

Through an Amishman's eyes, the days look like hand-crafted gifts from God – presents made of carved wood and string and parts that make a reedy whistle.

Consider Amos. I pulled into the lane tonight and had barely parked when the kitchen door opened and out he came, flashlight in hand, offering to help. I asked him to get the suitcase, so he picked up that 40-pound monstrosity the way I'd pick up a head of lettuce. Amos is a smart one. Calls me on the phone in the middle of the night and in his soft voice says, 'Would you like to come to the grand opening of the Baby Outlet?' I imagine his eyes really shone when he said that.

Ha-ha, I thought.

The Amish like to write 'ha-ha's' in their letters. I've grown fond of the ha-ha's myself.

It wasn't a bad line, especially for a farmer whose wife is in labor with their second baby and who had to walk down the lane and across a frost-crusted field to a phone kiosk to call the midwife. 'Oh, it was just something I thought of saying as I was walking along,' he says, delighted with himself.

Amos is a tease. Used to take his sister's dolls out behind the barn, put them in a shoe-box coffin, and bury them. 'I only did it when somebody pulled a stump over on me,' he says in idle defence.

'So you think you're going to get a baby out tonight?' I ask.

'Well, I wouldn't mind,' he answers, showing me the way into the darkened house.

Amos and Naomi are typically Amish, except that just now they're living in what will be their stable. All this land around here was woodland until three or four years ago, when a bunch of older Amishmen got together and bought it – it's about the last tillable piece of land in the county – now they're selling it at low interest to young Amish couples who want to have their own farms.

Amos and Naomi settled here after they were married a few years ago, and began to clear the land. Naomi, bandana on her head, black tennis shoes, bright-colored skirt clinging to her knees, black apron snapping in the wind, worked right alongside Amos – cutting, driving the team, hauling and all the rest. I practically had to tie her to the stove to get her to lay off at the end of her first pregnancy. They felled the small forest that covered the land and collected the logs into a mountainous pile for selling and then, with the help of their families, they began to work the land. Next summer they expect to get their house up.

An Amishman wants his farm more than anything. I've watched a man's eyes fill with tears when he talked about getting his own place. He wants to be with his family, to step over his children in the barn and work with them next to him in the field; he wants to have his father and mother in an attached house. He wants to be as intimate with his land as you and I might be with the palm of our hand.

Naomi put on a white batiste gown, lightly hand-quilted at the yoke. Her hair, parted severely down the center of her head and drawn into a knot at the back was covered by a white kerchief. At least an hour before, Amos had crawled up on the bed next to her, and since then, his massive farmer's fingers dusted with baby powder, he'd been rubbing her back. Her whole body loosened up from the heat of labor and from his massaging.

I asked her to pull her knee directly up to her chin. She buried her fingers deep into the thigh of her leg and sank into a powerful push.

Since Naomi had so little extra weight on her, you could almost see the bones of her pelvis giving way to the force of her pushing. They spread slowly, grindingly and firmly, the way plates of the earth would move during a quake; they allowed the baby's head to pass downward, the shoulders to turn along the spiralling route to the outside world. Naomi waited, breathed deeply, took Amos's hand, and threw all her strength into her abdomen again and, as if burying a heavy rock there, she gave another push. I could see the top of the baby's head.

She pushed again and, as the head crowned, the skin of the perineum stretched around it; the head moved closer to freedom and Naomi's skin thinned to transparency. I had worked the portal skin on the outside while the baby's head stretched it from the inside and between the two of us we eased in all the stretch available. Naomi gave a series of short pushes, she panted, the baby's head shifted – and there was its forehead and the top of its brow and the face. The head made a quarter turn and Naomi – pausing only a moment – pushed out her new baby girl. I cut the cord, wrapped the baby quickly, and Amos grabbed it, cooing, chuckling and hopping from side to side like a father bird. Later, when I took the baby out to the kitchen for a bath and I sudsed her head, I told her about how a long shaft of morning light was reaching across the kitchen countertop and making the faucet handles glow; how the windmill was creaking to life, pulling water from the well. I showed her, once I had the towel fluffed about her head, how the lawn, through the panes at the sink window, was iridescent, and I watched while the long branches of the protective yard oak stretched and lazily flapped. The morning was lavender and frost.

It takes a long time to learn the ways of another culture. When I first began practicing in Lancaster County, Pennsylvania, I suspected the Amish of being a cold, unfeeling people. I heard a story of a doctor who worked all night long in surgery to save the firstborn infant son of an Amish couple. Shortly before dawn, the baby died and the doctor, wiping tears of exhaustion and defeat from his own eyes, told the couple their baby was gone.

Using very few words, they thanked him, said they believed they wouldn't be needed anymore at the hospital, and she put on her cape and bonnet and he put on his hat. Without crying, without calling out 'Why?', without rending the hallways with their sorrow, they walked out.

A few weeks ago, I delivered my first stillborn child at home – my first death in 1,000 births. Had it been five years ago, I would have been destroyed. I would have given up the work. I would not have known how to withstand the loss; I would have blamed myself; I would have known there was a way I could have prevented it. In those days, I did not permit what I considered imperfection – either in myself or in the universe. I would have thrashed out, railed and stormed at the skies, if death had had the nerve to cross my path.

But I've been here too long and even I – the most wilful of the wilful – am slowly learning to be as courteous to death as I have always been towards birth. Not at all have I learnt to be cold; rather, I've become more peaceful.

2

Home

Maybe Grammy strode into my dream. Maybe one more time she grabbed me by the arm, dug her knuckles into my shoulder and said, 'Don't try any of those little-girl tricks with me, young lady. You want something done, you figure out how to do it yourself. You make something of yourself.'

In any case, I woke up in the middle of the night with the answer. I sat up in bed for a long time, staring and wondering if it was as good as it seemed.

I walked downstairs, stoked up the fire in the wood stove, and paced back and forth in front of it.

'I think I'll be a midwife,' I mumbled. 'I'm going to be a midwife,' I said aloud.

I knew it was right, although not by reasoning – I was a long way from being rational about my future. After all, I had already gone to college, I had a decent job, one that had earned me enough to make payments on my very own tiny farmhouse. On weekends and evenings over the past three years, I'd knocked down the old warped interior walls and nailed up used barn boards; I'd brought in Vermont slate so the kitchen floor would look like the tide pools at Boothbay. I'd been to the dump and collected old bottles and set them on a dish rail. I'd bought my plates from my neighbor the potter and hung pots and pans from a rack made by my friend the blacksmith. I was at a point where I could serve a meal for friends.

Neither was my midwifery idea fashionable. I had my dream in 1974, and people didn't aspire to being midwives then. Widows in 19th-century novels did, a few leftover hippies maybe. People would think I'd been reading an unexpurgated version of the *Whole Earth Catalogue*.

But I'd met somebody recently who was a midwife and I'd been thinking about the idea. And besides, when I was in high school, I would wait until after everyone went to bed and then I'd crawl out the window, sneak out to the car, let it roll down the driveway, start it up and drive to the emergency ward of the local hospital so I could watch medical dramas. That must have meant something.

'Of course,' I said to myself, '"The Squire of Brentwood" proves it.' That was a paper I wrote in High School. We had sheep at home then (the Squire was a most prolific ram), and I wrote a paper in my English class about how I couldn't concentrate on writing a paper because I'd been up all night with my arm inside a sheep's uterus. 'All activities pale' – I remembered writing something grandiose like that – 'when compared to the excitement of the maternity ward.'

The heart of it was, though, that being a midwife went along with everything I believed in. If I became a midwife, I could help give other families a start towards being like mine had been.

In other words, it came out of Nana's kitchen.

Nana's kitchen was the way things were supposed to be. It had Nana's lap. It also had a rocking chair, a Seth Thomas clock, and it hummed with the lives of women who bustled, scrubbed, patted, mended and arranged. Women whose entire lives were concerned with their homes, husbands, children, family, friends and neighbors.

Nana and Pappy had started with nothing but their youth and Yankee values. In the winters, Pappy worked in the Maine woods, sleeping with eleven men on one long straw mattress, and in summers he hired out on farms until he had enough money to buy the land on Westford Hill, Hodgdon Corners, Aroostook County, Maine. The original white frame farmhouse, with its kitchen, parlour and two upstairs bedrooms, went up in 1912. My mom was born there; so were her brother and sister. I was there the night my brother was born in 1948.

In Nana's kitchen I learnt about woman's work. Nana taught me to garden, cook, bake and preserve. On long summer afternoons, with aunts, she-cousins and neighbors all moving softly about, bumping plump, pasty arms, I learnt the rich satisfaction of tiering pears and peaches in mason jars; I came to savour the sweet steam rising from the pots; and wandering away from the edges of industry, I developed an affection for the piles of pits and peelings whose colors grew deeper and darker throughout the sweltering afternoons.

The women were sinking values into my bones. Not with their words, but with the smell of bubbling butter, brown sugar and cinnamon; the rhythm of fingers turning and flying across a pie crust; the sound of their voices moving in and out of the sound of their work; the room underfoot and on step stools they made for me. I became like them, before words, before thought.

Nana formed me with abundant and unconditional love. At the kitchen table, she'd show me how to cut out and sew pyjamas with one snap in the front for my dolls, and while we worked she'd say over and over again, 'You can get yourself into any trouble whatsoever, young lady, go ahead and try. It won't make any difference. I'll love you and you can't help yourself.'

Fortunately for my patients today, my mother's ideas about responsibility more than balanced Nana's breakaway heart. Mother was interested in standards – stern ones, ones that did not give way to stories, excuses, or extenuating circumstances. When I did something wrong, she sent me directly to my room, where I could concentrate, undisturbed and uncomforted, about my misdeed. Gradually I understood that responsibility is absolute and personal; that there's no shrugging it off when things become difficult.

If there had just been Nana, I would probably be a plump, contented farm wife today. But I had Grammy. Grammy was my great-grandmother on my dad's side. Grammy, the woman who raised my father, had no interest in punch and cookies.

Grammy smoked a pipe, spit, wore rouge and bangled earrings and sang dirty ditties. She ranted and raged at the whole pissant, goddam mean world. She was massive. Her breasts were so big and so undisciplined that she had to hold them up with one forearm in order to get her belt buckled underneath. I thought she was spectacular.

We have one old brown photo of Grammy as a young woman. There's a log cabin sitting no-nonsense in the middle of the picture. Grammy's young family is lined up in front of it. Miserable, cold-looking leaves are straying all over the ground. Another bleak November in the Maine woods; nothing to look forward to but five months of life-threatening cold.

Grammy's husband is over to the right. Although he must have been a fairly young man, his shoulders had already eroded. He had his pants hitched up and cinched. He didn't exactly glare at the photographer, but it's no smile either. Posing for the picture was clearly only one more miserable activity in his scabby, itchy, cold, dirty and mean lifetime. Must be his 30-30 leaned up against the wall of the cabin.

A step or two away from him is Grammy. An Amazon. Her hair is drawn up high in a knot; her dress is a fortress, seamed with rivets from shoulder to ground. For the purposes of the picture, she'd set the butt of her gun firmly on the ground and rested her hand ever so comfortably on its barrel.

One of the little girls standing near Grammy would be my father's mother – but it wasn't she who raised my father. For involved reasons, Grammy did that.

I loved Grammy. I was absolutely fascinated by her. Grammy – crude, tough and vulgar – was a midwife.

3

Midwife

'Nurse Bradburrry,' she would say in her stiff brogue. 'Recite for me the mechanisms for a left occipito-anterior presentation.'

I would rise, step into the aisle to the left of my desk, smooth the hard white canvas of my nurse's skirt, fold my hands in front of me, look directly ahead, and respond to the instructor.

'Thank you, Miss Helms. The mechanisms for the left occipito-anterior delivery are . . . ' And so it went – right occipito-anterior, frank breech, footling breech, left occipito-posterior. We recited, repeated, and tapped the words into our skulls as if by mallet and awl.

By the time I could roll out the answers like that, I'd been at Highlands General Hospital in Scotland for almost eight months. I'd completed my preparation for midwifery training: a one-year intensive course in nursing in Saint Louis, Missouri, followed by six months of probationary nursing at Highlands. Of course, the six months had seemed more like an advanced form of hazing than a probation. When I first got to Scotland and the cabbie let me off at the dark medieval door of the hospital, he rolled his eyes and looked at me as if I were condemned.

A 'matron' greeted me. 'Block 37,' she said, jangling her keys. 'Follow me.' She led me to a cell fitted with a sink, four hangers and a beige clay jar, meant for warming my feet. I looked at the iron bedstead, undoubtedly left over from the early days of the maternity hospital at Highlands. I'd read about those beds.

> Throughout history most babies were born at home. Maternity hospitals were first started for homeless women and were really extensions of poorhouses. . . . These first maternity hospitals were convenient centers for medical students to learn and practice obstetrics, but infections were rampant, as doctors conveyed bacteria on their hands from one patient to another, and many babies and mothers died. They were possibly the most dangerous places in which women could possibly give birth.*

I crawled into the bed every night, bidding sweet dreams to all the women who had died of septicemia in it, and then, in the mornings, I would apply myself to perfecting my use of the sterile trolley. As far as I could tell, the sterile trolley was the one overriding ritual of nursing in the United Kingdom.

One did not nurse without the sterile trolley. Suppose for example, one wished to apply a Band-Aid to a patient's wound. One would pull out the trolley and fall upon it with a scrub brush and a noxious-smelling foam. Once one had scrubbed the trolley, one draped it. Once one draped it, one could set out one's bowl. Then one could set out another and another. The bowls were followed by scissors, gauze, syringes, needles, clamps, calculator, butterfly nets, tubs of margarine, and I cannot remember what else, except for the Band-Aid. Once this procedure had been observed, one could apply the Band-Aid. Needless to say, if one touched anything while one was setting up one's trolley, if one broke the sterile field, one started over again – 'straightaway'.

Each day I took my maidenly trolley into the male urology ward, where the sun didn't shine. I must elaborate. The sun didn't shine for five months. It was a filthy, smelly and dingy place. Every few days, they dragged a cold mop down

*Sheila Kitzinger, *The Complete Book of Pregnancy and Childbirth* (Alfred A. Knopf)

the center aisle, leaving wax curled up like old men's toenails in the corners of the rooms and under the beds. They never washed the windows, as far as I could tell, and there were no screens, so when the days grew warmer, the flies came in and settled on the patients' wounds.

The men lay in bed after bed – ten down one side, nine back up the other. Nineteen iron beds and 19 iron grates. I gave 19 sick men – victims of strokes, men with cancer crawling from the inside out – baths every day. There wasn't one shower for the entire ward. They each peed for me in glass urinals, which I placed in a wooden cart and pulled, rattling, behind me. Then I tested the nineteen samples and scrubbed the urinals clean.

I learnt a new nursing vocabulary, one made up of singularly revolting words. For example, an IV was no longer called an IV; it was to be called a 'drip'. Gastric suction was called – I do not invent – a 'suck'. Which made the treatment for gastric distress a 'drip and suck'.

The rain and wind blew directly down off the Highlands and rattled the window of my room each day for that entire time. The other students ignored me, and my energy, generously inspired though it was, dwindled. Fortunately, in June, five months after my arrival, they announced that I would be granted my licence as a nurse in the United Kingdom, and that after a summer holiday in America, I could begin midwifery training. I'd made it to the good part.

By the time I returned to Glasgow in the fall, I had read and reread Maggie Myles's *Textbook for Midwives* so many times that I knew her words backwards and forwards and I ached to talk about what I'd learnt, to challenge and question. I found, to my great frustration, that there was to be none of it. Not only did the system discourage inquiry, the students themselves seemed to resent it. When I'd mention something about what we'd learnt to one of my classmates, I'd be dismissed with a look of annoyance. Finally, I realized that the typical student at Highlands was there because it gave her a chance for a promotion at home, or maybe a chance to get to America; she was unlikely to have much interest in midwifery itself. It was best to go about one's work dull-eyed and perfunctory.

Since I couldn't find someone with whom to share my enthusiasm, I retreated into myself. I ran every day, and on holidays I rode the bus to the Highlands, and while reviewing the positions a baby could take in the birth canal – left occipito, right occipito – I walked endless miles through heather. I pictured every turn, every bump on the road in the birth passage. I imagined changes in pressure and the way they would feel to the baby's head and shoulders passing by. I imagined the mother's muscles weaving supple, powerful slings to help her child out. I would come back to the library from my walks and search for answers to questions I'd discovered while making imaginary deliveries.

I went to class and recited my lessons. I tried to eat well. I hung around the delivery room. I read Maggie Myles again. Like the woman whose baby I would deliver, I roamed restlessly in the last weeks before my first baby.

Finally, they called me to meet the woman. Her long, angular face reached at least a half a head higher than her husband's. She had a bristly thatch of hair on her chin, uneven brows, big bones and dark blotches on her skin. Her eyes bulged slightly, and later, when she pulled in her breath during contractions, her cheeks sank into graceful hollows, as if they'd been carved by a slow-running waterfall. Her legs were ribbed with strength. I thought Janet was very beautiful.

She'd put on a freshly starched and ironed smock to wear to the hospital and since she was very nervous, she held tightly to her husband's arm. He stayed with her throughout. 'It's our first, you know,' he said, patting her hand. In his shirt pocket were two three-by-five cards: the first one had the choices of the baby's names; on the second, Janet had written the names and phone numbers of all the relatives he was to call. He pulled the cards out and showed them to me.

As her labor progressed and the contractions increased, she began to whistle through them; she'd be talking, then she'd slow down, roll up and over and perch on her right elbow, suck in her breath and whistle a few bars of a tune I couldn't make out. She was a determined girl. I don't think she had the faintest idea she was whistling.

Her husband let her pull on him, tug at him and dig her fingernails into his palm. Once or twice towards the end she said she couldn't go on, that it couldn't be done, but he'd stroke her hair and tell her softly, 'Don't look now, gal, but you are already doing it.'

When she got to the point where she wanted to push, we moved her to the delivery room and before long she was at the last of it.

I watched the top of the head coming towards me in laps, moving forward during a contraction, then dropping back. I had studied it so much, I could feel the mechanism of the birth canal – the rhythm of turning, burrowing, climbing, clenching and easing – as the baby secured his path. I longed to put my hand on Janet's belly to assure myself that the way I knew it felt was the way it felt.

She gripped the sides of her cot. I massaged the perineum. The head crowned. I touched the tips of my fingers to the creamy scalp and felt the pulse. Time stopped and I stopped and my hands joined with the baby's head. The baby's face crept out from under its mother's covering of skin. As the head came, my fingers eased along the cheeks almost as if a groove had been worn there to guide me. My fingers slid beneath the chin. The world turned then, one time and one time only on the axis made by the baby's head and body. Then the baby floated out into my hands.

Janet whistled ever so lightly and beneath my mask I smiled, because from the moment I touched the child's head I knew I had been born to be a midwife.

4

Wifie

Even though I hated the place, I learned a lot at Highlands General Hospital. I delivered babies. I thought nothing of working a seven-to-four shift, then sleeping and eating and coming back for an eleven-to-eight. I talked them into giving me extra time in labor and less time in the nursery. I lived my life at the doors of the delivery room hoping they would need an extra pair of hands. Happily I was part stewardess, part nurse and part general delivery mechanic. Contentedly I scrubbed up, set up and tore down. Eagerly I delivered big babies, little babies, flat babies, eager babies, preemies, twins. I did three breech deliveries in my first 20. By the time I left Glasgow, I'd caught 40 babies.

I learnt one skill poorly taught in the United States – how to use my hands to best advantage – but I worked under a medical style that I vowed to combat wherever I encountered it.

At Highlands Hospital, form ranked above everything else, including the well being of the mother and child. Form, indifferent as it might be to need, was the thing. I should have figured it out from the sterile-trolley business.

In the first place, a woman was to have her baby on time. Not when her body indicated, not when the baby had matured, but when the calendar prescribed. If a woman hadn't delivered by her due date, 'Pop you go into the hospital, girl, and we'll get this wee motor revved up now, won't we?'

The machinery started. It was incredible. There's not enough money in all of Scotland to bring in a bunch of fresh broccoli, but every last obstetric gadget in the modern world is automatically hooked up to a woman having a baby. First they put a catheter to her bladder. Then they put two wiry probes into her vagina: one is placed in the uterus to measure contractions, and the other is screwed into the baby's scalp to measure the fetal heartbeat. Contractions and beats follow the wire out to a metal box, which translates them on to a continuous band of paper. When the doctors come in to check a woman, they do not look at her, ask her questions, or feel her belly; they read the graph paper coming out of her machine.

Finally, she is given an IV with Pitocin, a drug that causes contractions to start or grow stronger, and once it's going she has until the end of the shift to get into action. If she hasn't had her baby by then, they give her an anesthetic and boost up the Pitocin – a combination which, incidentally, slows down the baby's heartbeat. In the second shift, she is to be ready to push. If she isn't, she's posted for cesarean section.

If she is ready to push, however – if her body should choose to be in harmony with the schedule of Highlands General Hospital – she goes to the delivery room. She doesn't actually go; she rides lickety-split on a metal trolley, crashing into walls and doorways on the way – a kind of permanent hysteria rules the corridors – and then she is lifted from the trolley to the delivery table, to which she is secured by tethers and ties. Her private parts are scrubbed. Her unscrubbed parts are covered with sterile draping.

The midwives scrub, too: hot water, a soft brush and iodine for fifteen minutes. We hold our hands up the entire time to keep the soiled water from dripping back onto them. Assistants help us with gowns and we dive our hands upward into sterile gloves. Then we set up the sterile trolley: 40 instruments in order. And if we fail to do that just so, then, yes, everything comes apart again, never mind the woman having a baby.

No one asks what one is to do if it is a choice between the

sterile trolley and the life of the baby. The idea is not to deliver babies, but to become a perfect mechanism in the delivery room.

Sister directs everything. We do as we are told. We do things we have never heard of, we do things we know are harmful. I had one baby whose face showed deep blue and whose neck was bound by three tight loops of umbilical cord: a baby in severe distress. I slipped clamps under the cord to cut it – a proper procedure, but, as Sister took pains to point out, done from the 'wrong' side.

Never mind the oxygen loss to the baby. Never mind potential brain damage. Sister insisted that I remove the clamps and put them under the cord from the 'right' side. So I did.

I watched while another student midwife tried to free a baby whose shoulder had stuck behind his mother's pubic bone. Like the baby whose neck is noosed by the cord, this baby was also suffering from oxygen deprivation. He needed the help of extraordinarily deft, strong and experienced hands, but Sister was not scrubbed so Sister did not intervene. She gave instructions from the doorway while the student midwife groped and the baby suffered damage.

Most of the babies, having been drugged through their mother's bloodstream, were sluggish at birth and we had to blow up their lungs for them before they were willing to breathe. I thought all babies were born like that, resisting birth, having to be convinced to live. Subconsciously, it must have made some sense to me. Who would want to be born in Glasgow?

By and large, the women came from hideous lives. Some of them knew instinctively that their children's lives would be too brutal to be justifiable. So, in ways that were eruptive, gross and thick – the only way they knew – they resisted reproduction. 'Poor wifies' we called them, poor women of Glasgow who would reach down with their hands and try to force their baby's head back into the womb when they could feel it being born.

Some fought with all their strength.

Margaret, a thin, rodent-faced creature, came to us filled with loathing. Her sister and mother pulled her through the door, explaining and re-explaining to anyone who showed even vague interest: 'She says she don't want no baby; she always said she never did want no baby. Said she never did have anything for herself when she was growing up and she was going to have something when she was grown. All she ever talked about was saving her money so she could move to London and live decent. I'd say she thought she was a little better than the rest of us, but I guess she found out she was just the same.'

I was kind to her, thinking I might give her a small measure of the respect she so desperately sought. She screamed back at me how she didn't need any consideration from people like me. She'd taken care of herself just fine without my help up to now and nothing would please her more than if I'd just go hang.

As the labor progressed, her raving and kicking grew more violent. She'd hiss and spit and beat us away when we tried to go near her to examine her.

'I won't have this baby. I won't have it. Never. No one can make me.' And she'd swing out at anyone who dared close in on her bed.

I saw her baby's head crowning and thought she'd be enough distracted by the pain so that I could dart in to catch it, but in a moving show of will, she jumped from her bed and ran down the hall. I followed, pace for pace, my hands held up for sterility. Nurses in the hall backed up flat against the walls in shock.

I chased her a half a block down the dimly lit hallway, the baby turning out as we ran; I chased her until she reached a dead end. She turned towards me, preparing, I could tell from the snarl on her lip, to fight dirty. I thought, How could

I get the baby out without hurting it or her? I turned around too, and backing up against her, pinning her to the wall, I reached through my own legs and hers and – as if in a reverse football 'hike' – I took her baby from her. We walked back to the room, both of us silent, the baby in my arms, the cord between us, the placenta still in her.

For six weeks of our training, we did 'district' postpartum care. We checked in each morning at the hospital and, wrapped in massive blue cloaks, high-black shoes and starched white hats, we took our list of addresses for that day's follow-up visits.

We wandered through all the back streets and burnt-out tenements of Glasgow.

We carried rolls of newspapers to spread out in the flats we visited, to protect ourselves, our babies, and whatever open wounds we found. We wore huge rubber aprons. That way, when we went to homes where there were no basins in which to wash the babies, we could fill our laps with warm water and bathe the babies in them.

I'd reach the base of some dark staircase, putrid with filth, and call out the name of the woman I was seeking. Generally, a man's voice would hurtle back like a rusty missile, 'Who's there?'

'Nurse Bradbury,' I'd respond.

His voice would change. Our position gave us protection. (We were highly respected. We seldom paid for coffee at the counter or for bus fare. Drunks would raise up on an elbow to salute us as we passed. We appeared to be bold, but we were safe in the jungle.) 'Come up, Sister,' he would say.

Unfortunately, what I had to say and teach my new mothers was not similarly respected. Teaching was impossible. Poverty, ignorance, and brutality preceded me and my lessons. What I taught dissolved instantly in the foul inheritance. Standing at a greasy sink, a baby in my arms, looking for a spot – any spot – to put down newspapers, a timid wifie crouched at my elbow and a vile man saying, 'She doesn't need to know how to wash the bairn',' I vanished into a memory of Nana's kitchen, with its white starched and ruffled curtains, its Seth Thomas clock ticking, its rocking chair. Nana's kitchen lived inside me, gave me comfort, and guided me towards the way things should be.

Then I looked at the man standing there, his pants half zipped, his bare white hairy arm leaning on the countertop, his eyes puffy and red, and tried to remember that his mother probably knew to try to push him back in.

We counseled women on family planning; we fitted them for a diaphragm and carefully explained how important it was to use it every time they had intercourse. A month or two later they'd be in the clinic, pregnant.

'What happened?'

'It was my neighbor's turn to use the diaphragm,' she'd say, 'and my husband, he didn't want to wait.'

Men, using kitchen knives and claiming their 'rights', would cut open their wives' stitches.

I was as kind and gentle as I could be while I was with the women. I talked to them about how to keep the baby warm and its tummy full. I answered their questions as best I could. That was all I could do. The system was fixed; everybody had to stay and do and be what they were, and had been now and for ever, in the hospital and out.

5

Booth

In Philadelphia, driving down City Line Drive from the north, you'll notice a change from ordinary city to blue-blood suburbs. Notice Saint Joseph's College* on your left, its entry fronted by a well-kept half circle of lawn, trimmed with flowers. On the right, down along, broad sidewalk shaded by elms, is the Jesuit sanctuary. A stone and iron fence lines the sidewalk and the grass rolls comfortably back into havens of silence, meditation and profound thought. Farther along are domesticated glens, ravines and meadows where sunlight puddles and splashes.

America. Soft, bountiful, sunny, generous, democratic, land-of-fresh-vegetables America.

I was coming home. I had certification as a nurse-midwife in the United Kingdom. I had yet to be licensed for practice in the United States; that would take 16 weeks of training at Booth Maternity Center on City Line Drive in Philadelphia.

Booth began as a home for unwed mothers, with a maternity hospital attached. Birth control pills, safe abortions, and tolerance for single parents forced Booth either to change its services or go out of business. A physician, John Franklin, proposed a plan for family-centered maternity care.

His idea, considered radical in 1971 when he offered it, was that childbirth was a normal event for the body and a normal, important event for the family. Believing that medical technology was used too commonly and casually in

*The names in this chapter have not been changed nor have any of the events been altered.

childbirth, he argued that it disrupted the harmony between the mother and her body, her baby's birth and her family. 'We wanted to support the mother's own heartfelt instincts for her baby and to see if we can graft on care as good as the maximum-intervention kind of delivery service.' He proposed a hospital delivery style, using a nurse-midwife/physician team, which he thought would be healthier for the mother, the child and the family. The local Maternity Center Association, the Salvation Army and the people at Booth joined with Franklin and created one of the most innovative and caring maternity hospitals in the nation.

I flew home at spring break at Highlands and interviewed with Sue Yates, Booth's Director of Education. I approached the crumbling old Main Line mansion. At the entry, there is a circular drive with a weedy bed in the center. A dogwood tree thrives there now, nourished by placentas planted by students of a graduating class after mine. Two or three steps lead up to the Queen Anne porch. The hand-plastered walls are the color of egg cream; and the tiles, where they haven't slipped away, are red. In winter, there's just the massive oak door facing you. In summertime, a wide, swaying screen door would be banging open and shut.

I went into a parlor. The mantelpiece was buffed; the fireplace appeared to work; and gray couches were filled with fluffy pillows. Sun streamed from the adjoining rooms, where Sue Yates had her office.

'The Booth experience,' Sue Yates said, 'is very demanding. You have to have your eyes open and be ready to go. You can't be depressed, or upset, or distracted by any other major responsibilites.' She wanted to know if I could arrange my life around such a program.

From where I sat, I could see a wall full of books, periodicals and texts. I knew that in the next room there were shelves filled with more books, periodicals, tapes, plastic models of women's bellies with doll-babies to go in and out of them, and videotaped lectures on all aspects of childbirth from experts around the world. This included my old friend Maggie Myles making her world-famous 'Hands Off the Breech' speech.

My mouth watered. Could I arrange my life? Could I arrange my life to be in a place where they wanted me to learn everything that I could about delivering babies? Sue Yates had no idea how easily I could do that.

'It is not only the schedule,' she said. 'There is – no matter what one's training – professional culture shock. If your experience has been in a high-tech hospital, then our laid-back ways make you question our performance standards; if your experience has been laid back, then precision is irritating.'

The student midwives at Booth come from all over the world, most of them to get their certification in America. Each one, she explained, has certain personal and cultural limits to overcome. One Irish woman, 'a lovely, elegant, long-necked girl', was extremely competent in the delivery room, Sue said, but she balked and crumbled when children attended a birth. The prospect of giving sex counseling or discussing venereal disease gave her a sick headache.

'A Chilean woman,' she continued, 'who had practiced independently for many years had a deep interest in therapeutic touch and holistic healing. She was initially offended by our use of technology, which she thought barbaric.'

'Finally,' she said, 'we demand self-reliance and self-criticism of our students. We find that nurses are accustomed to deferring to physicians, so they have difficulty in assuming complete responsibility for the outcome of their work, let alone the responsibility of advocating for patients in the face of an unsympathetic medical community. This business of being independent and professionally responsible is even more difficult for midwives coming out of more hierarchical settings – like those in the United Kingdom, for example.'

Amen, I said to myself, thinking of Sister standing at the door of the delivery room with her hands clasped politely in front of her while that baby degenerated.

I felt wonderfully, blissfully at home. I told her calmly and convincingly that I was strenuously self-reliant. I told her I wanted the premium training that Booth was reputed to give. I told her I had made considerable sacrifices to go this far, that I had a demonstrated record of singleness of purpose, and that I intended to be excellent. Booth could help me be excellent. I told her I needed the certification.

I didn't tell her that the most attractive man I'd ever met had just taken a job flying for a commuter airline out of Philly.

She said I could come, and so, six days after I returned to the United States from Glasgow, I began my course at Booth.

Booth *was* demanding. It *was* a culture shock. As given as I was to being independent, to running my own show, to making my own decisions, to an emergency-room mentality, I found it wrenching to transform myself immediately from delivery room wind-up nurse to professional midwife. I even wondered in that first week or so if I shouldn't have waited for the next class. But the feeling didn't last. Instead of taking strength out of me, Booth nourished me, gave me confidence and rewarded my skill. The people there wanted me to learn and to take good care of mothers – the very things I was most determined to do well.

First of all, they let us learn everywhere and under any circumstances. Not only in the library in the house, but in the hospital, too. There were funky cubbyholes, closets really, with coffee and ashtrays, tables and chairs where we could sit, talk, sketch anatomies and manoeuvres on the tabletop, and fight about how such and such a delivery should have been done. We debated the degree of technical intervention that was best. Do you drug them or not? What do you do, for example, with a Bryn Mawr type who isn't willing to give herself up to you; women who, instead of saying, 'Oh, Penny, you can get me through this?' would say, 'You have no right to push me through this.' We were constantly plotting and analyzing the way different women would have their babies.

Everything was different here. It was human. Everybody – mothers, babies, siblings, midwives, doctors – all of us were supposed to be regular people with lives around us. Our families, our hobbies, our busted radiators, impossible mothers-in-law, floated in and out of our work. Our human side was allowed to show: take Sue Yates giving introductory slide show about siblings at a birth. She was the consummate professional; she was in charge, in control, and I expected her to behave that way – formal, highly disciplined, and always to the point.

What happens? She's giving her lecture when up comes a slide of a kid who'd just watched his sister being born. Does she say, 'We've included this slide so that you can see that children who attend births can feel comfortable and relaxed about the experience'? No. Instead her voice starts zooming along like a roller coaster on a downhill turn.

'Look at that kid,' she says, as if she'd never seen the likes of him before. 'Would you look at that kid?' She walks up a little closer to the screen and looks herself. The kid, a sibling of the newborn, is looking cute, that's for sure. He's sitting in an oversized green hospital smock, in an oversized chair, with a brand-new baby comfortably in his lap and with his scruffy old mud-puddle tennis shoes sticking out at the bottom of the smock. 'Look at those feet!' she says, like it was her first grandson or something. She just liked the kid; that was her 'professional' point.

The people at Booth had thorough respect and affection for women, for their families, and for their way of life. The women came from every imaginable local culture: Philadelphia Main Line, Black Muslims with their robes and beads and bongos, revolutionaries, blacks, Chicanos, Puerto Ricans, macrobiotic types, hippies and preppies.

The prenatal clinic was a showroom for the maternity art done by the mothers: sketches, photographs, and watercolor washes portrayed women in labor, in delivery and taking care of their families. Sculptures lined the windowsills – some wooden and primitive, totemic in quality; others troubled. I remember a small, bound-up female figure, for example, made of twisted and layered wire with a twisted-and-layered-wire fetus inside her. A square wooden pregnant woman, not much different in liveliness from the square wooden chair she was glued to, was painted shiny, like a disco-dancing boot, in white acrylic.

Birthing style was mother's choice. You could have your contractions in a standard hospital bed where the mattress would go into modifications of the rickrack position by the mere pushing of a button, in a room where there were fetal monitors, belly bands, epidurals, spinals and locals. When you were ready to deliver, you could ride from there to the delivery room with its oxygen, stainless-steel rolling carts, plastic hoses, readouts, clamps, sutures and shiny lights. Or you could have your baby in the birthing room, in an ordinary old Salvation Army bed with flowered sheets, friends massaging your back and with your toddler sitting cross-legged beside you.

We meant for the woman's birthgiving to strengthen the identity and unity of her family and her way of life. So, for example, Southeast Asian families were welcome to move into the hospital with the patient. They lived on mats on the floor and cooked the mother's food. I remember especially a Korean woman whose family stewed up her afterbirth so she could drink the broth and, according to her belief, return the strength to her body that was lost in childbirth.

Although we couldn't accommodate crowds, we tried to fit in whomever the woman wanted at her birth. One woman wanted her boyfriend to bring his entire reggae band. Since there wasn't enough room indoors, the band played outside on the patio and the drummer stayed inside with us and beat his rhythms on the fetal monitor.

As in Glasgow, we delivered the babies of angry, hurt

women. Viciously angry women. Women who probably had been having sexual relations since they were ten, but who had not had a vaginal examination until they arrived at our doorstep. I would explain about how I was going to examine them and then as gently as I possibly could, I would reach my fingers into their vagina.

They would scream, 'Rape! Rape! She's trying to rape me!' and then kick and hit. For some of them, the fury persisted through prenatal care and all the way through delivery. They would hurl obscenities at the babies' fathers. 'That son of a bitch did this to me. I'll kill him. I hate his baby. Take this fuckin' baby out of me and get rid of it.' And once again, as with the wifies, there was a solid logic in their fury.

We had women who tried to make it work with their partners and brought them to the delivery, only to have them pass out from an overdose on the delivery room floor.

It wasn't much of a compensation, but we did work especially hard with those young inner-city mothers, girls of 14 and 15 who would let us help them. Booth's philosophy was to try to give them a good birth experience; to give them perhaps an altered view of what having a family might be like; let them see that it might not all be brutal. We stayed close to these girls, we avoided doping them up and wiring them up, not because they were less entitled to intervention, but because they were less informed consumers.

If a well-educated middle-class woman came in to have natural childbirth and she decided halfway through to throw in the rag, that was her business. She'd read the baby manuals; she knew that some of the drugs would be passed on to her baby. But an inner-city 14-year-old couldn't really give an informed consent. She'd never taken Physiology 101 and didn't know that drugs travelled through her to her baby. She didn't know that she might be losing the first moments of touching her baby and having him or her look back at her with bright eyes. We coached the young girls, put cool cloths on their brows, brought them juice and massaged their backs. We got to know them. Those of us who were able to, cooed to them. We helped them respect their bodies and its way of doing things.

I couldn't have given you any hard evidence, but it seemed that their births went better.

What was true before birth – the most homelike atmosphere possible – followed afterwards. The postpartum floor – in most hospitals, a quiet, 'hush, the babies are sleeping' twilight place – was jovial and hearty. Women would be padding up and down the halls or sitting in rocking chairs in their rooms with their babies; men would be wandering about at all hours, helping out, looking for things, smiling stupidly into space, taking their newborns for a walk down the corridors. The nursery, instead of being draped and closed up except for hospital regulation viewing hours, had no curtains. Typically a soft, shapeless, white-haired old woman in a calico apron would be there puttering around and talking to the new mothers, showing them how to bathe their new babies. The prints on the walls were taken from old children's storybooks from around the world: 'Then hush a bye, sweet to the spell and song of the dream shell.'

In the aftercare program, the same attitude prevailed. The women – single, married, rich, poor, battered, loved, in babushkas or feathered hair dressings, ignorant of being a parent or over-read and over-educated – were treated (with their babies, their partners and their other children) as an honorable institution. They were a family, and that, at Booth, was the important thing.

If the women were respected, if their bodies were respected, so were we. Midwives at Booth delivered the babies. We needed the doctors there; we wanted the doctors there for complications and medical problems; but we handled the normal births. They would put their head in the delivery room door and ask if everything was okay; would they be needed?

We learnt responsibility, some of us with difficulty, others easily. We did learn to be self-reliant. We were our patients' advocates. We had to assume professional responsibility for their wellbeing, even if it meant challenging the physicians. And we would have to do that. All of us. They didn't let us forget it. The American doctor, they taught us, was not keen on our opinions or our ways of delivering babies.

6

Paradise Visited

It would have been all right to have stayed at Booth as a resident midwife. Not only did I like Booth, but I had Richie nearby; he even went to Midwifery Association meetings with me. He was settled in a comfortable room in a big old boarding house and pretty much thrilled at the idea that he was driving people around in the sky. While Richie flew, I got to do a lot of deliveries in a humane hospital.

The trouble was, Booth had taught me to question what I was doing. For example, in our cubbyhole discussions at Booth, other midwives would sometimes argue from a book called *Spiritual Midwifery*. 'They say don't rupture the membranes until . . .' or 'They say there is no such thing as an arrested labor.' I learnt that *Spiritual Midwifery* was a book written by a hippie midwife for a colony of hippies who'd followed 'Stephen' in a bus from Berkeley and settled on farms in Tennessee. I knew they intervened in deliveries far less than we did and they depended a lot on the relationship of the midwife to the mother. In hippie talk, that was a 'birthing energy' issue.

I'd consciously avoided buying the book. I suspected the author understood some processes better than we did in the hospital, but they were things I didn't want to have to work out while I was studying at Booth. Also, I had a good idea that 'spiritual midwives' might be flaky; I'd seen too many flat babies – babies who were slow to breathe – so many mothers whose labors had just plain stopped, to believe that you could safely and sensibly deliver babies on somebody's porch.

But I kept thinking about how *Spiritual Midwifery* said that a woman did better if her birth people stayed with her all the way through: 'The Vow of the Midwife has to be that she will put out 100 percent of her energy to the mother and the child that she is delivering until she is certain that they have safely made the passage.'*

I didn't care for the hippie vow, but I was having a terrible time leaving women before they had their babies. I'd just get to the point where the woman's body and mind were intertwined with mine and she was trusting me and we were beginning to work together like we'd been at it for a lifetime, and I'd look at my watch. 'End of my shift, girl,' I was supposed to say in Glasgow style and then walk off. Every time I had to do it, I felt as if I'd wronged the mother and her child.

I was leaning on the counter at the nurses' station staring blankly into space, when the phone rang, a nurse talked for a minute, then put her hand over the mouthpiece. 'Some GP out in the boonies wants to know if we have any midwives who want to come join him in his private practice, including home deliveries. Anybody here want to talk to him?'

'Why not?' I said.

I had never been to Pennsylvania Dutch country. Amish, Mennonites, Hutterites, plain people, farmers, cultists, whatever – it was all the same to me. I had seen pictures in *National Geographic* of women wearing below-the-knee dresses and aprons; of men with beards who farmed with horses. Everybody was supposed to drive around in buggies instead of cars. One image stood out – a line of buggies in

---

*Ina May Gaskin, *Spiritual Midwifery* (Summertown, Tenn. The Book Publishing Company). Gaskin and other midwives on 'the Farm' are lay midwives; that is, their training is empirical or based on first-hand experience. The certified nurse-midwife, or CNM, on the other hand, must complete an approved course of study in both nursing and midwifery and be licensed to practice in her state.

procession across a hill at sunset. I thought the whole thing was a little overdone, but what could I say? At Booth I'd learnt some tolerance.

I drove out the Pennsylvania Turnpike on a cloudless morning. I was contented, looking forward to a break in routine. I buzzed along, cutting in and out of traffic. An hour later, at exit 23, I pulled off the turnpike. A matching pair of two-story brick houses with Federalist porticoes and green shutters faced me across the intersection. In this part of Pennsylvania – that is, anywhere within a 50-mile radius of Gettysburg – you feel like you're about to see either an 18th-century cannonball hurtling over a stone wall or George Washington himself. What I saw, actually, besides the Revolutionary homes, were gas station signs and restaurant billboards.

I was on my way to Intercourse. Dr Kaufman's office was in Paradise, but I figured that as long as I was coming out this way, I would go to Intercourse, which is a village in the heart of Amish country. It's impossible not to be curious about a place named Intercourse.

On second glance, the restaurant billboards didn't look the same anymore; they were simpler and cruder than they would be in Gettysburg. That was serious indication that I was getting near the country. I drove past a row of trees, a few more brick homes, a vacant lot – and then farmhouses started appearing by the side of the road.

These weren't just any old farmhouses, they were white two-story farmhouses like in the old Maine – farmhouses with barbered lawns and immaculate flower beds. Grape vines, not yet showing any leaves, were pinned in swags to porch roofs and were waiting there patiently for warmer days. Neat concrete paths led in a straight line to each front door and even here, along a major thoroughfare, the dirt between the edge of the roads and the edge of the lawns was marked by the teeth of a neatly handled rake.

Billboards and store-bought signs were fewer; pieces of plywood painted white and hanging from a simple post-and-arm affair replaced them. In black hand lettering, the signs read CABINETMAKER, APPLE CIDER, BLACKSMITH, HANDMADE FURNITURE, EGGS, HOMEMADE BREAD AND HONEY, QUILTS, VEGETABLES. Most of the signs had a note at the bottom: NO SUNDAY SALES.

A black buggy, pulled by a leggy and spirited horse, bounded along the edge of the road.

I was softening up.

Then I got to the village of Intercourse.

Well, now. It wasn't that the village wasn't fine. In fact, it was just what you'd hope for in a charming country village: a quilt shop, a candle barn, a couple of general stores, a post office, Brubaker's Garage, old oak and maple trees lining the street and (as all tourists learn), a hitching post out in front of the converted-to-computer bank.

What startled me were the Amish women; I'd never seen anything like them. White, stony faces, one after another along the sidewalks, in the general store, going in and out of the fabric shop. Each and every last one of them – girl or ancient – marched purposefully along, as if conscripted for duty. Each wore a massive black bonnet with a huge black bill that all but encircled her face and stuck out maybe an inch and a half from it. Most wore black shoes, black stockings and a black cape worn over a black apron, which was worn over a black dress.

Not one smiled or so much as looked at me or anybody else. They had their eyes drilled into the sidewalk. All of their faces were very smooth, as if they'd never been broken in by laughing or kissing or crying. It was a wonder to me they would ever need a midwife.

Frankly, I didn't think I could deliver their babies. Midwifery is an intimate profession. In order for me to help a woman have her baby in the way that is easiest and healthiest for her, I have to see some of her interior composition – her physical and emotional strengths and weaknesses – and I need to see them quickly and surely. My whole manner – my touch, my words, my knowledge, my joking, my gossip, my instruction and my silence – adjusts to her and to what I learn about her as we go along, and so each delivery is different since each woman has her own way to strength. The more a woman trusts her body and trusts me, the easier things are. The less obstructed the woman is, the less shielded she is from her body and from her emotions, the better her delivery.

That's why the births of those inner-city girls went so well. Being so young and so clearly in need of help, they *had* to trust us. They revealed themselves, gave up control, and allowed us to guide them to their bodies.

These Amish women – as cold, joyless and ascetic as they seemed to be – would shield themselves from the intelligence of their bodies. Not only did they keep outsiders at a distance, but judging from their scarlike lips, they kept themselves at a distance, too. You would probably have to use dynamite and a pickaxe to dislodge their babies.

I was glad I'd taken a half-holiday attitude towards this trip because the chance of my taking a job with Stephen Kaufman, doctor to the stony-faced women, was very slim. Not only would the deliveries be difficult and the babies reluctant to live, but I would have to spend my time with these dreary types. No thank you. Give me back my reggae mamas.

Still, I thought I would go ahead and talk to the doctor. No reason not to. I left the commercial roads and cut over to Paradise on farm roads.

The farms stopped me. They were perfect. They were absolutely exquisite. Each one was minutely cared for, as if the rows were pulled up straight each morning and the corners tucked in at nightfall. The soil was looser than at other farms; it was lighter, fluffed up, as if it had been given a good beating in a copper bowl.

I drove along a stream bed bounding with spring rains and watched where it widened into a pool by a farmhouse. Ducks sailed across the pond as if in serene possession of their affairs. I watched. There was no traffic and so few sounds. I rolled down the window and let the smell of the earth fill the car. I thought I could hear a duck paddling across the pond. I was awestruck.

I stared at the ploughed earth, at the breathing, fertile soil all around me. And then I began to cry. After the assaults I had felt and seen in the cities, assaults of man against woman, woman against child; after the endless asphalted city floor; after the heavy metal-dust smell of power coursing along boulevards and into dark buildings, here – here, all this time, these people had been taking care of the soil.

I drove around a curve of a hillside. On it, a boy of ten or eleven years, barefoot on an unsaddled white mare, was riding up ploughed rows. The horse pulled a plough and behind the plough, the boy's father walked. He carried a little girl on his back and stepped, barefooted also, up the rows of newly turned earth. I continued, afraid to breathe for fear of disturbing what I saw on the road to Dr Kaufman's office.

Amish couples sat side by side in matching costumes in Dr Kaufman's waiting room. In addition to their black pants, the men wore black coats with hook-and-eye closings. Their black, flat-brimmed hats hung from pegs by the door. The women had taken off their outdoor bonnets.

Here I need to explain something. Indoors, each woman wears a white organdy 'covering', a gathered and banded cap that is shaped like a heart at the crown and covers the back of her head. It is secured to her hair with a straight pin, which is driven through a narrow band of organdy that runs across the top of her head and down either side. The combination of the straight pin and the severe stretching of the hair away from the center part often causes a pool of baldness at the top of a woman's head. That these women were able to secure their covering to the few thin remaining hairs seemed impossible to me at first. I was fascinated; I found myself studying the pins and bare skin, and stray hairs the way a child studies the first deformed person they ever see. 'What is that, mama?' or, in this case, 'Mama, does she put the pin in her skin?' Like the child, I was uncomfortable in seeing this unnatural arrangement, but more than anything, I was brazenly curious. I stared at every opportunity.

Just so you'll know, the caps are fastened without causing bleeding.

For more formal times, like going to the doctor, the Amish woman is sure to tie the ends of the bands of her covering not tightly under her chin, but loosely, so that a small white bow rests on her chest just below the hollow of her throat. The effect is sweet and virginal. When she's busy or just around the house, she often leaves the little bands running free, instead of tied, and they blow and play about her shoulders.

The Amish, Dr Stephen Kaufman explained, were quiet and reserved around physicians, as they were around any English. They go to a doctor, it was glibly said, for 'birth, death and when they cut their hands off.' Dr Kaufman didn't know much about their beliefs, and, like a lot of people in the area, he thought of them as a simple, plain people without any education who, he observed, didn't always take his advice.

His idea was to build a bigger general practice among the Amish by delivering more of their babies. A midwife was a way to increase his access to them and they seemed to like the idea, he said. I was to talk to some of his prenatal patients after he was done with them.

'Are you thinking of coming here?' Priscilla asked. She had no scar mouth. She had no captain's face, no infantryman's single-mindedness. Instead of black, she wore a bright blue dress. She smiled gaily, her face shone with eagerness. It seemed as if the idea of my coming was quite wonderful to her.

'Yes, I am,' I said and waited, wanting to get her purest response.

'Well,' she said, 'we'd be glad to have a woman to deliver our babies again. Dr Kaufman is a good doctor, but it's different with a man. Men don't understand. Ever since Dr Ruth had her accident, we've had to have men. And then some of us would like to have our babies at home. Dr Kaufman said you might deliver babies at home.'

And then she asked me if I knew how she could get her figure back again.

When I asked Stephen what he told the women about weight, he said, 'I didn't think these women ever thought about things like that.'

Men! I could certainly understand that these women got doughy and didn't like it. It was being a farmer's wife: too much cooking all the time and no one probably ever bothered to explain about calories to them. It would be easy to help these women lose a few pounds.

We drove out to visit some patients.

Since it was Monday, we stepped under the weekly wash. In each and every farmyard the wash snapped on the lines in the same order: black pants from big to small; shirts – lawn green, sky blue, lavender – from big to small; dresses, the same; and then on to less distinguished items – shorts, socks, sheets and dozens and dozens of diapers. Stephen warned me to be careful not to drive over the buggy shafts (the long poles that attach the horse to the buggy) either coming in or, more likely, backing out.

Each Amish kitchen we visited was immaculate. The floor, always of linoleum, shone back at us. The countertops were clear, the sink scrubbed, and all the dishes put away. The walls were painted green – the same color they used to have in hospitals – and the cupboards were pine. The kitchens were big – the center of virtually all activity in the house – and furnished with a big table in the center. There might be a couch and a chair, too, but the table was the thing.

Children assembled willy-nilly at the corners of the room and stared wide-eyed at Dr Kaufman and me. After a while a little one would break ranks and come over to his mother and crawl determinedly into her lap. The woman would talk quietly and cheerfully but without show. She would laugh and smile and stroke her children's hair. Shortly after we'd arrive, her husband would come in from the barns or fields, and pulling up another chair, he would talk with us, too. They'd offer us ice cream, custard, cookies and pretzels. We'd slow down and talk at a farmer's pace – with more space between words and ideas. I liked it; I remembered it from Westford Hill, Maine.

Over and over again I heard about Dr Ruth, the woman who'd been doing home and hospital deliveries for the Amish for 30 years. She'd had an accident and ended up in a wheelchair, and the women were stuck. 'Dr Ruth was rough sometimes. She'd give the babies a hard pull sometimes, and she made mistakes,' they told me, 'but she was terribly busy and she worked hard. We feel she cared about us and our babies. She'd get us to the hospital if there was going to be a problem, like if there were going to be twins or something.' Dr Ruth delivered 5,000 babies before she retired.

'Now we only have these other doctors not Dr Kaufman, but the other ones – and we're not sure they always handle things the best. My cousin had her labor start early – she was only seven months – but she was having contractions. She called the doctor. She and her husband, they thought maybe they should go to the hospital, but the doctor said that it was okay and he came out to her house and delivered the baby. It weighed just a little more than three pounds.

'My cousin and her husband, they wanted to know what to do about the baby after it was born because it was so tiny and they thought maybe they should go to the hospital with it. The doctor said just to put it in a box on the oven door and don't worry about it anymore.'

The woman spoke softly, without rancour.

'Their baby died in the oven. And that was after the husband had carried the placenta out of the house to bury it. He found a second baby in the placenta, which the doctor had never bothered to check for or deliver. They had a hard time giving themselves up to that.'

Stephen and I stumbled out of the house after hearing that. We looked at each other in shock. Stephen said it made him ashamed of his profession and it made him think that sometimes it wasn't such a good idea that the Amish don't sue.

At the last house, the husband said to me, 'Is it true that if you came here you would sit with the woman through her labor?'

7

Paradise Considered

I stayed two and a half days with Dr Kaufman, talking, seeing the local hospital and visiting patients. He showed me the rec center, set up an appointment for me with a real estate agent, explained about the school system if I should ever want to get married and have children. He showed me where the Chinese restaurants were. If I came, I would handle pre-natal care office visits, I would labor-sit with the women at home and would deliver those babies, too, although Dr Kaufman would be present for the actual birth. He would handle hospital deliveries until such time as we were successful in getting me hospital privileges. Then I would be able to do midwife-attended hospital births and also follow home delivery patients into the delivery room in emergencies. He couldn't pay much, but we would renegotiate in a year, and besides it's cheap to live in the country.

Dr Kaufman – Stephen, that is – was smart and he seemed to be trying to be a good doctor. He didn't know much about pregnancy – because he was a man, I suppose, and because in medical school they don't teach much about healthy, pregnant women. I thought I could do a good job for him, treat the women well, whether Amish or English. At the least, I could help protect the farm women from doctors who were killing their babies and I could teach them new ways, ways in which modern medicine could make their deliveries safer and more comfortable.

I drove home slowly along back roads, looking at farmhouses. These were country women; they cared about their gardens, their quilts, their children and their homes. I understood them. I could give them good care.

What about Richie? I knew Richie was, without a doubt, the best of the males of the species and, besides, we had made what he called a 'conscious decision' to live near each other. Richie had to fly; and after years of yearning and plotting, he got probably the only crew seat available to an old fellow – he was 33 – in the entire country. It was about an hour and a half from Lancaster county to the north Philly airport. That was too far. Maybe it wasn't. Maybe it would be all right. What if Richie really didn't want me to do this? What if he didn't want to move? What if we decided to live an hour and a half apart and I lost him?

Richie wasn't at his place when I got there. I let myself in, washed, scrubbed my face, changed my clothes. On the bureau I set a fresh-from-an-Amish-kitchen, molasses-based shoofly pie. Richie loved pie. There was a big white wicker rocker in the corner of his room, the kind with the high, peacock-tail back and wide woven arms. I'd gone out the week before and got a blue-and-white polka dot pillow for the seat of it; he said it was a waste of money and I thought it made things just right.

I wrapped myself in a blanket, rocked in the chair, and waited for Richie to come home. I looked at his shirts, lined up like a drill team marching blindly towards the closet wall, and at his shoes, toed up against the wall beneath his shirts. His books now included *Zorba the Greek*, Fritz Perls on *Gestalt Therapy*, as well as something like *The History of the Wing of the Airplane from the Sand Dunes at Kitty Hawk to the Salt Flats on the Mohave*, 'with drawings of the major structural advancements'. The books were arranged alphabetically by author along the top of his bureau. There was nothing hanging on the walls of the room except a narrow pine shelf that Richie had designed, built and finished expressly to hold his grandfather's fiddle. It had been in his parents' attic in Island Falls, Maine, for years, then had gone astray. Richie, hearing that it was about to fall into unappreciative hands, made a special trip to Massachusetts to retrieve it. It rested securely now against the columbines and nasturtiums on the wallpaper of his room in this boarding house in suburban Philadelphia.

Richie and I had met – well, met wouldn't be the right word, more like exploded into each other's lives – at my parents' summer cabin on Pleasant Pond in northern Maine during that summer break from school in Glasgow. For three weeks, Richie and I spent our days paddling from cove to cove on Pleasant Pond; talking, swimming, picnicking, and visiting every last Maine character with a moving jaw – all of them Richie's friends. At night we curled up by the wood stove at his cabin and talked some more.

Richie'd grown up in Island Falls and had gotten a degree in engineering from the state university. When I met him, all he'd seen of the world was Maine and parts of Vietnam; all he'd known of work was potatoes, sewer-plant design and runway construction. True, he did know how to fly, but he hadn't flown far, and the time had come, he said, to break out, to open up his consciousness, seek truth and all that. Richie'd worked up these ideas while reading *Siddhartha*, the *I Ching*, *Walden* and *The Greening of America* in a construction trailer on the edge of the Frenchville runway. I was impressed.

He'd get up from his rocker, stir up the fire, walk out on the porch and kill a bat with his tennis racket, bring me a dish of ice cream and one more time, he would laboriously explain that he did not want now, nor did he ever want, a dependent woman in his life. Never could abide them. And at the moment he was ploughing himself into this self-discovery business. He'd arranged a leave of absence from work and found just the car he'd been looking for; he had the route mapped out. He wanted to spend lots of time 'standing around tumbleweed in Texas and,' he said, 'there's a place in California where you can sit in hot tubs that are cantilevered over the Pacific Ocean. Think of that, Penny. Not lobster shacks and death-cold winds, but hot tubs by the sea!'

After he'd finished up self-discovery, and if he could find somebody who could fit him with proper contact lenses, he was going to become a commercial pilot, or if that failed, he was going to Oman and make lots of money as an engineer.

Then and only then might he consider allowing a totally self-sufficent woman in his life.

Assiduously I went over my entire past for proof of my self-reliance. I told Richie how I'd navigated white water in the Sierras; had taken pregnant criminals on outings around California; had built a VW; put up all that weathered barn board in my farm in Maine; not to mention cooking, canning, sewing and lambing. I mentioned how I had single-handedly put myself through a crash nursing program in Saint Louis, one of America's most dangerous cities. (I described in blood-chilling detail how I drove through the city one night with friends when I had the flu and had to throw up, but we all knew we could not stop the car for fear of being victims of random attack, so we continued driving through the streets, while I hung my head out the window, vomiting and thinking I would be lucky if no one took a pot shot at my head, hanging as it was like a tetherball from the car window.) Furthermore, I went on, I had endured the dismal and morally debilitating days in the male urology ward in Highland General Hospital and I told him how, when I got my midwifery degree, I would plunge directly into Maine's remote parts and deliver babies all by myself.

I also told him about A. Robert Peterson, a contact lens magician I knew in California.

Richie reached over to me and pulled me close to him. He said the same words then that he would say when he put me on the plane to Scotland. 'I just hope you are what you seem to be.'

Since then I'd been trying.

* * *

By the time I'd finished my work in Glasgow, Richie had been west and back, and these days he talked to me, he helped me, he got a hot water bottle for my back when I had cramps, he put his arms around me and held me. He was funny, he certainly had no fear of teasing me and he was always wandering off to places like Albuquerque in the back of a plane and then coming home to tell me absurd stories about how he was taken hostage by a gang of marauding women who wore yellow lipstick and lived in a cave deep in the shadow of the Grand Canyon, but loyal to the end, he'd won his escape by splitting their sides with stories of folks from Island Falls, Maine.

Richie wasn't perfect. For one thing, he was too organized – I had made more mess since I arrived at his place that afternoon than he had made in the six months previous. Furthermore, he was a man and probably couldn't be trusted. And finally, he couldn't understand why I got hysterical about some things. But I loved Richie.

Richie's room was only ten minutes from north Philly airport.

I started to think again about Lancaster County. My second day there, Stephen and I stopped at the home of a woman whose husband kept running away. (Actually, we had tried to visit the first day, but the yard had been filled with black buggies and Stephen said we shouldn't intrude.) Some Amish, even though they want to join the church and do, even though they get married and have their babies, can't stay within the community. I'm sure there are all kinds of reasons for running – all the ones that make those of us on the outside do it, plus some that are peculiar to the Amish culture.

Ike, Lydia's husband, was that way. They'd had their fourth baby and Ike had run away again, this time for so long that the Amish elders had to go to Boston to get him. He'd ended up at some church door, shaking and incoherent. Fortunately someone in the congregation knew about the Amish.

The elders brought him home, but he couldn't do his work and he was about to lose his milking cows for the lack of a decent roof on his barn. That first day when we drove by, the Amishmen from the neighborhood were crawling all over the barn roof; they had it finished by chore time. The women were inside making a meal for the 30 or so men who were working.

When Stephen and I saw Lydia, Stephen asked her how Ike was doing. She thought he was better. He was eating something and he'd slept the night before. In the time we talked, she never said a word against him; she never complained about the work and worry he caused her; she never said, 'If he loved me, he wouldn't do this to me.' She stayed at the farm, looked after their four babies and waited for him to come home and to get better. She did wonder sometimes, she said, whether he should go someplace for help with his mental problems. But now that he was getting better, she didn't think of that so much.

Back in Richie's room, I sat in the wicker chair and watched the sky wash pink in behind the twigs and branches of the elm trees. For a while I thought about the pots and bottles I had in storage in Maine. I got up and had a piece of Richie's pie. Then I read for a long time and, dragging myself in my blanket, I curled up and went to sleep on Richie's bed. He didn't come home until much later; there had been some kind of a delay in Boston.

In the morning I told him I wanted to go work with Dr Kaufman.

He wanted to know how long this moving around was going to go on. Yes, he wanted an independent woman. Yes, he wanted me to have a career of my own. Yes, he admired me. But ever since he'd known me, it was one stand after another. Maine, Saint Louis, Glasgow, Philadelphia, not to mention white-rapids riding in California, and now, of all places, Paradise, Pennsylvania. Perhaps I would never stop. We finally had a place where we could do the work each of us wanted to do, where we could be together, where we could make a home if we decided to, but no, I had to go a 100 miles out in the country, work for peanuts, and deliver babies at home, which, he reminded me, I had said was ethically unacceptable. 'I don't suppose you remember throwing yourself against the wall and shrieking "ethically unacceptable"?' he asked, licking his fingers and serving himself another piece of shoofly pie.

'Richie, I want you to come and see.'

'I've seen cow manure.'

'Please, Richie.'

We drove out the next weekend in his 1965 VW beetle, which had gaping joints and no heat. Richie had a cold; bitter winds and rain darkened the landscape and shrivelled up our skin and bones. Richie drove with a blanket wrapped around his shoulders and blew his nose. He saw nothing that interested him. 'A bunch of dirt farmers dressed up in Walt Disney costumes,' he said.

I called Stephen Kaufman the following Monday morning and accepted the job. I didn't understand quite why I did it, but I did.

Three weeks later I delivered my first baby at home.

I was overwhelmed with the responsibility. I'd delivered a lot of babies by then; that is, enough to know that things went wrong. That was my job – knowing about things that went wrong. As a midwife, I could help a good, healthy birth be a relatively comfortable and probably a richer experience for a mother but, by and large, she could do it by herself with her husband or a friend. What she needed me for was to anticipate problems and to handle emergencies. By the number of them I'd seen, I had no trouble justifying my presence at a birth.

At Booth, I had backup: not only fetal monitors, intra-uterine pressure monitors, X-ray machines, ultrasound scans, suction, oxygen, drugs, IVs, blood transfusions, but also anesthesiologists, obstetricians, surgeons, neonatologists and skilled nurses, not to mention a scrub basin and a sterile trolley.

But what do you do about emergencies when you're standing in somebody's bedroom in a farmhouse in the middle of a cornfield, in a place where the fanciest technology is hot and cold running water, and your medical team is composed of a farmer who – at best – had delivered his own calves.

Take flat babies. They have poor color – that is, they are blue or gray and their bodies are limp; they show little or no enthusiasm about breathing. It was my clear impression that most babies were flat. In the hospital you automatically cleaned out air passages with a suction tube that's piped right into the room; then, without breaking rhythm, you leant in the other direction and grabbed for an oxygen mask so you could, if necessary, 'bag' the baby, that is, pump oxygen into its lungs. You could stimulate its heart. You could turn to the neonatologist and have him or her take the problem off your hands, especially if the mother was having difficulty.

Suppose Stephen was late for a delivery, the baby was flat, and the mother started to hemorrhage? How would I resuscitate the baby, keep the father from fainting, get the emergency team on the road and stop the hemorrhaging all at the same time? And how long does it really take for one of these country emergency teams to respond to a call? Women die in childbirth, for heaven's sake. If the placenta breaks away from the uterine wall in just the right place at just the right time, a woman can lose enough blood in fifteen minutes to die.

And I was off to deliver babies where there might not be any electricity and the nearest phone was either in the chicken coop or across the pasture.

* * *

My first delivery was in an Amish cottage, fenced in with an honest-to-goodness white picket fence. I turned into the drive just as Enos, the father, was tucking his two-year-old onto the seat of an open buggy. Enos – with dark wavy black hair, a square jaw, eyes the color of a mountain stream, six feet tall and broad-shouldered; in other words, a picture-book husband – waved, grinned, and said he'd be right back. He prompted his horse and pulled off down the gravel drive to take little Johnny, the two-year-old, to his aunt's house.

Thinking I would find Katie stretched out in her bed, I turned to go up the steps to the back porch. Just then she popped out the back door. She had a paintbrush in her hand.

'Oh,' she said. 'Hi. Oh, my goodness, I'm not quite ready. I was putting the final coat of lacquer on this rocking chair when I started to have stronger contractions. I just wanted so much for it to be done, so I could rock the baby in it.

'Then I decided that I'd better call Enos. He works out at the machine shop, so I went to the neighbor's phone, and I didn't want to call you because they'd know, but I just called Enos and said I thought he ought to come home.'

She'd cleaned the brush and now she laid it down on some neatly folded newspapers spread out on a corner of the porch. Not only did the rocker look freshly lacquered, but it appeared that the porch floor had been scrubbed and waxed not long ago. She stopped talking for a moment when she stood up, put her hands on her hips, and stretched out her back.

'Is that a contraction?' I asked.

'Yes, it is.'

'Is it pretty strong?'

'Yes, I believe it is, and I haven't put that plastic thing on the bed yet.'

We walked through an immaculate kitchen and a spotless living room. She'd gotten her husband off to work, got her toddler up, washed, fed and dressed, cleaned up the breakfast dishes, straightened up the living room and painted a rocking chair. I think it was about 8:30 in the morning.

I had my small bag in my hand.

'Before we make the bed, let's see how dilated you are.' I was thinking that this woman couldn't be too far along since she was running around like she was getting ready for her first date.

Wrong. Nine centimeters.

'Where's that plastic sheet?' I said. 'Looks to me like you're about to have a baby.'

She chattered her way off to the linen closet and back. 'Oh, I'm so excited,' she said. 'I can hardly wait. Every night when I go to bed, I say to Enos, "Maybe tonight I'll have the baby. Maybe by tomorrow morning it will be lying right here between us." And then in the morning when I wake up, I'm so disappointed because it didn't happen and I've been thinking I would have to wait all the way until the next night before there was even a chance again. I never even thought I could have it during the day. Enos keeps telling me not to be so impatient. He says he has to remind me that he believes the baby really will be born.'

She stopped again for another contraction, and as soon as it passed she went back to spreading out the plastic sheet over the mattress cover. I was supposed to be helping her, but I had trouble concentrating. I kept staring. The woman was nine centimeters dilated and she was bustling about furiously.

We finished making up the bed, then she thought maybe she'd change from her dress into a gown. Next thing I knew, she'd hopped onto the bed. Her face was flushed and she was ready to push.

Stephen's office was only a quarter of a mile away. I'd put a call in to him on my radio as soon as I checked Katie that first time, and he pulled in just as she was getting serious about pushing her baby out. Enos followed right behind him.

He went to Katie's side and grabbed her hand.

The three of us attended quietly. A couple of times Katie said it hurt and she called her husband's name, and he got closer to her and held her so she could push more easily.

The baby, a boy, popped out as if he were on his way to the outfield to catch a long fly. I put him on the bed at Katie's side and she curled herself around him.

'Oh,' she said, 'look at him. Look at our new baby. Oh, I wonder what Johnny will think.'

Enos stroked her head and said, 'So now you have your baby.'

And she said, 'Oh, my, look how beautiful he is. Just look. Oh, Enos, I love him already.'

I checked Katie to see if there were any tears in her perineum. There weren't. For a moment Stephen stood back with his arms folded and watched. 'I couldn't have done it like that,' he said to me and then he went on to check the baby. In a few minutes, he left, giving me responsibility for the aftercare.

I cleaned Katie up, washed the baby at the kitchen sink and got him started at his mother's breast. Then I went out into the kitchen to give them a chance to be alone and to do my paperwork.

Pretty soon Enos came out, opened the desk and started riffling through papers. He pulled one out, looked at me, and smiled peacefully. 'I never want to choose a name before the baby's born,' he said. 'I write down a list of names that I think of, but then I wait until I see the baby before I choose one. No reason,' he said softly, leaving time between his words the way these people do. 'It's just my way.'

I went back into the bedroom just as Enos was getting ready to go back down the road for little Johnny. A buggy was passing by and you could hear it slow down as it came near the house. 'Oh, I know who that is,' Katie said. 'It's my sister. We were supposed to go together to our appointments at Dr Kaufman's today. I guess she'll be surprised I don't go with her. I guess Enos will tell her how come I'll stay at home today. Oh, I hope she stops by on her way back from the doctor.'

I was staring again. This was not a hyperactive person, just a cheerful, enthusiastic young mother. But she'd just had a baby and she was still full of energy. Next thing I know, she says, 'Can I get up? Just for a minute. I just have to try something. I just need to go in the other room.'

I couldn't think of a reason to say no but, then, I was pretty stunned at the time. I helped her stand, made sure she wasn't feeling dizzy and watched her go to a bureau in the second bedroom. She came back with a tiny white baby cap.

'I just have to see how he'll look in this. I made it for him and I just can't wait to see him in it.' She plunked herself down on the bed and picked the baby up. The baby, now a good 45 minutes old, went into her lap and she busily put the little bonnet on him. 'It fits perfectly,' she said. 'Look at him, look at our baby.'

I waited until Enos returned and then left. A buggy was coming from the direction of Dr Kaufman's office. I waved as I passed by and they smiled and waved back.

I was totally bewildered. And euphoric. I'd never seen a birth quite like this one.

8

Spring Road

'Penny speaking.'

'Is this Penny?'

'Yes, this is Penny.'

'The wife, she has a pain.'

'What fer pain is that?'

'Why, it's the pain down low.'

'Does it come and go?'

'Yah.'

'Is it time for me to come?'

'Whatever you think.'

'Who would this be?'

'Elam Stoltzfus.'

'Oh, would your wife be Mary over on School Road, then?'

I quickly learnt the way to ask questions and to identify people, but it took me a long time to get used to phone calls from Amish fathers-to-be. They just didn't seem to want to tell much. In the first place, an Amishman isn't likely to go in for much detail when talking with outsiders. But put him on the phone and he'll clam up even more; he's not used to it. After I'd been in the community for a while, I got a letter from an Amishwoman that helped me understand the whole thing. She wanted to thank me for something, but she explained that she had never learnt to enjoy the phone – mainly because she never used it much – and besides, she was afraid the person on the other end couldn't understand her.

If you're going to be nervous that your message won't get

across when you're making a thank you phone call, you're likely to be in real difficulty when you have to call somebody up and hope they understand you need them to come deliver your baby. And if that isn't enough, this Amish husband is standing in a phone kiosk, his wife is at least a quarter of a mile away, and I start asking questions he doesn't know the answer to, like how far apart the contractions are and 'what fer else' would I want to know anyway. What he does know is that he's scared the baby's going to come roaring out of the channel before I get there to catch it. All of these things make him forget that his wife may not be the only woman in Lancaster County due to have a baby.

Not that I hadn't been waiting for the call from Elam Stoltzfus. Only a few days before I had been with Elam and Mary Stoltzfus in Stephen's office. We sat with our hands folded reasonably in our laps and decided what to do when Mary went into labor. She was likely to be early and by as much as three weeks; she always was, they told me. It always went fast but smoothly, and she wanted to have this baby at home. Stephen got up, walked casually over to the window, looked out for a moment, turned around, leant loosely against the wall, slipped his hands in his pockets casually the way doctors do when they're trying to tell you that some things that seem like life and death to the rest of us mortals are nothing at all to be concerned about.

'I can't think why you shouldn't have this baby at home,' he said.

I can, I said to myself, unable to conceive of doing a home delivery unless conditions were textbook perfect.

What about the special risks of prematurity, Doc? I wanted to say. What about hypothermia? The baby might not stay warm enough (preemies don't have enough body fat to keep them warm). And what about Respiratory Distress Syndrome? ('Get the baby to special care,' is what the midwife's texts read.) And that was just for starters.

'There are, of course, some risks associated with prematurity,' Dr Kaufman went on, 'specifically hypothermia and

Respiratory Distress Syndrome . . .'

Mary and Elam listened and nodded thoughtfully. Mary was quiet, dark-eyed, soft-spoken and dutiful. She wouldn't panic; Mary wasn't the type to panic, I said to myself, anticipating the direction of this discussion. Mary's already had three babies. She probably delivers leaning against the wall with her hands slipped casually in her pockets. And her husband – take one look at him and you'd know everything was going to be all right. He appeared to be one of those men who could fix anything, make anything work – the type who could milk a cow and paint the barn at the same time. His children probably came out singing 'John Henry, he could hammer . . .'

'But these are unlikely to occur and I believe we are well equipped to handle them if they do,' he concluded.

Mary and Elam looked at each other for a moment and then Elam said, 'I believe we'll have our baby at home, then.' That was all. It was settled.

Naturally, I didn't sleep after that. Besides going over in my mind the subtleties of delivering a premature child, I had to stay awake to test my radio every five minutes.

The plan was that Elam would call me first, I would call Stephen, and we'd both go over to Mary's; but I would get there first because I was closer. I had memorized and practiced the route; I figured seven minutes. This was Mary's fourth baby; the last one had come in three hours – this one wasn't likely to take much longer.

The night the call came was bitter cold; ice crept all over the roads. I hadn't planned on icy roads in late April. It took me about 15 minutes to get to Mary's house, instead of seven.

My headlights flickered on the ice that had formed on the gravel in the drive. Elam came to the door, poker in his hand. Thinking it was going to be a normal spring night, he'd let the stove die way down, and when I got there at about 3.30 he was stoking it up. He apologized.

The kitchen was starting to warm up, but the bedroom –

way in the back corner of the house – was still freezing. Walking through the dark hallways to the bedroom, I prayed for time; but after one look at Mary I gave that up. The baby was waiting neither for warmer weather nor for Dr Easy Does It.

I had on my down vest and long johns and so I stopped noticing the cold quickly enough. As for Mary, well, you can't be cold when you're pushing out a baby; it's impossible. And I suppose we managed to keep Elam running back and forth for one thing and another so that he stayed warm. Anyway, by the time baby Joel's brow showed, we had all forgotten how awfully cold it was in that bedroom.

Until his little body followed. He weighed only five and a half pounds and as I lifted him and went to set him on his mother's stomach, I saw steam rising from his body like breath from a horse's nostrils in the dead of winter.

I threw a blanket over him, reached under it, clamped and cut the cord in one move, bundled him and handed him to his father. 'You go downstairs and you hold this baby over the stove.' Elam smiled, put his giant farmer's paw under the wee bundle, stuffed it affectionately in the corner of his arm, and started out towards the kitchen. 'It is very important for the baby to stay warm,' I said with great firmness.

I heard no crunching of the gravel, saw no headlights through the bedroom window. Dr Kaufman was nowhere to be seen.

I stayed with Mary to deliver the afterbirth, got rid of the wet and bloody sheets, wrapped them up, washed her, helped her change her gown, tucked the blankets up under her chin and went downstairs to find Elam and the baby. It had been about 20 minutes.

I'll never forget the sight in that kitchen. Everything was in order, as usual. There was the kerosene lantern going on the kitchen table. Elam was standing in the middle of the kitchen in the halo of warm light, a grin on his face, sweat pouring down his face in a stream, his arms outstretched straight over the coal stove and the wee baby held in his hands above it, like a blessed offering.

'I guess if he's warm as me, he'd be warm enough' was all he said.

Dr Kaufman's car had skidded on the ice and he got stuck for a while in a ditch. He came in about the time the back bedroom began to warm up.

Joel's four now and thriving.

9

The Country Hospital

By telling you about Mary and Elam and how Stephen didn't make it until after their baby was born, I'm afraid I might be giving you the wrong impression of him. As I said, Stephen is a fine doctor. His decision to do the delivery at home was a sound one and his not getting there in time was just one of those things that happens in a rural practice. We skid on ice, get stuck in snowbanks, our beepers go haywire, we drop our supply of sterile gloves on the path leading up to a house.

Take, for instance, another delivery, on another freezing night, that became nothing less than a series of emergencies. The mother, whom I had carefully interviewed in my office, chose the last minute to remember to reveal to me that she hemorrhaged after her births. She waited for just a second or two to let that sink in and then she delivered a baby who didn't want to start breathing. I called the ambulance and though fearing the mother might start to bleed at any moment, I had to begin working on resuscitating the baby. I carried him to a spot near the stove. Like that night at Elam and Mary's, I had on my down jacket, only in this case I had it on simply because I hadn't had a chance to take it off.

So I kneeled in front of the stove, sweat pouring off my body the way sweat poured off Elam's, breathing for the baby, and every now and then skipping a beat to call into the other room, 'Is she bleeding at all?' She wasn't.

This went on for about seven minutes, until the emergency crew arrived. I didn't have to call in to the other room any-more, but I did have to go on breathing for the baby for another 13 minutes.

The little fellow, so long pleaded with, so long breathed for, was finally convinced to join us, and he then took vigorous hold. Within minutes he was pink and warm; his reflexes were excellent. We relaxed for about 30 seconds, everyone rejoiced about the baby's liveliness, then I waved off the emergency crew, reached into my bag for a prefilled Pitocin syringe so I could give the poor mother a shot and she could more quickly deliver her afterbirth. The Pitocin, having been out in my car under the icy sky, was frozen solid. No matter, I thought. I would simply put the syringe on the stove for a moment to melt the liquid inside while I went over to check the mother.

I put the syringe on the corner of the stove, went into the other room to the mother, felt her uterus, talked to her for a few moments and by the time I got back to the syringe it had been transformed into a molten, bubbling puddle on top of the stove.

That's the sort of mistake that teaches us to be humble in our work.

I was able to stimulate the uterus by massaging it from the outside, and she delivered the placenta with no difficulty, although more slowly than she would have with the Pitocin.

As we were cleaning up I asked her why she supposed she hadn't hemorrhaged.

'It's simple,' she said with downcast eyes. 'I was too scared.'

Stephen was a genuine ally.

When I accepted the job with him, we agreed that I would immediately apply for hospital privileges, that he would sponsor my application and energetically support it. We both knew there would be opposition from the other doctors, but we also felt it could be managed.

Getting privileges was important to me. I had told Stephen that I had no great desire to do home births. 'Every single baby,' I said with great conviction, 'deserves optimal birth conditions.' At the time, I felt strongly that a hospital was more likely to provide those conditions.

I must say that after I knew Country Hospital* better, I was less absolute. I hadn't practiced in a level-one hospital, like Country Hospital, before coming to Lancaster County and so I didn't fully appreciate their limitations. Designed to serve rural areas, level-one hospitals are equipped to give only the most basic care. They tend to have more general specialists working in them: internists or cardiologists. An important part of their expertise is in emergency intervention and referral.

At Country Hospital, then, there was a room for delivery and there was one for surgery; there were nurses, needles and telephones. They did have a fetal monitor, a gift from a local benefactor, but no one knew how to use it, so it was parked in a remote basement closet with its plastic cover still on. There was no intensive care nursery, no pediatrician, no obstetrician, no neonatal specialist. If a baby was in danger, you had to rush him or her to the level-two hospital, Infants and Children's Hospital, 50 minutes away.

The big advantage in having a maternity patient in Country Hospital, from what I could tell, was that she was closer to emergency surgery, should it be needed. That and the fact that, for the professional, the hospital is a reassuring, supportive environment; you are surrounded by a system that has been invented to help you give care. If I were, for example, to do something reckless like rest a plastic syringe of Pitocin on a hot radiator, there would not only be other

*I want to remind the reader that I've invented the name of this and every other hospital in the book except for Booth. I've also changed the names of places and, with the exceptions mentioned in the preface, people's names. I have no interest in exposing a particular institution, because I don't believe individual institutions are the issue; the issue is a philosophy and style of care that is, in my experience, found in many hospitals today.

syringes of Pitocin to replace it, but there would be someone to go for them and someone to clean up after me.

Anyway, I wanted to do midwife-attended hospital deliveries and I wanted to be able to stay with home birth patients who, in an emergency, might have to be transported through the surgery doors – a barrier I couldn't cross without privileges.

So immediately after I arrived in Paradise, we made our application and they – that is, some of the doctors – began their resistance.

Stephen threw himself into our side of the effort. He got himself seated on the proper committees. He showed them data proving that midwives are good for babies and mothers. I don't remember exactly what evidence we chose to include, but it's likely we cited a rural Madera County, California, project in which the death rate for newborns dropped by more than half when nurse-midwives practiced. We educated, we wrote letters and we answered questions. We documented my education, training, licensure and skills. Stephen took his colleagues to lunch. He put on a gigantic poolside party (complete with cameo appearance by the highly respected Dr Ruth in her wheelchair), so that the doctors and their wives could meet me in pleasant surroundings.

After five months of effort, we succeeded in getting a resolution passed that gave me privileges to practice in the hospital as an 'allied health professional'. We went out to dinner to celebrate.

And the next morning we read the newspaper account: 'Midwife Joins Hospital Staff, Five Doctors Quit.' That is, they gave up their staff privileges; they refused to work in a hospital that allowed me to work. One of the physicians was quoted as saying that he just felt the decision was 'a step backwards'. He implied that care from a midwife was lower-quality care, that it was somewhat primitive.

Now that was absurd. Aggravating and infuriating, too. But basically absurd. Of all the arguments one might level at midwifery, that one, applied as it was to the nurse-midwife practising in a hospital setting, is poorest. Think about it: the hospital is there and the doctor is just down the hallway. The midwife, an expert in normal labor and delivery, stays by the mother's side for the course of labor the way a nurse can't (the nurse has half a floor to patrol), and the way a doctor can't (the doctor's overhead would never allow it and, besides, it's a waste of skills). If anything looks irregular, the midwife can push a button and all the high-tech intervention available can come rolling in the door.

But he said it, and, of course, everybody started to wonder if maybe it's true: maybe midwives are a throwback; maybe they practice with hangers and fishhooks; maybe they do wear layers of petticoats that they never change. Oh, they might tear them up occasionally and stuff a strip or two into a mother's mouth to keep her quiet, but they don't take them off, wash them and hang them in the sun to dry. Have you heard that midwives never pare their fingernails except into cauldrons of swamp brew?

I lost my temper.

In calmer moments, I understood the doctor to be saying that midwives were not highly trained enough to orchestrate the array of machinery and drugs that were necessary, in his opinion, to deliver babies.

We had to try to answer the challenge – that midwifery was lesser care – even though we knew it meant beating through a tangle of misconceptions about women, medicine and childbirth. We now understood that our statistical demonstration that the midwife-attended childbirth was healthier for the mother (not to mention less costly) was wholly insufficient. The resistance to midwifery was more than a century deep; it went back to when science and technology were first applied to health care.

Let me explain. It used to be that midwives – female midwives – attended births. Their training was informal, that is, handed down from midwife to midwife and learnt through experience. Their therapies were herbs, their interventions during labor were walking, positioning, massaging and perhaps bathing.

Then, in a development independent of midwifery, came the application of science and technology to the healing arts. Then came modern medicine and with it the rise of the physicians in a profession dominated by men. Medicine and male physicians gradually engulfed midwifery.

The overtaking was gradual, of course, and if you dip into the past, you'll find times when female midwives had more patients than male physicians and times when things were in balance. There was even a period when American doctors were advocating the kind of system Dr Kaufman and I wanted to install at Country Hopital in the 1970s.

> From 1750 to approximately 1810 American doctors conceived of the new midwifery as an enterprise to be shared between themselves and trained midwives. Since doctors during most of that period were few in number, their plan was reasonable and humanitarian and also reflected their belief that, in most cases, natural processes were adequate and the need for skilled intervention limited, though important. Doctors therefore envisaged an arrangement whereby trained midwives would attend normal deliveries and doctors would be called to difficult ones.*

That didn't come to pass. Instead, we Americans became more enamoured of technology and we American women, for complex reasons, became more passive in childbirth. Male doctors started taking all their tools and tricks, including forceps and cesarean sections, and applying them liberally (under the name of advancement) to passive women – made more malleable by the introduction of anesthesia.

*Richard W. and Dorothy C. Wertz, *Lying In: A History of Childbirth in America* (New York: The Free Press, a Division of Macmillan Inc., 1977)

Americans, more than people in other cultures, were enamoured of technology and intervention in childbirth, and we got in the habit of intervening so much that the natural birth process became masked and we, the whole society, began to think of 'birth as a potential disease.'* When that doctor at Country Hospital 'just felt' that midwifery represented a lower level of care, he was expressing a commonly held belief. He, and much of the rest of America, treat birth as if it were pathogenic, that is, as if something were wrong, as if it required corrective action, not to mention rescue. And, of course, midwives are not doctors.

Stephen Kaufman and I tried to explain that midwives attended normal births, that a major part of their professional training was in learning to screen out high-risk patients, and that they always had doctors backing them up. By demonstration, by articulation and by our patience, we tried to explain.

At least we could tackle that doctor's objections; it had some substance buried in it. The other arguments just wore us down. Another doctor was quoted as saying that he objected to the decision because of some procedural flaw in the decision-making process; and another implied that you only used midwives when you didn't have enough doctors.

Stephen stayed with the effort, soothing, talking, educating. In newspaper interviews he spoke politely and patiently. He explained that many physicians hadn't had the opportunity to understand nurse-midwifery, or other allied health professionals, for that matter. He said he felt that once they had some firsthand experience they would accept these other professionals and find their skills useful.

Meanwhile, I tried to do my part. I remained well groomed, cheerful and professional; I answered all the questions the newspaper reporters asked me, factually, pleasantly and simply. I explained that doctors and midwives did do

*Ibid., p.236.

things differently – that we were more likely to have a woman up and moving around during labor; that we would give her something to eat; that we were less likely to use medication and technology; and that we were less likely to cut the opening of the birth canal. Instead, we worked the tissue and stretched it.

I worked in the hospital. I behaved. I was quiet and unobtrusive in my practice. They gave me a small room for natural childbirth and they allowed my women to walk the halls and let me give them something light to eat so they could keep their energy up. I didn't do shaves and enemas routinely, I did fewer episiotomies than doctors and I was delighted not to hook women up to the machinery because it prevented them from walking around and that helps keep a labor moving along.

Both Stephen and I believed that if we did a good job, if we were reliable, if we didn't make much of a scene, then the hospital and its doctors would realize we meant no harm and midwives could, with appropriate intervention by physicians, give mothers excellent care. We believed that women would actually be attracted to Country Hospital because it had midwifery services.

But the resistance held. One of Stephen's colleagues virtually abandoned his practice so he could devote full time to the cause. He filled a briefcase with midwife horror stories and stood at the front door of the hospital and handed them out as the doctors came in to work.

And the more I thought about it, the more peculiar the resistance seemed to me.

After all, Country Hospital was not a high-tech, high-intervention hospital. It was unusually simple and probably because of the people it served. A great many of the people who used Country Hospital were Mennonite families; certainly, Mennonite farm women dominated the labor and delivery patients.

Some of the doctors were Mennonite, too, and they

seemed to be less enamoured of technology and more humble about their own skills. One of my most vivid memories in that hospital was watching one particular Mennonite surgeon prepare to perform a cesarean section. He would, each time before he cut, lift his scalpel – delicate instrument that it is, capable of saving the baby and mother, capable also of cutting a wound across the face of the unborn child – and hold it for a moment, poised on the tips of his thumb and forefinger. He regarded it ritually before he dropped his hand to cut. I liked to think he was investing the scalpel with a prayer.

I was working in a hospital where technology and intervention were not dominant; where the habits were not to over-anesthetise, not to overcut, not to overdoctor women at childbirth. Yet even here, the doctors were foaming like mad dogs because a midwife was delivering babies.

That five doctors quit the hospital just to protest my practice surprised me and then, as months went by and I delivered babies quietly and healthily and still the battle raged, I began to realize that the reaction to my presence was far greater than the apparent threat. This was not a thoughtful acting out of society's debate on intervention and quality of care. This went to the root.

I believe now that many male doctors simply did not want a woman, especially a nondoctor, doing life-and-death work. By my success in giving good care, I was regularly showing that the doctors' knowledge was not sacred knowledge, that it was not inscrutable to all but the high priesthood of physicians.

Then, too, I was taking fees they thought should have been theirs. And finally, I was taking from them the power to control women who were having babies.

I remember talking to one doctor at Stephen's poolside party. A charming talker and a literate man, he loved especially to talk about himself. 'From the moment we enter medical school,' he said, 'we are trained to think we are gods.'

10

In the Fields

When I first moved to Lancaster County, I camped out in an apartment. I threw a mattress on the floor and slept in a snarl of bedclothes. I swam laps at the rec center every day to keep my nerves from igniting and then rushed to the whirlpool. Usually I had the little whirlpool room to myself and I'd turn the power on to dynamo strength, take a deep breath, and dive into a tuck at the bottom of the small plastic tub, where I vanished for a merciful 45 seconds into a warm, pulsing, pounding, rolling, tingling vortex of nothingness. In the beginning in Lancaster, while I was on trial for a murder they were hoping I would commit, I had to calculate and recalculate every action, every decision, every attitude, twitch and gesture of my body and face. My sanctuary was one minute of oblivion in a swirl of shooting bubbles.

Richie came to see me. He never said anything more about my leaving Philadelphia and, in fact, I'm not even sure he thought about it anymore. We were both shocked by what I'd done. Shocked and sobered.

We had thought we were only talking dreams, talking as lovers, we had thought our conversation flowed because of finding each other, we had thought we were suspending belief. Why should we, away from one another, opening the car door, sending away applications, or putting away the silverware, be convinced that I would stay with my enraptured vision of working as a midwife?

When I drove out to Lancaster County that first time, I

should have known better. It was clear to me that my being a midwife for these people had always been true; this part of my life had been waiting for me. All the suspense, the anticipation, the agonizing decisions, the wondering if I was or was not going to make it, had been mere accompaniments, diversions and embellishments, which distracted me and made me believe I had some choice in the matter, when in fact I had none. Quite simply, I had come home.

I believe Richie felt it, too. When he eventually came out to find me, to figure out how to share a life with me under these circumstances, he was conceding humbly to an absolute.

It couldn't have been that easy for him, making the adjustment. He hadn't wanted any change and now here I was putting every morsel of my being into thinking of how to handle the problems of home deliveries, into keeping calm and behaving while I was at the hospital, and into planning strategies to win over infuriated doctors. That didn't leave much of me for him.

Yet, within a few weeks he began looking for places to live between the airport at north Philly and the delivery room at Country Hospital. When he grew tired of hunting for rooms, he'd come and see me.

Sometimes I took him with me on house calls. I got him used to following buggies on the road and to the point where he, like me, began to hope one would appear in front of us and we'd be forced, like the buggy passengers, to go slow and look out the window.

One house in particular fascinated me. It was a regular two-story farmhouse with a broad low porch across the front and a massive oak tree spreading protectively over the front yard. The first time I passed the house I saw a bent, skeletal figure in the yard. She stood so still as to seem hung in the air beneath the tree. She wore a bonnet and an Amishwoman's dress, but was so frail that her body seemed to be of neither sex.

Unlike all other Amish farmhouses, which gleam with fresh white paint, hers was gray. Instead of the usual green garden chairs on the front porch, there was a couch with humps on it where springs were breaking through. The outbuildings were covered with tar paper instead of white siding.

I made a point to go by the house whenever I could. Obviously the woman who lived there was ill and poor, but there was something about the house that made it different. It haunted me, but not in a bad way. I was drawn to it as if something special and good were there.

I eventually realized it was the way the place was kept. The lawn, balding though it was, was trimmed crisply each week; its edges were barbered like any prosperous lawn. The tar paper on the outbuildings was patched in squares, each one nailed neatly into place; there were no ragged edges flying in the wind. The small garden was maintained. The window shades were drawn evenly each morning. The place was immaculate.

On these roads, apparently, poverty failed to poison either dignity or responsibility. Here one tended the little that one might have with as much discipline and order as one tended the much that one might have. Being stewards of the earth as the Amish say they are apparently meant being a steward of any part thereof, however great or small. Of course, the woman couldn't have done the work herself. Her family and her neighbours must have done it.

I drove Richie by that house.

During the first summer months that I was in the County, Richie and I would drive during the day and then, when the sky turned its usual, amazing mothwing pink, we'd go for a walk through the covered bridge to an old stone mill. We'd sit and listen to the water slip by and wait for the legions of fireflies to arise, court and bedazzle one another among the rushes.

Then we'd go home and eat roast chicken. I'd got into the habit of roasting a chicken for Richie. Elmer Ebersol started that.

One of our first times out, I took Richie over to make a house call on Elmer's wife, figuring that he would want to kill a chicken for us. Elmer was happy with the way his wife was treated before his baby was born and to show it he had started bringing me a chicken every time he brought her in for an appointment. In the last month before she delivered, I'd stop by the house to check her – it was too long a ride in a buggy to our office for a woman eight months pregnant – and sure enough, Elmer would put aside what he was doing and go out and get me a chicken while I waited.

I had barely pulled in the driveway and introduced my friend Richard Armstrong when Elmer, Amish romantic, said he thought I might want to roast a chicken for my friend the airline pilot. There was more than a hint there that if I did that up right, Richie might be willing to marry me.

'Would you like me to kill you a chicken?'

'If you'll let me give you a hand,' said Richie, who knew how to be well mannered on a farm.

Elmer leant against the car. 'You sure you want to?' he said, looking at the city slicker and letting a slow smile unfold over his face.

'Why, yes. I believe I would,' said Richie, getting more laconic by the word.

'A lot of folks lose their interest in eating chickens after they've seen one killed,' Elmer said.

'I guess I'll take my chances,' said Richie, and we followed Elmer into the house so that he could tell his wife to get the water boiling. At Elmer's house, the chicken-killing chores are divided up this way: Elmer's wife boils the water, gets instructions from the midwife on how to tend to the new baby, and keeps the older children occupied by allowing them to crawl all over the back of the sofa to the windowsill, where they can see kittens playing outside in the tree. Elmer's mother, Elizabeth, called Lizzie, comes over from her adjoining house. Lizzie makes the decisions on chicken-killing matters and she also cleans the chickens. Elmer catches the chicken, drops the hatchet on its neck and does anything else he's told.

Richie and Elmer disappeared outside, and pretty soon Elmer came back in, saying that they'd captured the chicken and didn't I want to see Richie tying it up? I could tell I was supposed to be the audience for this affair, so out I went, to see Richie putting the last bow knot in the legs of the chicken.

It's hard not to love a man who can catch and bind a chicken.

Next thing I know, Elmer picks up the stunned chicken and lays its bitty white neck right between two ordinary nails hammered into a log. Thwock.

The head went to one side and the body of the chicken, blood spurting out of its neck, to the other. Its wings flapped, it ran around, and the bloody fountain gushed while Richie and Elmer calmly talked. I turned my back and walked around the farmyard for a few minutes. Make of it what you will, I do not care for the sight of blood. Elmer went on talking about how his mother was an expert with chickens. She'd been gutting them since she was a child; the family used to make part of their living that way. They'd load their chickens on the back of a wagon and drive it right through Intercourse, selling chickens off the back as they went.

Couldn't do that anymore, that's for sure. So many regulations about refrigeration. A farmer couldn't afford to keep up with those regulations.

Lizzie had come out by then and she sent Elmer to fetch the boiling water, which he did. She told him to pour it into the tub and he did, and then she dunked the chicken into the scalding water.

I remembered that smell pretty well from when I was a kid, and I guess Richie must have, too, but neither one of us said a word. We both bent down and started pulling off feathers in hunks. When that was done, we backed off. Lizzie did the innards.

She pulled out the windpipe, careful to cut it clean at the bottom first; then she scraped off that gland at the tail – she wasn't sure what it was or why the chicken pecked at it, but her dad had told her to cut that off right away, so she always did. She was careful in handling the stomach; if you were careful, she said, you could pull out the lining of the stomach and its contents all in one fell swoop and that was more pleasant for everybody. 'Do be careful to cut out the place where the throat tube connects to the stomach,' she went on. 'A lot of people get upset when they recognize a hole in something they're eating.'

I tried to show enthusiasm for the gizzard and the heart and the lining of the stomach; I even initiated a search through the entrails to find a missing lung, which Lizzie wished to comment on. Then we rinsed the whole thing off and Lizzie directed Richie and Elmer to go off and bury the entrails in the yard.

The Ebersol family scurried about, gathering up corn, pole beans, lettuce and cantaloupe to go with our roaster, and then they stood around in the farmyard – old Lizzie, Elmer and his wife, each one with a baby in their arms – and waved us off.

Richie used to say that going around with me was like being a groupie. It's true. When the midwife arrived, children would start crawling out from holes and corners of the houses, barns and other outbuildings. Sooner or later their father would appear, smiling happily like I'd done him a big personal favor. The mother and I would start the conversation. The children stood around smiling shyly, they'd giggle and the small ones would tug at the larger ones' dresses. After you visited for a while, you were a member of the family.

I remember when Richie and I went over to visit Rebecca and Reuben just a few hours after baby Benjamin was born.

That was late in the summer – a busy time to have a baby, what with filling silo.

As we walked up to the house, we watched the mounded loads of corn jouncing along to the silo on a flatbed wagon. We watched the three gleaming, thick-limbed horses – their flesh the color of the earth and the earth the color of gold dust. The warm, juicy smell of the cut stalks filtered through the yard.

Another wagon was in the field working the rows. Another team pulled it and right alongside it there was a binder – a machine that cuts the corn stalks, lays them down in clumps on a short conveyer belt, binds the clumps with twine and then dumps the bound clumps into a waiting Amishman's arms. The corn stalks are cut one by one; the teams go about the field in one direction, working in a square, in the dust, patiently going row by row by row. Standing on the back of the wagon, even for an afternoon, you begin to see the land intimately, as if it were the palm of someone's hand – with wrinkles, cavities and mounds.

The binder, as I said, is pulled alongside the wagon by the horses; its blade is powered by a small gasoline engine. Reuben, who looks more like a rabbi than an Amish farmer, loped back and forth along the back of the flatbed wagon, catching the clumps of corn as they came off the binder at the front end, carrying them to the far end of the wagon, and stacking them there.

Dr Kaufman had done the delivery that morning while I'd been on another delivery. Well he didn't actually 'do' the delivery. This baby, the sixth in the family, a 10-pounder, and the first boy, had things pretty well under control. They said the baby had insisted on cleaning up after himself, but Dr Kaufman felt he should do something to earn his pay.

When we arrived Rebecca was lying on the couch. She was dressed in her Amish blue dress, the green shades were all pulled way up, the windows were open and white sheer curtains luffed in the summer air. She seemed slightly subdued, but otherwise no different from the Rebecca who'd been putting up apple sauce two days before when I'd stopped by.

I'd just picked up the baby when the other children came flocking in, raising a cloud of dust and noise about their father. The oldest girl had taken over the management of the house. She had magnificent dark, intelligent eyes, natural elegance and poise. She looked like she should be the doctor. On the outside – among the English – she would become a doctor or lawyer or college professor, probably the latter. When she was younger, her mother said, she'd sneak off to the barn and read books instead of doing her chores. 'She's learnt better now,' her mother said. 'She doesn't do that anymore. Her sister does it and now this one knows what it's like to miss a pair of hands.'

Two of the little girls tumbled onto the couch near their mother, boring instinctively towards her lap. She restrained them from a direct attack on her belly, patted them and talked to them in Pennsylvania Dutch, the language the Amish use in their homes. The remaining toddler, unwilling to make the dart in front of us to get to her mother, glommed onto her father's leg and all but strapped herself to it.

The younger children, having found their respective safe corners, stared at Richie and me with steady concentration. To be sure, they do not see or talk to that many English and we must have seemed very strange to them. Think of the elementary facts – my hair is short, short as Richie's sometimes; I often wear pants; I talk fast; I make faces that Amish women don't make; I drive around in a car. And the toddlers would know, in some dim way, that I (or Richie and I) was associated with this new baby, and they must have been assembling the pieces: new baby, English woman, small case, mother's flattened stomach. Perhaps I had something to do with the baby being a boy. Jesus came in there somewhere, too, they knew. Jesus brought babies. Bewildering.

The older children, having had several opportunities in their lives to get the puzzle pieces together, stood quietly with sage little cat smiles on their faces.

Richie spoke up.

'Filling silo, are you?' he said to Reuben.

'Yeh. Picked my day, didn't I?'

'Can I help?' Richie asked.

'Can you drive a team? One of the men has to go off this afternoon.'

'With some instruction, I believe I could,' and Richie followed Reuben out to the fields.

I had not seen many women like Rebecca yet; I guess there probably aren't many Rebeccas in the world, not in any population. She was a master of her profession, a housewife and mother of perfect grace. Soft-spoken and unprepossessing, she directed this intimate multitude deftly and joyfully. She had simple dignity and invisible but formidable strength.

Would somebody please bring her something to eat? Cornflakes and a sandwich maybe?

It was 1.30 in the afternoon and she'd already done a morning's work, including having a baby, and it was about time she wanted her breakfast and lunch. The two older girls vanished round the corner to prepare the food.

The cornflakes were quite soggy when they arrived and there was purple stuff glopped all over the top of them. This was grape slush – concentrated grape juice. It appears on all manner of incompatible but otherwise fine food in Amish households. I began considering a vow never to watch an Amish woman eat her first meal after a delivery. Stewed placenta is one thing, decomposing cornflakes with grape sauce is another.

The sandwich came out. Peanut butter and jelly, she'd said. I saw the brown layer and the red layer, one for peanut butter, one for jelly. What was that white layer oozing out between the brown and the red? It was a mayonnaise layer.

I turned away, went to the window and looked out. Richie was standing, legs bent loosely at the knees, at the front end of the flatbed wagon, a mountain of corn listing from side to side as he guided the team down the lane. He tugged the reins and the team went around the corner of the field and towards the silo.

Rebecca, meanwhile, must have realized that the children had gone wrong with the mayonnaise because she soon called for a piece of bologna (our salami). 'Don't try to starve me,' she said. 'I can eat the kitchen clean.' I didn't know how she was going to make the correction in the sandwich, but at least she had all the right parts now: peanut butter to go with the jelly; and bologna to go with the mayonnaise.

She stuffed the bologna right into the sandwich, cheek by jowl with the peanut butter and jelly. She was such a graceful person, a woman of such dignity. Why was she doing this to her food?

One of the children asked for a bite. Another one had to show her mother a toy. Ruthie, the second-oldest girl, came to ask where the box of crocheted hot pads were; two or three other questioners came and went. Rebecca spooned food in her mouth as she could.

These women do not get much of a break from their responsibilities. I remember saying loudly to one woman shortly after she had given birth. 'Why, you look so good, you could jump right up and get back to your chores.'

She looked at me very crossly. 'Hush. Don't you let a soul hear you say that. I feel just fine and I intend to enjoy myself lying here; this is the only vacation I get in a year.'

Rebecca's cornflakes were mush, I tell you, warm, spongy mush. The woman could endure anything.

I could see Richie jumping off the wagon. He was now unloading the bound clumps of corn stalks and dropping them on a short conveyer belt. The belt carried the stalks forwards through a modest opening into a narrow metal chamber, which was fixed with a mouthful of whirring, glistening blades. The blades shredded the corn and stalks, and then a blower shot the cut silage right up to the top of the silo. The whole business was powered by a tractor motor, to which a belt was attached.

An Amishman will use a tractor this way, for its power, but not to work his fields or get from one place to another.

Rebecca, who hadn't finished her cornflakes, now asked for a chocolate cupcake. Well deserved. Wise choice, I thought, assuming the woman would politely set the unfinished food aside, letting her children realize the inadequacy of the meal without faulting them in front of an outsider. The oldest daughter brought the cupcake. Rebecca stripped it of its paper cup, broke it in half, and dropped it directly in the cornflake-grape slush swamp.

That appeared to be the ticket, for she energetically cleaned up the contents of the green bowl and began vigorously scraping away at the bottom of her plate – a traditional ending to meals among the Amish. She smiled enthusiastically. I sighed.

I left in a short while, waving at Richie in the fields with the draft horses. Just think, my Richie the airline pilot and three Amishmen bringing in the crops.

When I came to pick him up later he told me that the boy at the next farm over had an accident while he was working with the corn chopper. He was dead.

I thought about how Richie had been feeding the chopper.

'Seems like if the corn gets stuck on the conveyor belt, the only thing to do is to step over onto the belt and jump up and down to loosen things up. Thing is, if you don't jump off in time, or if your foot gets caught among the stalks, then you fall and get sucked right into the opening and your legs get chewed up right with the corn stalks.' Richie paused and looked at me. 'Doesn't take long to bleed to death when your whole leg's whacked off,' he said.

I tried to be matter of fact: 'How old was the boy?'

'Fourteen or fifteen, I guess. He's the youngest in his family. It was his first year working full time in the fields. There'll be a viewing tomorrow night. I told Reuben I'd be happy to drive them over.'

11

The Viewing

I was over on Stone Mill Road making a house call the day I had my first viewing. I think it must have been soon after I got to Lancaster because it was spring. My patient had just had her first baby girl and thought that she was the most wonderful thing in the world, and that I was a close second. I was basking in my destiny.

So I was in this woman's kitchen wiping cookie crumbs off my face and hugging and chatting with the fat baby on my knee, when an Amishwoman knocked abruptly at the door and walked in. Her face said nothing. It had that flat look, the one the women use when they're shopping in Intercourse, the one that means, 'Don't come near me.'

By this time I understood the function of the look: it's a way of keeping distance. The Amish use it occasionally among their own, that is, with certain private situations; and they use it regularly with the rest of us. They do not wish the world to know their problems or their joys or even their shopping list; they do not elect to concern themselves with the world.

The woman asked me if I were Dr Penny, which is what some call me. I said I was and she said, 'Maybe you'll be stopping over at Sarah Riehl's on your way home?'

Sarah was eight months pregnant with her second child. Every indicator was healthy. I couldn't imagine why she would have anything wrong, but I'd learnt by this time not to ask questions in this sort of situation, mainly because I wouldn't have gotten answers.

You see, Amish do not acknowledge one another's pregnancies. No one has told me why; it's 'just their way'. When I first came, I would say to my women – who keenly loved news of one another's families – 'Do you know so-and-so over in Leola? She's got the same due date as you do.'

And they would look at me as if not understanding a word and turn away.

Finally one of the older women grabbed me by the ear and took me aside for instruction. 'Hush, dear, we won't be needing any talk about who is going to have a baby. You'll have to learn to stay quiet until after the babies are born.'

I had a pair of sisters who rode together 45 minutes in their buggy to Stephen's office for antepartum checks and 45 minutes back to their houses together every month. Day came that the first one delivered, I was sitting on the bed, tucking a baby girl into a pink receiving blanket, and I said to the new mother – figuring an exception would be made in this case – that I wondered whether her sister might be having the twin to this one that same day.

I might as well have suggested that we all go out ice skating. 'Now what would you mean by that?' she said, and from then on I conformed to their way exactly.

When the Amishwoman came to say wouldn't I be stopping by at Sarah's, I could only assume it had something to do with her pregnancy and that it was an urgent matter. It meant 'Sarah's pregnant and she's in trouble. Go now.'

I left quickly, nothing spoken, everything understood, and drove to Sarah's. The barnyard was jammed with buggies and more were turning in. Team after team were hauling husbands and wives to somebody's parlour when everyone had fields to plant.

I parked my car in the forest of black buggies and went to the side of the main house. Sarah and her husband, Joel, as is typical for a young couple, didn't have the main house. They were living in the addition, the part that had been added at some time or another for somebody's parents. These 'grossdaadi' houses are typical in Amish country. The old people, the grandmas and grandpas, when they retire from farming, move out of the central house – the one that's built for six and seven children and for having church for 50 and weddings for 150 – and into an attached apartment. Actually, it's a smaller version of the central house. It's got built-in china closets and everything.

Sarah and Joel had one of these smaller versions. It was fully equipped. Besides the shiny linoleum kitchen floor, on which all Amish home life takes place, besides the china closet, the scrubbed countertop and shining sink, the long table for eating on, for cutting out squares for quilts, for shelling beans and folding clothes, for changing babies – besides all this there was, centered on the long wall of the room, Sarah's clock, the one that Joel gave her when she agreed to marry him. (Girls will not say they are engaged, but they will say they've got their clock.) Over a small sink in the corner was a mirrored cabinet and below it a rod with a towel hanging from it. The towel – white and elaborately embroidered with green thread – was wrapped in a plastic covering. She would have given it to him as her token when she accepted the clock. Also on the wall there was a lumber store calendar that had a photograph of a stream running through a glen; there was a board with hooks and dowels for guests' hats and cloaks; there was a blue felt painting, which had Joel's name on it and Sarah's and the name and birthdate of their first child. There was plenty of space left underneath the first child's name.

Joel worked at the farm here where they were living and he was learning blacksmithing to make more money so they could get a place of their own. What with all that to do, Joel still always brought Sarah to the office in their buggy. Once they insisted on sneaking me out the back door to show me the buggy; it was lined with green crushed velvet and was equipped with a matching blanket. (Joel the rake, I began to call him, in memorial to his courting days. His hair was red and I could tell he trimmed his spiffy little beard.) He always asked if he could go into the examining room with his wife and he'd lean over the table, inspecting things, pointing out where the baby's elbow or bottom would raise his wife's belly like a mole raises the earth, and generally he asked a hundred questions about what was going on. He wasn't doing it like he was a plant manager, he wasn't checking to be sure I knew what I was doing; he just didn't control his curiosity and enthusiasm.

That's one difference between Amish and city people, especially those who are having home deliveries: the questions they ask. The Amish are reasonable.

I think it's because they're used to the idea of birth and to taking care of things at home. It's a home- and family-centered culture, and the way they have babies is an extension of the way they live. Newborns, for example, live the early months of their lives on the kitchen table – everybody passing by talking to them, squeezing their tummies, picking them up for a bit of carry-around. If the baby's awake, you'll find him at the table for meals, his food stirred right up with the whipped potatoes, his swing sitting there next to the bench, his gurgles mingling idly with the silence and the talk of his brothers and sisters, his mother and father.

In a couple of years, he'll come running into his mother's room within a couple of hours after the new baby is born. Birth is routine: it doesn't happen every day, but it happens often; and it happens in the barnyard, so it's normal and people have an idea of what it's about and they ask a reasonable number of questions.

Joel and Sarah knew about having babies from their own experience, and Joel's curiosity about the whole thing was just that. He thought having a family was terrific.

Sarah was maybe 22. That day when I stopped by I found her standing quietly in her kitchen, her arms folded in front of her the way the women do. She was in black and she was surrounded by men and women dressed all in black. As the women arrived, they shook hands with the others and nodded. I stood there for a little while, pleading internally with somebody, anybody, to please tell me what to do. Finally, somebody came over.

'Joel was building a silo this morning with three other men. They were near done and Joel was up on top when the brickwork collapsed. He fell and was crushed. Must have died right away. We thought maybe you would check to see if Sarah was okay.'

Oh, sure. And I sucked my breath through my teeth.

About that time, the door swung open and in came six Amishmen carrying a wooden casket. Plain wood with a gray stain on it. They slid it onto the kitchen table, opened the lid, and the viewing started up. Believe it or not, I'd never seen a dead person. All that time in hospitals and no corpses. That had been just fine with me. And this wasn't just a dead person. This was Joel.

A couple of Amishmen walked over to the coffin, looked into it, said things like, 'Yep, that's Joel. Doesn't look like he felt a thing.' And, 'I suppose he has some questions saved up he'll be wanting to ask.' And then they stepped aside. I forced myself to get in line. What else could I do?

Sarah, seeing that I was quaking and pale, came and took me by the elbow as soon as I got past her husband. It had been Joel, all right, his red beard brushed up.

Sarah gestured for me to follow her.

When we got to the bedroom Sarah said that she wondered if I would check to see if the baby was all right. There was to be a full viewing tonight; hundreds would be coming. She wanted to know if the baby was all right and that it wouldn't hurt it. Calmly she lay down on the bed so I could examine her and listen to the baby's heartbeat. I did that and I asked her the right questions, but I couldn't concentrate. I was staring at the bed.

Not only had Sarah changed into black mourning clothes, not only had she made the house immaculate for the people

coming to the viewing, but she had removed the second pillow from her bed.

12

The Home Delivery

Over the months, I worked out the problems associated with home deliveries.

Take the ten-minute sterile scrub. I was accustomed to scrubbing in the hospital and, in spite of my impatience with it, I knew it was for good reason. One of the major discoveries of modern medicine was that women were dying in childbirth not because of having babies, but because of germs carried by the people helping them have their babies. Since that discovery, we have all scrubbed up to get the bugs out from under our fingernails and skin cells and, thereby, to keep the mother's wounds safe from infection.

Lying awake in those early months, tossing and turning at night, I figured out how to do a home-made sterile scrub. Even though there would be no nurse standing at attendance. I could still scrub for ten minutes at the kitchen sink, leave my hands dry in the air, take my gloves from their sterile packing and slip them on with minimum contamination.

That plan was good except if the baby started coming fast and if I needed something right now, something that lay deep in my medical bag, and something that could not possibly be described to an Amish farmer. Then my sterile scrub was in jeopardy. I tried to be careful, but I felt bad at the idea of having to commit infractions of my rules.

Then I went to a house where they had no running water. Now, here's the problem: I would have had to prime the pump, scrub up, prime the pump again with my elbow to get water for a better lather, scrub some more and prime the pump again with my elbow, and rinse my hands. And I was supposed to reserve enough strength to deliver a baby.

Not a chance.

I finally talked to a woman who also did backwoods deliveries and asked her, somewhat frantically, I admit, what she did about the sterile scrub.

'Think about it, dear,' she said in a kindly way. 'Where do the germs in the hospital come from? They don't come from healthy mothers, now, do they? Healthy mothers have their own immunities; they have immunities to their family members and to germs in their homes. Hospital germs do not come from homes and husbands, they come from people who are in the hospital because they are diseased.'

Oh, yeah. It dawned on me. Oh, yeah.

She went serenely on: 'Pump the water with your hands. Wash up with soap and water. Pump with your hands. Rinse your hands. Put on the sterile gloves before you do a vaginal exam, change them if you have to paw through your bag or go out to the barn, change them more frequently if your mother's got a tear, and stop worrying, dear.' She put her hand softly on my arm. 'Stop worrying. Women can have babies at home; they've been doing it for centuries.'

I saw virtually no postpartum infection among my home delivery patients.

My patients and I also survived emergencies. I had one terribly shy woman; she blushed at the slightest bit of attention. I had arrived when she was going into labor. I did my routine investigation and found the cord coming down before the baby.

Prolapsed umbilical cord. It means that as the baby's head moves down the birth canal, it presses against the cord, which carries life-supporting oxygen. As the baby's head moves even farther down, the pressure increases until the baby gets no oxygen. The mortality rate for a baby with a prolapsed cord is about 50 percent.

I would have to send the Amishman to phone for the emergency team, put my hand inside the mother's vagina, and push against the baby's head, holding it back from its descent, and hoping to keep it off the cord until somebody could do a c-section.

So I assigned tasks: he was to get things ready to go; I was to keep the head held back, and she was to pray. I told this woman, with all her painful modesty, that I was going to keep my hand in her vagina during the ride to the hospital and to surgery. She, looked me in the eye and, without a blush, said, 'Do what is necessary,' and I took a breath and inserted my hand into her. Then, to give us some privacy, I had her husband throw blankets over the two of us. I suppose we hoped we'd look like a bundle of laundry when we arrived at the emergency room door. We stayed that way, lumped together, while we got her on a stretcher, into the ambulance, and all the way to the hospital. She continued to have contractions. She never complained; and what's more, she never blushed.

I regret to say that when we arrived at the emergency room door, a brisk wind snatched away the blankets and left this poor woman and me peculiarly and nakedly attached, in the middle of a parking lot beneath the light of an illuminating moon.

I moaned.

She looked at me directly, as if to say, 'Don't you dare start up now.' What she actually said was 'Don't give it another thought.'

Fifteen minutes later she had a baby girl by cesarean section. I had held that baby back by continuous pushing for 40 minutes – up to the moment they put her on the delivery table and it wasn't until she was safely delivered that I remembered I'd been nursing a wrenched shoulder. I remember it vividly because that, probably more than anything, reassured me. Apparently, these things had been arranged so that strength would be there – both in my patients and in myself – when we needed it.

Eventually I noticed that my home delivery statistics were spectacular. I hardly did episiotomies. At first, I thought it was a fluke – that I'd had a run of women with Olympic-class birthing bodies. In those first months of doing home deliveries, Stephen and I nudged one another black and blue as we watched women, eight centimeters dilated (the baby drops out at ten centimeters), bending and bustling, stoking up the stove, making the bed, and stepping into the bathroom for a quick shower. We were used to English women, eight centimeters dilated, who believed they needed help to sip juice.

But the run kept on and I started looking at my Apgars. An Apgar is a rating scale that measures the condition of a newborn. You consider the baby's heartbeat rate, respiratory effort, muscle tone, reflex irritability and color, and you give the baby a number between one and ten. Remember all those flat babies in hospital? The ones that had to be suctioned, bagged and jiggled about? They averaged Apgars of five or six; my home birth babies: eight or nine.

I carried oxygen to bag the babies. I carried a DeLee's suction to clean out their air passages. I could do episiotomies. I could stitch up tears or cuts. I could give shots for pain. I could get emergency help when I needed it. I was just about positive that I could do anything for these women that a class-one hospital could do – not a big town, city hospital – but a class-one hospital like Country Hospital. It was getting to be a decided possibility that I could do it better.

I had a friend at one of the bigger hospitals in Philly who arranged for me to conduct an experiment. I thought if I could see a city hospital delivery now, as an anonymous observer, with nothing to do but think, record and evaluate, I would better understand my growing preference for these Amish home deliveries. Were they – as they seemed to be – better for the mother and baby? Or was I just infatuated with the gentle people?

My friend made it possible for me to watch a delivery. I was not to do anything; just watch.

At City Hospital, I entered into a vast room, brazenly white, with fluorescent panels overhead. Waxed floors, empty of humans, stretched away in the distance into disappearing arteries of linoleum. A floor buffer whirred in one of the corridors. Two or three women in white dresses and white caps were posed behind the massive, curving, chest-high desk that centered the room. Their heads turning in one uniform movement, their eyes followed me as I shuffled awkwardly towards the elevator.

I felt like a spy.

The maternity ward looked considerably friendlier. Bright yellow walls and rust-colored carpeting took the hospital edge off the hallways; a waiting room, fitted with a fish tank and trees, was relaxing.

I went to the lockers and changed into a pair of anonymous blue scrub pants and V-necked shirt. I'd get a hat and slippers, as would the father, before we went into the delivery room.

'She's at seven,' the duty nurse told me, as we walked back to the woman's room, 'but when they ruptured her membranes, the water was green, very green, very meconium, you know. I'm surprised they're willing to have an observer with that kind of a problem.'

Meconium-stained fluid meant that the baby had had a bowel movement while in the uterus and it could also indicate fetal distress. In my experience, however, if the heartbeat was good, real alarm was inappropriate. Many fine, healthy babies were delivered with meconium-stained fluid. Alertness, yes; alarm, no. In the hospital, meconium staining meant automatic intervention.

As we approached the room, I could hear the hollow pounding of a baby's heart – it sounded as if it were beating inside an empty refrigerator. The fetal heart monitor, a metal box standing on four metal legs, stood directly to our right as we walked into the room. It was attached to the infant by way of red and green wires that ran along the mound of the mother's stomach and disappeared into the birth canal.

The nurse turned first to the machine and, picking up the long strip of paper that issued from it, examined the graphed lines that ran its length. Absently she asked the mother how she was doing, absently she acknowledged the small sigh and a humble 'Okay', and then, finally, having satisfied herself with the paper, she turned her attentions to us. She introduced me, smiled at the father, and said something about things being just fine. He looked at me, winked to let me know that he had everything under control in here, and resumed watching the basketball game. For a moment, his wife tried to find me with her eyes, but gave up. The nurse adjusted the band, about two inches in width, that went the girth of the mother's belly. This belly band is another device to measure and record contractions. Like some of the other trucking tools, it inhibits the mother's movement and therefore tends to slow labor. The nurse patted the woman on the arm.

'The doctor will be here shortly,' she said, and then left.

The night before I went to City Hospital, I'd delivered Susie and Ephraim Glick's baby. Susie had a bunch of things yet to do before she had her fourth baby, and she was especially determined to get into a quick bath. She had her husband running here and there, looking for some plastic bottles to put hot water in – Susie had varicose veins and we would need to put some heat on them after the delivery. I asked her if she felt like pushing yet and she said no, she didn't, and besides she needed to have a bath. She'd been working in the strawberry patch right up until I'd arrived and her feet were dirty.

I'd set out my things in the bedroom, and sat down to read a magazine article about growing tomatoes in a raised bed. Susie's husband, Ephraim, marched placidly up and down the stairs with a flashlight, bringing down plastic bottles. He moved the 18-month-old out of the bedroom and brought in some things I needed, and just before he sat down, Susie called from the bathtub, 'Ask Penny if she wants any tea, Ephraim.' I didn't so he sat down to read the *Botschaft*, the weekly newspaper that serves Old Order Amish communities. There wasn't a sound in the house except for the ticking of Susie's Seth Thomas clock. Occasionally, in the distance, we heard the rumble of thunder. A storm coming our way. That went on for about 20 minutes.

She came out scrubbed from being in the bath and damp from being about ready to push.

'Come on, Ephraim,' she said. 'Let's go and have this baby.'

At City Hospital, the woman in the belly band looked slightly confused, then turned to her husband. 'Am I having a contraction?' she asked.

He leant over her and looked at the machine. 'Why, yes, you are, dear. Now then, let's push.'

One thing you had to say for the father, he had cared enough to memorize the natural-childbirth book backward and forwards. 'Breathe,' he said, eyes on the monitor, 'that's good, now push, now breathe again, now push.' He was so well prepared with book learning that after this child, his perfect son, was born, he would refer to his wee arms and legs as 'extremities'. 'The extremities are normal, dear. Now I am counting the fingers and toes: one, two, three, four . . .' He'd read that this verification of fingers and toes promoted bonding between mother and child. The mother wants to know if her baby has everything it's supposed to have; his intention was to produce this information for her. He didn't attempt to touch the baby himself; he did not address it directly, nor praise it aloud; instead he assessed it.

I don't imagine he was an unloving man; but what I've seen time and again is that the technology of the hospital overwhelms patients' natural instincts; they are intimidated, afraid of appearing stupid or clumsy or sentimental in a surrounding that seems so efficient and immaculate and intelligent.

His wife screwed up her face and grunted.

She didn't feel the contractions. Because of the regional anesthetic she'd had, the only way she could tell that her body was proceeding with its labor was by the machine. Her urge to push was so numbed that she had to fake it – 'Just imagine you're making your bowels move, dear,' the nurses would say.

A couple of times during her labor her husband told her, 'It's a contraction, dear. Now then, let's breathe. Push. That's good.' And then a nurse or other official would come in the room and say forget it. She stopped instantly and resumed her fuzzy stare into space. Her husband pecked her on the forehead and lifted his eyes back up to the television.

Susie and Ephraim's bedroom was too warm, and Ephraim went about and opened a couple of the windows just an inch or two. Great drops of rain began to fall to the earth outside the window, the wind gusted, the white dotted-swiss curtains billowed at the window and the smell of wet earth filled the bedroom. There are always deliveries – count on it – on nights with thunder and lightning. Something about the barometric pressure. We got Susie settled in her bed, arranged her pillows and her husband lit a bedside lamp. For the next contraction, I rested my hand on Susie's belly; when it was past, I would do a vaginal exam. For a while, I massaged her feet and legs; her husband dusted his hands with talcum and rubbed his palms into the small of her back.

When Susie's contractions got more serious and closer together, I moved right next to her, one arm resting on my knee; the other, now gloved hand resting on Susie's knee. 'Push into your bottom, Susie,' I said. 'That's good. Now breathe. I can see the baby's head now. I can see your baby's head coming.'

* * *

The doctor arrived at City Hospital. Tall and artfully gray-ing, he eased in, put one foot on the bed rail and stared at the screen monitor. He didn't touch the woman. 'Let's get her into the delivery room,' he said pleasantly, walking out.

The delivery room walls were dark green shiny tiles with white grouting. The floor, an intaglio, was shiny black with gray and white pebbles floating in it. Shields of stainless steel hung on the far wall; some were punctured by electric recep-tors, others had metal clips that held stainless-steel instru-ments, some had ropes of rubbery black cord hanging from them, black cords that swooped down on the floor and coiled loosely around the base of flat-faced lamps that sur-rounded the delivery table. It, too, was of stainless steel. It seemed so narrow, like a camp cot, and a thin mattress exag-gerated the impression. Metal stirrups – which had the shape of moulded leg guards – rode the air.

The woman was lifted from a rolling bed onto the delivery table. The doctor, nurses and onlookers slipped on cap, slip-pers, gowns and masks. The attending nurse became a doughy clump of blue. The husband took the shape of a blue monolith near his wife's head.

The woman's body, drugged and heavy, was rolled awk-wardly onto the delivery table. Her legs were sunk into huge canvas socks that tied at the knees, and then they were lifted into the leg stirrups and bound with belts and buckles, twice on the foot and twice on the thigh. Once she felt a push breaking through the anesthesia, and then she was asked to pant her way through it so that they could get her bound up. The nurse spread a drape over each leg and then the doctor stepped forward and cast the last drape over her body. It cov-ered her to the neck. From his view, there was nothing of the woman to be seen except for the small area of pale, jellylike flesh with two dark hearts – the vagina and the anus. The great lamps in the room flashed on.

The woman was secured in the lithotomy position. Someday in the future this position will be cited as an example of how our civilization got its technological cart before its medical horse. The lithotomy position – convenient for medical intervention in childbirth – works against the physics and physiology of childbirth. In it a woman can seldom push effectively. She hasn't got any leverage, she hasn't got gravity on her side, she's not in a position to help her pelvic bones spread out and, what's more, the baby's head is pressing for the entire ride on one of the largest blood vessels in her body – thus slowing down circulation when the baby needs it most.

Because she cannot use gravity, because her labor is tempered by immobility, because she hasn't had anything to eat and her blood sugar is low, because she can't let her body follow its unique musculoskeletal formula, because she has assumed that she is not delivering this child but that the doctor and hospital are doing it for her – for all of these reasons, her body does not labor as well as it might. And then, of course, the need for surgical intervention increases.

Susie knew her stuff. She rolled over on her side for a while, then onto her back. When the contractions came, I just stood back. Energy rippled the surface of her skin, her arms and legs pounded against the mattress with the leftover pulsations. 'Okay, Susie. Let's get you up on your knees. We need to take some pressure off those veins and also give those bones the best chance to spread for the baby's head.' Susie sat with her bottom resting on her heels.

The doctor picked up a syringe. It was five inches long. With his back to the woman, he flashed the point of the needle, squirted some of the fluid in an arc in the air, and then turned, not warning the woman that she would feel a prick and a burn. He reached into her, pulled away the exterior flesh, and twice drove the needle deep into the flesh of her perineum.

The woman's husband hadn't said anything since we came into the delivery room. The woman, the tip of her nose barely visible above the mountain of drapes, said nothing. The baby's head was crawling persistently out of the birth canal.

The doctor hadn't touched her except to put the needle into her.

Now he picked up a pair of scissors and cut from the birth canal towards the woman's left flank, through five muscle groups and an inch and a half to two inches into her. It was a textbook medio-lateral episiotomy.

At Susie's, I worked the perineum with my fingers, helping it stretch. The baby, held and squeezed by its mother's muscles, came bounding down the birth canal. It turned, ground under the pubic bone and then its head began to bulge. The perineum thinned. I put my fingers on the cap of the baby's head to keep it from coming too quickly, to give the perineum a chance to stretch. I asked Susie to pant, which slowed the baby's coming.

Left medio-lateral opens the birth canal up, all right. Flesh hung loosely from the cut. The vagina was wide open and lazy and the baby's head rested like a beached whale on the vaginal tissue and in a dark pool of blood. Fresh blood seeped into the drapes.

'Pant,' I told Susie.

'Hoosh, hoosh, hoosh.'

The baby's head rotated, showing its slant of forehead, then more and more. The perineum slipped over the brow of the face. 'There now, there, Susie, there's your baby's head.'

Ephraim couldn't stand it anymore, he had to have a better look. He dropped his wife's hand for a minute and came over to look over my shoulder to see the head.

* * *

The doctor stood back and reached at arm's length in the general direction of the baby's head. He slipped fingers under the baby's chin and pulled it out. 'There,' he said dramatically, 'that's what caused the trouble. This baby was trying to push his arm out in front of his head. He's fine now.'

'One more push for the body,' I said.

Susie, not losing any momentum, surged one more time, and the baby was out. It started crying right away.

'It's a girl,' I said, putting the baby on the bed next to Susie and covering it with a receiving blanket while I cleaned fluids out of her nose and mouth with a syringe. Susie stayed on her knees, a small amount of blood puddling about her, then – giving its standard warning with a narrow rush of fresh blood – the placenta followed. Susie said little. She had one arm free and, drawing the baby towards her, she cuddled her at her side. Ephraim said, 'This will make Grandma's 108th grandchild – that is, if somebody didn't beat us to it.'

The doctor handed the baby to the nurse, who carried him to a small metal table in the corner of the room. A heat lamp went on and the baby kicked slowly; he was uncovered and exposed for the first time in his life. The delivery lights came on. 'He's cold,' the doctor said. 'I'd like to warm him up under the heat lamp.' The nurse put a plastic suction tube down the boy's throat, a machine hummed, extracting mucus. Without talking to him, she trimmed his cord, wiped his face and weighed him. His mother had not seen him yet except at a distance; she hadn't touched him.

The doctor delivered the placenta, settled down on his stool, flashed his needle in the lights and began stitching. He would stitch muscle for 15 minutes.

* * *

Ephraim cut the cord, we wrapped the baby a little better, and I gave her to him to carry about – 'leave her head a little lower than the rest of her body so that she won't choke on any mucus' – while I washed Susie up and placed the bottles with hot water in around her legs. Her muscles were shaking from having used up all her sugar supply, so I covered her up with piles of family quilts and got her some apple juice.

The doctor finished stitching. He pulled his gloves off, walked to the baby and, gripping the boy's chin between his thumb and index fingers, said, 'You're quite a boy.' He went over to the father, shook his hand, told him he'd examine the baby in the nursery, and stepped out.

The nurse started undraping the woman who was shaking and complaining of being cold. Her husband said, 'Yes, dear, you're supposed to be.' The nurse said nothing and continued unbuckling the straps that held the woman in her stirrups and untying the giant canvas socks. Finally, the nurse said, 'As soon as I've finished here, we'll let you hold your baby for a minute,' and finally she got a light flannel blanket and put it over the woman's body.

Susie and Ephraim's baby would be called Katie. I washed her up, amusing her with my conversation as I did, weighed her and then put her back on the bed to check her. Discussing whom she resembled, how good her color was, and who the grandparents were, I dressed her and wrapped her in a receiving blanket. I put her under the crook of her mother's arm and she started nursing.

The nurse left the husband and wife in the center of the now echoing delivery room and took the baby down to the hall into the nursery. When I left at 1.30 am, the baby was on a metal table under bright lights and heat lamps. A woman in the nursery was measuring him. As she left the delivery room, the nurse had said, 'Mother can see baby in the morning after doctor makes rounds.'

I left Susie and Ephraim's house after the baby had started nursing at the second breast. 'The best thing to do,' I said, 'to keep the baby warm and to help her get gradually accustomed to the outside world, is for the three of you to sleep together tonight. Don't worry, you won't roll over on her – you'll know she's there.'

13

Getting Married

Neither Richie nor I liked the idea of getting married. Everybody we knew had already been married and nastily divorced. I couldn't stand others' horror stories, let alone the chance of having one of my own. We both thought the wedding ceremony was ridiculous.

But I wanted to go to a midwifery convention on the West Coast and if we were married, I could fly on Richie's pass. And since I had stopped being a student, I didn't have any health insurance, and if we got married I could be on Richie's plan. And then we'd about decided to rent a house together and that would be more convenient if we were married. But I hated the idea of getting married and so did Richie, and I was busy delivering babies and I didn't care to think about it.

About that time, I delivered my first primigravida at home. A primigravida is a girl who is having her first baby. Lizzie was especially proud of the fact. Just by the way she carried herself, she implied that she expected to be awfully good at having babies. She also gave the impression that she tried just a tad harder than everyone else to be sweet and that she was kind of successful at that, too.

When her labor started, she expected undivided attention, and she gave me no peace. Her water broke; shouldn't I come right away? No, not yet. Her contractions were starting; should I come right away? No, not yet. And so on. I finally gave in about 5 am and went to her house.

The bedroom was still dark when I came in, but I could see the crib, with its doll-baby smooth sheets. One infant gown was arranged in the center of the mattress; next to it were two diaper pins, closed and clipped together, diapers and an undershirt with ties. A blanket, banded in green ribbon and embroidered in that red, pink, yellow, white, pastel running thread, was folded to show the words *Our Baby*.

Our mother-to-be was sitting up in bed, hair tucked into a white scarf, pillows plumped nicely around her. She had one hand resting gracefully in her lap and the other in her husband's hand. She looked a great deal as if it were Mother's Day and I was there to serve her shirred eggs and blueberry scones in bed, and then the children would be permitted to come in, give her kisses and run off to play nicely.

She smiled to assure me she was going to be mature, then she spoke, explaining that she was counting on having her baby by sunrise. The pains had been very hard already and she knew it must be just about time. She tucked her lips in with finality, raised her eyebrows and looked at me as if to pat my acquiescence into place.

She was so bright, so ready, so sure of herself, that I knew we were hours, if not days, away from a delivery. I put my hand on her stomach and waited for a couple of contractions. They were miles apart and mild.

'Well now, Lizzie,' I said very seriously. 'I'm afraid it's going to be some time longer than that.' I had to bite my lip so as not to smile. Not that it's funny, but you see it again and again, and you know what they have ahead of them, what they have to face up to in the next few hours – especially ones like this who are thinking about dolls – and you can't help but smile and shake your head a little.

She took it pretty hard. She looked abject.

'Maybe by noon,' I said, nodding encouragement, 'maybe by noon.'

Her shoulders dropped a trifle, she looked at her husband as if asking him to make me understand, her eyes started to water up, but then she took a big breath, gave her shoulders a shake, and looked back at me as if to say that she was a grown-up who was prepared to take life's major setbacks. She was a good girl, I could see that. She had planned on being brave through the hard parts, and here, she said to herself, it was.

Fortunately, the mite hadn't the faintest idea of what hard was.

I gave her some blue cohosh – a herb that stimulates labor – told her to drink juice, get in the bathtub for relief from back pain and, when she felt like it, get out and start walking around the house. The labor was slow; something was keeping it from picking up and the odds were it was because she knew – for all her bully front – that she was just a child and children can't be mothers.

Lizzie needed time to grapple with herself. I went and got some breakfast.

When I got back, the pain had begun its inevitable education. The rigidity in her shoulders was eroding, and pride was washing out of her face. For a while, she sat slumped in a chair to make a mild show of her suffering, and then, getting no satisfaction from me, she rose and started walking timidly about the room. I told her, 'What a good idea,' and she perked up, walked with more conviction. When a contraction would start, she'd find her husband's face with her eyes, then go over to where he was sitting in an armchair, squat next to him and put her head in his lap. Time after time he cradled her head in his lap and with his hand he rubbed the small of her back.

Sometimes, she would look up at him, imploring him, just as the pain started up. Her lip would tremble. The boy would say softly, 'There now, there now. You're doing so well.' Then he would look at me for reassurance and I would nod.

He turned to me, 'She always wanted babies. Ever since I knew her, she wanted babies. It was all I ever heard – babies, babies, babies – way before we were married.' She smiled modestly and this time when the contraction came, she stopped next to him and curled up into a self-contained ball.

She put one fist on her knee, rested her forehead on it and let the contraction boil out of her body. He watched her, trying to stifle the look of pain that crossed his own face as he heard her moan. He waited for her contraction to subside and he stroked her shoulder once, tentatively, reverently.

He believed in her. He believed she knew about babies. He believed her big talk. She was his wife. He loved her and couldn't see at all that she was taking new and sorry measure of herself.

She doubted herself. As if the physical pain wasn't enough. She knew she was not being magnificent, transcendent, which was what she had planned. She wondered if maybe she wouldn't even be able to push it out the way any ordinary girl would.

Neither of them had had the slightest idea it was going to be like this.

I sat with them and waited.

There's at least one time before the final appearance of the baby when inexperienced mothers decide for the first time in their lives to give themselves up. They are tired, they have been brave, they've used themselves up and they cry out, 'I can't. I just can't. Make it stop. Help me.' When the young women say it, I celebrate inside. Because then, if only for a split second, they capitulate to the independence of their bodies and the awesomeness of this business they are joining in.

The ones who are new at having babies, the ones who had darling little figures like this one, adoring parents and special attention – especially them – they war with their bodies, they keep control. Because they are young and strong and wilful, because their fathers adored them, because the boys used to flirt with them, these young girls believe they are clever mistresses of their destiny like no mistresses before them, and they try to run the labor with their minds, with their school-book ethics of how brave women behave. And then, as the labor proceeds, their strength ebbs and they have to give up. For a while they despise themselves for having failed, and then, finally, they know it's beyond them. They abandon themselves to the force that has overtaken them. They give up their special place in the universe, surrender themselves to those who are helping them, and see themselves in a truer light – they are no more and no less than any struggling woman in labor. The secure ones feel release and throw themselves with grace and abandon into the current that so far outpulls them; the more frightened ones resist the power; they flail and hold themselves back.

Lizzie had been resisting; trying to be brave and trying to look good when having a baby. As she gave way, her labor progressed. She'd let her shoulders go, her mouth was now unpursed, her legs fell randomly on the bed when the contractions were over.

She was tired. She'd been at it nearly 12 hours. A searing contraction came and, finally, she cried out, 'Help. Help me. I can't do it anymore. Make it stop. I can't go on anymore. Penny, help me.' She looked with terror in her eyes to her husband, gripped his shirt, and pleaded with him. He looked at me. 'Hold on to Ervin,' I said. 'Hold tight and, yes, we can do it, you are doing it, your body is guiding you, your baby is coming. Follow your body, put yourself into your pain, bury yourself in the pain. Listen to me: the more you push, the sooner you can put your baby in your arms.' I looked at her husband.

'Come on, Lizzie, come on,' he said. 'Our baby's almost here. It's our baby coming, Lizzie. Our baby's coming.'

She had her baby about 12.30; a nice baby. Later Ervin helped me out to the car with my suitcase. I looked out my rearview mirror as I drove off. He skipped the pathway and jumped up over the three steps to the front porch. Coming towards me down the lane was a buggy carrying a woman. It would be Lizzie's mother. I'll never figure out how they know when to come.

Lizzie and Ervin had their people. When Lizzie shattered the first time because she couldn't quiet her baby, when she became frantic when a high temperature hit, when she first felt that anguishing suspicion that the baby was changing things between her and Ervin, then she could look to her parents' lives and to her people for help – people who dressed the same way as she did; people who performed the same chores in the same order in a day and in a life; people who prayed the same prayers and applied the same rules, people echoing into the past and into the future, showing the way in an endless succession of mirrors.

Black buggies file unevenly across the soft-webbed November morning. Grass and roadside weeds lay down heavy with the weight of the early winter damp air. Small square windows of the buggy frame a husband in his black frock coat and black, flat-brimmed hat. He's been up since four to get the milking done and his face is soft and at rest. His wife, black bonnet in a dark halo around her face, is by his side. She pulls her shawl snugly around her.

In November and December in Lancaster County, on Tuesdays and Thursdays and taking all day, the young people marry. By eight the yard fills up with buggies, and husbands and wives climb out for the wedding ceremony. They enter, the women shaking hands and nodding in fellowship. The marriage sermon goes on for most of the morning – men and women listening on benches on different sides of the room – and, plying verses from the Bible, it is instructive of marriage duties.

Bride and groom, dressed in new but otherwise ordinary Amish clothes, listen – I imagine – the best they can. Through their excitement, they will hear some of the obligations recited to them. They needn't worry too much; what they'll miss at their own wedding, they'll hear at another's. Since it is the custom of the community to honor the teachings of the church, the instructions will be used again and again.

Their minds, I'm sure, concentrate as best they can on the promises, but as much as anything else, it is the singing voices of their brothers and sisters, voices like shuttles working open and shut, each voice crossing over the bride and groom again and again, that probably weaves them into being married.

At the bride's house, supper for 100 or 150 is nearly ready. Family and neighbors have been killing chickens, chopping celery, cutting up cabbage, scrubbing potatoes, building tables, and setting up temporary wash stations for days. Now, young men, some of them dressed rakishly in white shirts and black string ties, pose casually in the bride's yard or lean against the side of the barn. They're conscious of the young women – sequestered upstairs in the bride's house – watching them, and so they exaggerate their ease. In a bit, they'll choose a partner whose hand they'll hold while walking to the wedding supper.

More guests come. The women carry in desserts and treats from their kitchens. Cookies, candied popcorn, taffy and cakes – cakes trimmed to look like pandas, cakes ringed with flowers made of icing, high cakes, low cakes, flat cakes, mounded cakes. The women, modestly getting one another's name and road and cousin or aunt until a family connection is rooted out, file along the display of sweets and admire the kitchen work of others.

Bride and groom, holding hands, go to their corner, called the 'Eck', for the wedding dinner. Long tables, covered with blue-and-white checked oilcloth, stretch away from them in either direction, and through the other rooms of the house. Celery stalks, standing up in clumps, are the center of the tables, marking the distance off. A 100 or more water glosses are lined up; silverware, napkins, salt and pepper shakers, containers of apple sauce fill the tables. This will be the first sitting.

At the married people's table, men sit on one side, women on the other. They chatter and gossip, men as well as women, until the sound dies down. Somewhere in the room a head drops and instantly all 100 heads drop in silence.

The silence is thrilling. Whatever one's belief or lack of it, the silent prayer before and after each Amish meal does feel holy. It may be that silent prayer is generous to the stranger; it invites him in.

Suddenly, the meal is in full swing. Women and men scoop up their slaw and mashed potatoes – no time for talking now – beets, bread and butter, stuffing, doughnuts, celery in egg and vinegar cream sauce (a wedding special), coffee and cream, eating as if eating were a hoedown. Servers – more cousins and aunts and uncles of the bride – carry bowls and trays to the table, shovel food on empty patches of plates, and chide those who don't eat enough.

Somewhere in the room there is the sound of one plate being scraped; then the sound of all the plates being scraped. Then that one invisible head drops. All heads drop and there is silence again.

Within minutes the tables are cleared and the dishes, silverware, cups, glasses, serving dishes, spoons are splashing through a washtub in the corner of the room.

In a while, after a second sitting, men will pick up the benches and line them up, and for the afternoon, men and women sing. The voices thicken and dry and begin to sound like wood grain, if wood grain could sing. Then men wander in and out of the house – talking in the yard, talking in the barn. They smile and laugh above their beards. The women talk about laundry and babies, gardens and other weddings this fall. They nurse their babies in the corners, carry one another's cranky baby on a walk. It goes on this way; they will have supper together, too, and there will be more singing.

Late in the evening the young people go to the barn and play games, dancing games with no instruments; they flirt and pair off, getting going for another round of marriages.

The bride and groom spend their wedding night at her home and they spend the next couple of months of weekends visiting family and friends to make themselves known to the

*brotherhood as a married pair. Then they will set up house-
hold.*

Lizzie, my child-mother, could marry in trust and begin to
take her place in the adult world even though she was not
ready. I, Penelope Bradbury – worldly, independent and self-
sufficient modern woman – could not.

Where I came from, the idea of belonging, of carrying and
being carried by others, had been sacrificed or lost. No, it
was worse than lost, it was considered bad. To trust others,
to follow an instruction, to ask for help with the burden of
one's life, was to show oneself a fool. It showed you didn't
know your way around.

Each of us pretended that we could manage life's events –
births, deaths, sickness and transcendent joy – on the
strength of our personalities. Like that girl pretending – with
her face all ironed and posed – that she was going to have a
baby by sunrise.

Richie and I, if we married, would have to be married by
ourselves, alone; if we faltered, we would have only our own
peculiar strengths to guide us; and if, between the two of us,
they didn't happen to be the right strengths or if they didn't
happen to be enough and if we gave ourselves up to others in
a moment of trial, as Lizzie had to Ervin and me, others
would bear no responsibility for us. We realized that we
would be taking our risks alone and the trouble was –
although we never talked about it – both of us valued a last-
ing marriage so much that we truly didn't want to take the
chance of having one and losing it.

One morning about 10.30 I got back from a delivery and
Richie was standing in my living room in his blue jeans, a
faded LL Bean chamois shirt and a pair of sneakers. He was
holding the phone book in his hand. 'Justice Douglas K
Wenger of Paradise – metropolis of the farmlands of
Pennsylvania, home of one stoplight, one gas station, an ice

cream parlour, and the Paradise Hotel with country music every other Saturday night – Justice Douglas K Wenger has agreed to marry us in half an hour, so if you'd like to change . . .'

Richie's often a joker in moments of anxiety.

Not talking, I changed from one set of dungarees to another, put on my BMW T-shirt, my LL Bean chamois shirt, went out, got in the car, slammed the door shut, and looked straight ahead.

Richie tried to make jokes as we drove along and I tried to be pleasant. Not that I didn't love him; I just detested this.

Judge Wenger, seeing that I was tense and that Richie was trying to make light of things, got into the spirit and said he sure hoped we didn't want a lot of talking at this wedding because he had just been fixing to go fishing when we'd called.

We finished in about 10 minutes, paid our 15 dollars, and took time to go the extra miles and take a honeymoon drive through Intercourse. Then my beeper went off and Richie had a flight to make anyway, so we went our separate ways.

We told hardly anyone that we were married for a year. We did tell Richie's mother and father. They had done the same thing back in Island Falls 35 years earlier because she had been a nurse and they would have fired her if they knew she was married. After another year, when we felt we had a little record of success behind us, we gradually told others.

China

After we got married, Richie and I rented a house over on Cowpers Road. We looked landed because we were surrounded by other people's cornfields, but all we had was a small triangle of lawn and a garden plot not much bigger than the back of a farmer's hand.

Did I care that it was small? It had been five years since I'd had a garden and I thought every dirt clod was a diamond. I went out in broad daylight – fearless of the teasing likely to come from my neighbors – my shovel on my shoulder. I turned over the dirt and, over the months, turned in orange rinds, coffee grounds and lettuce leaves. I planted tomatoes, peas, corn, lettuce, onions and potatoes. Late in the spring our new neighbor, Eli, came to the door with four seedling tobacco plants in hand; a tribute, I like to think, to my courageous pretence of having a garden. He planted them for me.

It would make a good joke for the summer weeks, about how Dr Penny was a tobacco farmer. I'd put my hands in my pockets, lean back against Stephen's waiting room wall, and talk tobacco with the Amishmen coming into the office with their pregnant wives. 'It wonders me,' I would say, shaking my head thoughtfully, 'how our tobacco is going to take this wet (or dry, windy, sunny) weather.'

'Why' – they'd pause and think about it some – 'do you have tobacco already?' And new respect would fill their eyes.

'Why, yes, we do,' I'd say and smile, benign and peaceful as the Buddha.

I stretched my work in the garden. In the morning before

breakfast I wandered out to see in what new leaves the dew had gathered. In the afternoon I weeded, I dug, I pulled off imperfect leaves, I watered and sprinkled and cut sharp edges to the garden with my spade. I put up poles for beans, tied up string, and waited for the curling pale green shoots to make openwork against the Amish landscape and sky.

I worked and dug and thought. In the garden, nobody asked me questions, no one challenged me, no one demanded, no one second-guessed. In the garden I had my own mind.

In the garden I had to make the decision about how I was going to practice. I couldn't put it off much longer: the doctors at the hospital still resented me; they chipped away at Stephen every chance they could get and, naturally, that created tension between us. If we were going to continue to practice together, we'd have to put a lot of energy into a new strategy. Did I want to do that? I'd been trying to figure it out. How should I deliver babies? I couldn't choose for others, but I could choose for me. What was right? I'd done my comparative study at City Hospital. I'd read everything I could about births in other cultures: I knew about Native American baby-having, imperial Russian baby-having, old white South and old black South baby-having, not to mention the baby-having of Glasgow wifies and central Philly teens.

The fact was, it had been relatively easy to walk out of that hospital in the city and be glib about how the machinery of medicine was overpowering good sense and mother nature. It was easy to be seduced by the homemade-bread atmosphere of an Amish household. But leaving the practice with Stephen, leaving the hospital altogether, meant turning away from everything.

When I got down to it, there on my hands and knees among the radishes and carrot shoots, I found myself thinking about my women friends, my sisters-in-law, my cousins – all of whom went or would go to hospitals for their babies. I was trained in hospitals. Hospitals saved lives in miraculous ways. I wanted hospitals, English hospitals, to learn to treat my friends and relatives with gentleness and to treat their laboring bodies with respect. I wanted lifesaving technology nearby for them if they needed it. I didn't want to give up on helping get the two styles together, I didn't want to walk away. It didn't seem such an unattainable dream.

In trying to figure out my dilemma, I'd gone so far as to write to a woman who had been a missionary midwife in China before the revolution and who was planning a return tour. China, I thought, might give me some answers – there, I understood, they combined traditional and high-tech medicine; they might know the blend we needed. Maybe we could do what they do in China. If Anna Stone, ex-midwife to the Chinese, would take me with her, I'd pay the $3,000 and find the time to go. I needed answers badly.

I waited to hear from her. Meanwhile, working along in my dirt, my backside pushing up against my neighbor's rows of new corn, I would experiment with thinking about the problem of modern medicine and baby-having the way an Amishman would think about it. It was a question of technology, after all, and the Amish were experts in choosing technology.

Most people on the outside – the English, that is – believe that the Amish culture stays the same. It appears that if you're farming with horses, if you're driving around in a horse and buggy, if you're wearing long skirts, that you're living exactly the same life that your forebears were living in Switzerland in the 16th century when they first became religious purists.

The Amish do change. They use different standards from the English to decide how to change, how much to change, and in which direction. But they change.

For myself, I couldn't figure out the bathrooms. Why would Amish people refuse to have electricity brought into their homes by wire, do without phones in their homes, and yet have completely modern bathrooms? I tried making up my own explanations, but none of them made sense. So finally I asked, 'How come all of you have nicer bathrooms than I do?' It's because of the government, they said. The government said if they wanted to sell milk from the Amish cow to the English world, it wouldn't do to have outhouses. The Pennsylvania Amish decided they needed milk for a cash product so that husbands and fathers could stay home on the farm, and so, after long discussions and prayer among themselves and final ruminations and prayers by their bishops, the Amishmen installed spiffy new bathrooms in their homes.

For another example, in Lancaster County they use generator-run milking machines and cooling tanks – but they don't allow the use of pipes to get the milk from the cow to the cooler; instead the milk is transported in buckets by the children.

We outsiders aren't very good at reasoning through to these decisions in an Amish way. Some of them – like this one with the pipes and buckets – seem capricious. When I try to follow the train of thought, make it work in my English logic, I often lose my way. Then it helps to remember a typical Amish explanation for some decisions. 'It's just our way,' they'll say, as if it would be absurd for us humans to pretend that we understood all the reasons for our ways.

It also helps to remember that the brotherhood is conservative; they've found a good way to live and want to preserve it. As a result, there's a strong tendency to stick with the way things have been because that's the way things have been. I heard one Amishman criticize some of the others for worshipping the past – as unholy a worship, he said, as the worship of any other false god.

Most Amishmen, though, keep their heads turned away from the world and its innovations. It is the few, those irrepressibly curious and innovative by nature, who scan the rest of society to find ways to preserve the Amish life. These experimenters show, perhaps better than anyone, how an

Amishman makes decisions about technology and change.

I know an Amishman who has a generator-run computer in his chicken coop. He, a quiet, thoughtful, hobbit-sized fellow, agrees with many worldly writers that the computer – the cold, wired, electric-faced, non-organic computer – might be able to help a man stay at home and be with his family and with his community. He is testing his idea, without noise, without announcement. He just keeps his computer in his chicken coop and is teaching himself to understand its possible uses. He has thought most kindly about us non-Amish and hopes that the computer might help us stay home and be with our families, too.

Most of all an Amishman wants to protect his faith, keep his family close, keep his ways, keep humble before God, be a steward of the land, and make a living. If he needs a technology to allow him to continue, then maybe, he'll say, taking a long time to decide – debating the matter with his brethren – maybe he'll use it; but if it gets in the way of faith, family and stewardship, then he'll stop thinking about it.

About the time I was putting in the first lettuce in my garden, they brought in a new chief of ob-gyn at Country Hospital. He was, as they say, a 'take-charge guy', and he thought the thing to do was to make some ruling on every delivery where there was any sort of complication. He made his ruling only after jamming his fingers into the vagina of a laboring woman, needed or not.

Haseena, a sixteen-year-old translucent-skinned girl from India who dressed in a rippling stream-water blue sari, had just come to this country with her American husband. She knew virtually no English. Her husband found me to deliver their baby because in India men do not deliver babies. It is immoral, immodest and shocking to a woman if a man attends her at birth.

I was very gentle with this soft, murmuring Indian child. I wanted her to feel safe and welcome in her new country; I wanted to lift her, carry her, ease her graciously into being an American and into motherhood. Through her husband, she asked me for books about having her baby. I looked, but could not get hold of books written in Hindi, so I gave her books in English and her husband translated them and read them to her. With great pride, he complained about her, 'She keeps me up all night, reading and rereading the books. She is so amazed and hungry to know. Again and again she says, "Is that the way it is? Read it to me again."'

I found Haseena waiting at the hospital, at term, in labor and as calm, polished and beautiful as a cherrywood lily drifting in the late summer sun. She was so still, I thought her labor had just begun. Her calmness soothed me, and I thought that clearly all was going to go well. When I examined her, though, I found that she was almost completely dilated and I also found that the baby was breech.

I pulled the sheet back over her, told the two of them what I'd found and quietly we began to prepare ourselves.

I knew how to deliver breech babies vaginally. What's more, I was a *woman* who knew how to deliver breech babies. I knew to keep my hands off the breech. I knew how to let the baby's legs and body drop and hang, suspending its weight; I knew to allow the baby's head to notch out, nape hair by nape hair, from under the mother's pubic bone. For myself, I knew how to concentrate on watching the articulation of childbirth in reverse; to keep the ultimate discipline, that is, to observe while physics and mechanics, uninterrupted, synchronized the birth.

If the patient is ready, if the patient trusts, and if I could keep my hands off, it could go well. If it became necessary to intervene surgically, there was time, but there was time for the breech delivery, too, and that would have given us the possibility of leaving this smooth young girl intact and uncut.

The chief arrived. Without speaking and without apologizing for the intrusion, he pulled back the sheets, spread Haseena's legs apart and rammed his fingers into her.

'Breech!' he called out, as if he were yelling at a hockey game. 'Primigravida breech! Prepare for c-section.' He dropped the sheet, turned, and walked out of the room.

I watched them drop their scalpel into the doe-skinned girl, and all the time they were at her, I thought how an Amishman would have seen the situation; he would have known that it is wrong to use technology when it isn't necessary and especially where it violates stewardship.

I did go to China that summer. By the time I left, I suppose I had convinced myself that China would resolve my dilemma once and for all. I fully believed that in China the chasm between natural, traditional health care and modern medical technology did not exist. I must have begun to think of all China, its one billion people, its one-third of the globe, as a thriving Lancaster County taken one step farther. In this China of my mind, the practice of obstetrics was unimaginably rich in technique and wise in application.

Somehow in China, I imagined, they had figured out how to combine – gracefully and humanely – the past with the present.

Anna Stone, the certified nurse-midwife, had served with the American Friends Service Committee Ambulance Corps before the cultural revolution in China. For this, her return trip, she had recruited not only midwives, but old colleagues, people who had been medical service missionaries – including some who had accompanied the people while they fled from the siege of nationalist troops led by Chiang Kai-shek. Some of these Americans had carried X-ray machines on their backs the length of the Long March. In the days when China was ulcerous with crime, warfare, brutality and disease, Anna Stone and her colleagues were its healers. In China, they were thought of as being Western friends of the highest sort; they were heroes and heroines of China's 'darkest hour'. The Chinese would respect them and answer questions.

For three weeks we travelled through China by train. At each stop my companions were honored. Special signs went up; banners unfurled. We were treated to formal teas and were honored guests at multicourse banquets; my friends were applauded and bowed to.

At every stop we explained the purpose of the trip. We did not want to see the Great Wall; we did not want to visit the Friendship stores, and we did not want to see showcase hospitals. We wanted to see the miracle of modern China, how everyday health care and medical practice in China had scooped the Chinese people out of a scabrous, infested past and, combining traditional and modern techniques, had made life in China healthy. I, of course, hungered to see how China practiced obstetrical medicine in a way that preserved wholeness.

Stubbornly they kept us away from the people's China. Relentlessly, they took us to city hospitals equipped with labor beds that were hard and metal and were furnished with straps and stirrups. They showed us hospital layouts that made it clear that the father had no place in the delivery room.

I had anticipated learning about the application of herbal therapies in the hospital setting; instead I answered questions about the dosage of magnesium sulfate for preeclamptic patients. I expected to discuss how hospitals planned for patients to walk about and bathe during labor, to see labor beds that permitted delivery postures I had never dreamt of; instead I answered questions about techniques for inducing labor, about genetic research, about amniocentesis, about ultrasound, about every space-age, silicone-chip obstetrical device. Our hosts spoke without apology of high rates of cesarean section and high forceps delivery.

I was deeply disappointed. I had come around the world to find sanity and wisdom, and what I found was a people elbowing their way towards a medical technology I had already seen, one I too often had found brutal, stupid and mean.

I suppose the Chinese bureaucrats will remember it as an official gaffe, but one day our group did stop in a common-place farm commune – the kind of spot we had been begging to visit. We pulled up to a mud-walled, whitewashed, dirt-floored clinic where no Westerner had been before. With the others, I stopped and peered in the door. A padded cradle stood against the wall, rough-cut wood shelves held jars of herbs, and over in the corner of the room, casting a shadow on the chalky walls, was a pressure cooker – exactly the same pressure cooker that I used at home to sterilize my instruments. Next to it, instrument packs, packed in muslin, folded just the way I fold mine.

Curious children came skipping in from a nearby school-house; they poked and prodded one another as they made their way to the clinic to make a circle around the strangers. I repeated one of the few words I knew in Chinese. 'Midwife,' I said, pointing to myself. 'Midwife,' I repeated. 'Midwife, midwife,' until finally one of the older children ran to the fields.

In a while a woman came bouncing up the road from the fields on her fat-wheeled bike. I smiled, beckoned and walked towards the door of the hut. She followed me. I pointed to the pressure cooker and to me and nodded; she took my hand. I pointed to myself. 'Midwife,' I said in Chinese. I pointed to the instrument packs and to me and nodded; she patted my hand and nodded again. Again and again, we patted one another and nodded.

I didn't bother to think. I didn't compare her practice with mine or try to remember what I might transport to the United States. I was overwhelmed. I knew without question, I knew it from the bottom side of my stomach, I knew it with my head and my heart, 'This is good. This is right. This is the way.' Back in the United States, back in Lancaster County, back home among the Amish, apparently, I had been slowly finding my way through the distraction of high technology and politics, towards the center of the business. I was slowly rediscovering the universal, the truest methods of delivering babies.

15

Losses

I got back from China just in time to watch my neighbors start dropping the corn out in front of my house. It had been a generous summer. The stalks were heavy and when the wind hurried through them, it sounded as if the leaves, in unselfconscious enthusiasm, were applauding their own performance. Richie – now on his second silo-filling season – managed a team of mules casually, with the same loose joints, the same grace he had in the cockpit.

I didn't help with filling silo, but I did throw myself into tobacco spearing. Actually, I didn't have a choice. About a week after I got back, in the evening, just about sunset, I went out to visit my garden. I looked down and realized that my entire tobacco crop – that is, all four plants of it – had been harvested for me; cut and speared while I'd been off on a delivery. The crime or favor – I didn't know which – was still fresh; the leaves were just beginning to wilt.

I was standing there, shaking my head and wondering if there was such a thing as tobacco bandits, when Eli drove up in his farm wagon. Eli pulled on his beard a few times, studied the horizon with great care and then, apparently fully convinced it was true, observed that it was a fair evening.

I agreed.

He took a little while and then he asked, 'Any new babies?'

Well, yes, there had been, as a matter of fact. 'An English girl,' I said. 'Someone you're not likely to know.'

He rested and let the answer sink in.

He adjusted the reins, rested and then said, 'See you got your tobacco about put away.'

'Why, yes, Eli,' I said, walking over to tug at a spot on the horse's harness, 'it appears that I do.' I looked him in the eye, then back at the horse and then I waited. I stroked the horse's neck, ran my hand along his back and patted him lightly on the flank. 'I don't suppose you'd know how this tobacco got down, now would you?' I asked.

He smiled just a trifle, looking awfully pleased with himself for a man who was supposed to be concerned with humility. 'I just believe I might,' he said.

He adjusted the way he was sitting in the buggy, made some remark about how it was a terrible good year for tobacco and especially right here in this particular hollow, said he thought he ought to be going, and he turned his wagon in the drive.

After he'd turned his horse to leave, he looked around over his shoulder and he mentioned they'd be spearing the next evening over to his house if I would still be wondering how it got done.

So I helped put away Eli's tobacco crop.

Tobacco is a major cash crop for the Amish, a significant source of income for the families and for the entire community. If you're part of the community, you share in tobacco growing.

The cycle starts in November, as soon as the kitchen garden is picked clean of the last remaining beets. A farmer then leads a couple of mules into the backyard and gets them to drag disks through the earth. Using giant steam plates he sterilizes the plot, patch by patch, and then tucks it under black plastic sheeting. He literally puts the ground to rest for the winter months. In the spring, with a watering can, he sprinkles seeds over the plot and in June the family members carry the seedlings, which look a lot like heads of butter lettuce, out to the fields in cardboard boxes and nest them, by hand, one by one, in the dirt. From planting to stripping, each tobacco plant is tended by hand.

Over the summer months the beds are hoed, cultivated and weeded; then, in late August or early September, once they have achieved their full size – by now, they look like giant versions of romaine lettuce – harvesting begins; that is, the tobacco is 'put away'. The men lead the process; they go out with long-handled shears and they cut the fat stalks of the plants that are ready for harvest. (Transplanting is staged so that all of the rows don't come to maturity at the same time.) These lie flat, shrivelling slowly in the sun until the women and children arrive in the late afternoon or after supper.

I'd head over to Eli's in my blue jeans after finishing up office hours or house calls. Along with the other women, I'd pick up a lathe – a flat-sided stick about five feet long – and, slipping a metal tip over one end, I'd make a spear. I worked along the rows, picking up cut plants, spearing their stalks, and pulling the stalks down onto the lathe.

Mary, Eli's six-year-old, gave me a hand. Mary's not much bigger than a squirrel, but she was out in the fields dragging the plants to the grown-ups. If one of my plants got stuck on a lathe, she'd hang on it and swing like it was a gymnast's bar until it fell down. She'd look up at me, giggle, and scurry off to find another stalk.

We the spearers left the lathes on the ground behind us as we worked. Once we finished, Eli and his son would appear with the wagon and they'd walk up and down the rows, lifting the lathes off the ground and piling them on the wagon. They'd go from the field to the drying barn for hanging. There the leaves drape, gradually changing over the months from a moist fleshy green to a golden brown. In the winter months – November, December and January – families, and young people especially, get their big stove going in the stripping room in their barn. They sing, tell stories and strip the tobacco leaves; then they press, bale and ready the leaves for market.

It was during the harvesting of tobacco and the filling of silo, I remember, when Reuben and Rebecca came to Dr Kaufman's office with Benjamin on their lap. I was about to rush over and start to babble. I thought I might favor them with a dramatic rendition of how Richie was plying the corn-cutting trade he'd learnt at Reuben's side a year before, but I stopped myself. Something was wrong.

Benjamin's weight was terrible; there were hollow shadows around his eyes; his forehead seemed large and heavy, and worse, his awareness would blur and he'd drift away off, leaving us behind. I couldn't believe it. Baby Benjamin, baby boy after all those girls, a child whose arrival had been celebrated by so many light hearts, a baby like this was meant to be snooping through the kitchen cupboards or smacking his fat palm in a bowl of mushy cornflakes and grape slush; he was meant to be crawling all over his sisters, giving them hugs and yanking on their skirts. He had perfect, loving, generous parents; he came from a household robust with vitality and health. A mistake for this baby to be sick. Reuben and Rebecca sat calmly, answering questions, and we all agreed that the baby should be taken to Infants & Children's Hospital for a complete battery of tests. I agreed to drive them up the next day.

Unfortunately, I wasn't able to make the first trip. The evening of the day I saw baby Benjamin, while I was out spearing tobacco, I got fierce cramps and it was all I could do to get home and curl up in a knot on my bed. I didn't even have the strength to fix the hot water bottle. I lay in my bed moaning while great boulders of pain rolled back and forth over my abdomen.

I stayed there in torment for several hours before I finally realized what was happening. I was having a miscarriage. It took me the longest time to figure it out – had I been a patient of mine, I might have been quicker – but the fact is, my reproductive system gives little information from which to diagnose. It appears to be totally random. Some of the world's finest doctors said it 'defied description'; others said that if I ever conceived it would be a miracle, and that if such a miracle occurred, the resulting embryo could be expected to last about 30 minutes. By the time I'd put all the pieces together, I figured out that I'd been pregnant for about three months and this was a miscarriage.

Once it hit me, I felt an overwhelming sense of awe. Richie and I had made this little fellow who didn't pay any attention to prognoses of fancy East Coast physicians. Here he was, meant to live for no more than 30 minutes altogether, and instead, he had survived to be an old man, relatively speaking, an irascible old 10-weeker who must have fought death tooth and nail, as far as I could tell from the wrenching, dragging, stamping and storming that was going on inside me. How I admired him (I knew it was a boy). I rolled over, sputtering partly with the joy at the thought of the life that had landed inside me and, at the same time, stuffing one pillow hard against my stomach and jamming my face into another pillow, as if that would smother the pain.

I used to say to my patients that miscarriage – that far along – was often said to be more painful than normal labor. I say it with greater conviction now.

When Richie came home from his trip that day, he got the hot water bottle and the talcum powder, and hour after hour, he patiently massaged my back and kept my head tucked safely in his lap. Sometimes Richie can love me so that I become nothing but the warmth and safety of his arms.

We lost our baby together.

I know, you could say I never really had a baby, except during those few hours when it was already over and done with, but I guess these things aren't entirely logical. I loved my baby. Writhing on my bed, yes, absorbed in pain and self-pity, yes, still I was flooded with adoration for this tiny, not yet shaped baby who had lived in me. I was awed by him; awed by the spirit of the child who had lived so long where no child was meant to live. To have had such an amazing being alive within oneself is a great honor; to have been a vessel, a carrying basket – even for a while. Oh, God, I wanted him to have lived. I wanted to see him, wrap him, carry him, study his face. I wanted to raise him, protect him; I wanted for Richie and me to teach him what we had learnt about living. I would have respected this child. Oh, God, I didn't want him to be dead. I didn't believe he could be dead.

But he was and we named him. Together Richie and I buried him.

I rested a day. Richie worked around the house and brought me Chinese food for dinner, and then there was nothing to do but go back to work.

When I got back to the office I found they hadn't completed the tests on baby Benjamin. I drove him and Reuben and Rebecca back up to Infants & Children's. Baby Benjamin looked worse than he had two days before and now I was truly angry with him, angry because he threatened to abandon the earth, leave it, even though he'd been given such a ruddy start. He'd had a good chance for a full, strong life and he appeared to be letting it slip lazily away from him. I couldn't bear it.

I don't know what we talked about driving up to the hospital. The tobacco crop, I suppose. Corn crop. The other children. I don't know.

At Infants & Children's they found that Benjamin had an invasive brain tumor – one, that is, that had grown into the vital parts of the brain and that made removal virtually impossible.

At the news, the faces of Reuben and Rebecca rippled and stilled. Without saying anything, without touching each other, just exchanging looks acknowledging that each had heard, they rose and followed the doctor where he bid them go to sign some papers.

I stayed with Benjamin. He began to wail thinly when they left, and I picked him up and held him so he could lay his head against my shoulder and at the same time look out of the window on voluptuous green slopes and an autumn forest. I swayed back and forth, lightly stroking his back, and soon the thin wail died out.

I studied his ear and eye, his frail, translucent cheeks. With great care, I touched the soft hair on his head and patted his bundled body; I put my cheek against his sweet warm skin. Finally, I understood that there was nothing I could do for him, and because of that I succumbed to him as he was. I saw his exquisite beauty. I felt the perfection of his terribly imperfect body. He gave me great peace, little Benjamin did, because I could love him exactly as he was, exactly for the amount of time he had with us. For a short while, I was able to love him not for what he might have been, not for what he would give to all of us and become, but for what he was. I could love him for the moment, completely; I didn't have to measure love out so it would last. It seemed to me that the grandest thing I could ever do with my life was to treat Benjamin kindly while he lived; to try to give him all goodness and love while he was here. Nothing more.

Reuben and Rebecca took Benjamin home as soon as they could because he cried himself hoarse when he was in the hospital. They took him home because, although the doctors could operate, there was virtually no hope of it making any difference. When they left, one of the nurses said, 'I admire your decision.'

But the next day, Reuben and Rebecca started hearing from Baltimore doctors. It was a rare case, they said; perhaps they could find a way to help some other child in years to come if they could treat Benjamin. They asked Reuben and Rebecca to hand over the child.

At home, all the family took turns carrying and rocking Benjamin, who suffered horribly through the days and nights. They, too, wanted to give him as much love as there was time for.

Soon the doctors began to say they could prolong his life

for five years, and then, with suspicious quickness, they said they could cure him.

Reuben and Rebecca prayed, talked with each other, the minister, and the children, and decided that the baby had enough to endure without being put in the hands of strangers in a hospital where the family could only visit him. They said they didn't believe that God had given them Benjamin to be used in an experiment.

The doctors filed suit. 'They planned,' Rebecca said, 'to come take him out of our arms. We didn't know about this law. We didn't know they could carry our baby away without our saying, "Go ahead, take our baby from his family."'

The rest of the machinations aren't important. I know I ended up driving Rebecca, Reuben and Benjamin to Infants & Children's, where Benjamin died.

It was after that that I decided to leave Stephen and the Country Hospital. Up until then I'd limited my disagreement with hospitals and doctors to birthing issues, and each time they shocked me with their technological bluster, I reminded myself that if I really wanted change, I had to stay and act on what I believed.

But this was one too many interventions. They should not have intruded into the delicate sanctuary of Benjamin's family. There was defilement in that act. And then my feelings compounded, and I remembered how they had rent Haseena's body and raided the tranquility which had been so gracefully carried in her. I remembered how commonly they went to a laboring woman's bedside to read the print-outs from the fetal heart monitor and never even looked her in the face or stroked her hair. I thought of all the times they had put their rapacious need to accumulate medical knowledge before their respect for the people they were caring for.

In their great enterprise, too many of the doctors seemed to have forgotten that other people's ways could be worthy and deserving of honor.

I left Stephen and I left Country Hospital. I would go out

on my own. I didn't know if any woman would come and ask for my care. I just knew I wanted to take care of Amish women and their babies in a way that respected them.

16

The Office

We got the last of the tobacco put away about the same time that I decided to go out on my own, so it seemed right to promise everyone an open house and tobacco harvest party on the Sunday night before a Monday opening. I shouldn't say it seemed right; in fact, the whole idea made me very nervous.

After all, Richie and I had only to paint the entire downstairs of the house, furnish it and talk to insurance, accounting and legal people. We had to put ads in all the newspapers for used examining tables and lights and other equipment. That left making sure that every pregnant woman in Lancaster County knew that I was thinking – make that thinking *and* dreaming – about her pregnancy, her backache, her other children, her husband and her baby, and letting her know that I was willing to go to enormous lengths to give her sensitive care and the birth that she wanted.

I established a custom birth policy and, as it turned out, it gave me some of my best births.

Take the bus, for example. Martha Ann, a holdout from the hippie generation, was an earth mother of the sixties sort. She was a vegetarian, she wore beads, she made major decisions based on astrological forecasts; she was mellow, forgiving and loving. She had children from different phases of her life and that was okay.

When it was time for her last child, she chose to have it at home in her bus on the hillside in the woods of Pennsylvania. She came to me because most doctors won't deliver babies in buses.

She also wanted her last child to be Sunday's child, so late on Saturday evening, she fixed herself a 'California cocktail', which is the whole-earth version of Pitocin. At one o'clock on Sunday morning, then, she called me and I drove out to her place. It was one of those nights so startling in their beauty that I thank God I have a job that gets me up to see them. Stars pierced the sky. The moon lounged lush and full on the horizon. The fields rippled broadly under the night sky; they opened wide and spilt out on a down slope of the planet. I drove out beyond the trees, beyond the intersections, into the open field lands. The road meandered as if it had all the time and space in the world to get to where it was going. A stream shimmered beside me as I drove through the night, and then I crossed a narrow stone bridge and turned onto a gravel lane leading up to the woods.

At the top of the hill, in a small meadow surrounded by trees, was the old bus, settled knee deep in wild flowers. My headlights shone across its front and across the meadow, where they illuminated a tepee.

Pulling aside a drape of gauze and wool, I entered the bus. Inside there was a kitchen counter, sink and stove, a table and a master bedroom – that is, a wall-to-wall bed at the rear of the bus. The steering wheel and driver's seat were in their regular place at the front.

Martha Ann's husband, Chuck, had attached a shed roof to the bus lengthwise and set in walls and a concrete floor. This addition to the home was filled with tables and couches, which seemed to be pushed here and there depending on day and time or on mood or necessity. A child lay sleeping on a couch; another snored lightly from a hammock not far away. The room was toasty, heated by a stove. Moonlight poured in.

A huge jar of catnip tea sat on the counter in the kitchen, where I settled my things. Wood shelves sagged under sacks of oranges, barley, other grains and dried cereals. A three-

year-old blond dumpling of a child named Foxglove crawled
up on the countertop, composed herself Indian-style, and
confidently asked for more tea and honey, please, Gretchen.
Her friend, Gretchen, came from the tepee.

I had checked Martha Ann already. She decided to stay on
the bed – accustomed as she was to going quickly once she'd
started labor. I let her alone for a while while I got acquaint-
ed with Gretchen – my most likely candidate for assistant.
While we talked, Chuck awoke, growled contentedly,
stretched his great bear self and went for his clothes. He put
on a pair of Elmer Fudds and a fiesta 'birthing' shirt, hand-
embroidered with tropical red and orange flowers by Martha
Ann.

Gretchen had a grand, quiet smile and dark straight hair;
she was a handsome, soft-spoken woman. I couldn't quite
figure out how to ask her whether she knew anything about
baby-having because I couldn't tell how old she was. She
looked like she was in her early twenties, but she had a silent,
assured way, as if she knew a great deal more than 20 years
teaches. She patiently made tea and picked things up, put
them away and wiped the countertop. I kept trying to gauge
her age and experience. I didn't want to insult her, but if she
was unfamilar with childbirth, I wanted to prepare her. I had
no choice but to be direct. I asked her what she knew.

'Oh well, what I learnt from having five children myself.
The oldest is 18 and the youngest is 15 months. I had the first
two in hospital and I realized what I was missing.' That was
all. No political comment. No railing at the medical establishment. She just realized what she was missing and started
having her babies at home. She must have been at least 34
and she looked no older than 22. I had no idea how she could
have stayed so unharassed five children later, but I thought
she would be able to help if I needed it.

The final character was Chuck's mother; an oxford-cloth,
middle-class woman with streaked hair and button earrings.
Carrying a great tureen of soup, she stepped into the bus as

graciously and comfortably as if she were arriving at her lawyer son's suburban split-level; she appeared content, proud, and as if all she ever wanted was for her grandchildren to be born in buses. Foxglove got down off the counter, toddled over and climbed up on her grandma's lap.

Hearing changes in Martha Ann's breathing, I went in to be with her. Gretchen, who had agreed to get another of my cases from the car, was just leaving the bus when the lights flickered and went out. 'Under the front seat,' I called out to her, 'is a flashlight that might work.'

Chuck's mother lit the only candle in the place. I pointedly assured Martha Ann and Chuck, now sitting cross-legged on the bed beside his wife, that most of delivering a baby was a matter of handwork rather than eyework, so even if we had to do it completely in the dark, it would be all right.

Gretchen had just beamed the flashlight on the newcomer's point of arrival when, swoosh, the baby's head came zooming out of the birth canal like it was on a greased sluice. The top of the baby's head was covered with green meconium stain. Baby-alert.

But the baby's face rose quickly and with good color. I reached automatically to feel for the cord at the neck; it was wrapped twice tightly – a 'noosling' we call it, because as the baby moves down the birth canal, the tighter the cord becomes. I picked up one clamp, slipped it under the cord and fastened it. I picked up the other clamp, but there was so little elbow room and so little light that I was afraid of clamping Martha Ann instead of the cord. Tentatively, I put on the second clamp. Then I cut the cord between the clamps, setting the baby free.

Her body slid out quickly. I grabbed her, sucked the mucus from her mouth, throat and nose, and started to rub her back vigorously to get a good cry. At the same time, I noticed that the far end of the umbilical cord was vigorously spurting blood all over the walls of the bus; it thrashed around like an unattended hose going full bore. Apparently my tentative second clamp had not fully closed off the cord. Blood shot up the wall, across the front of Chuck's shirt, and spattered across my arm. I watched it, wondering how I was going to snare the thing, when Gretchen calmly reached over, took hold of the cord, and pressed it tight between her fingers. She said nothing. The baby cried, I clamped the cord a second time and went back to my routine.

Apparently all events were easily absorbed in this household – straight grandmas and errant umbilical cords – so it was an easy thing to settle the new baby, to give Grandma her chance to admire, to mop the blood off the walls and to get Martha Ann started nursing. Chuck climbed over his wife and the new baby, giving each of them a hug as he went and then he wandered on out to see if he could find out why the power had failed. Foxglove, who had finished her tea and honey by now, replaced him on the bed. As she sat, tentatively stroking the baby's head, we women – Foxglove included – talked names. Then Gretchen drifted towards the front of the bus; Grandma – who had to be up at six to get to a special church service – bustled off with her face shining. I gave my instructions, gave Martha Ann congratulations, and went to the shed part of the bus, where Chuck and Gretchen were.

The lights were still out. The moonlight, riding high above the pine trees, cast a shadow work of windowpanes on the concrete floor. Chuck, burly and composed, his arms folded comfortably across his chest, stood in front of the stove and watched his older children sleep. Gretchen was sitting a ways away, stroking the head of one child. It was still warm in the shed. I stood and watched them until I was absolutely quiet, too, and then I lifted the doorway of gauze and went back into the pure and perfect night.

But this – my night visit to the oneness of things – was yet to come. And if I'd been planning on a clientele of hippies, it would have been different in those weeks before I opened my office. But the Amish, as far as I could tell, were the reverse of the hippies. Instead of 'Everybody come in and do your own thing,' it was 'Do not taint us with your wordly ways.'

No matter how much I wanted to be with the Amish, to protect their women and children at childbirth, to be sensitive to the childbirth standards of their culture, I didn't know whether or not they would fully accept me, either as their midwife or as their neighbor and friend. It wasn't that they hadn't been cordial and pleasant; they had been. But that's something different from real friendship – friendship that would forgive me my mistakes and tolerate me even when I grew short-tempered or tired; friendship that would allow me to drop in unannounced at somebody's house, just to visit or even to ask sensitive questions, like what do you do if somebody won't pay or how do you get a woman to cooperate?

Besides, I wasn't sure about how they would accept me as a midwife on my own. Before they had the assurance of knowing that I worked out of the same office as a doctor. Would they trust me if I told them that I had a back-up doctor – which I had – even though they couldn't see her each time they came in?

Besides, we knew the Amish well enough now – it was about a year after we'd first come to Paradise – to appreciate that their way excludes outsiders.

It might sound as if I was suffering from simple start-up anxieties, which I was, but they were compounded by the basic fact of Amish life: that for four and a half centuries, the Amish had remained separate from the world. I was clearly of the world; I didn't go to church or claim a faith. 'Be ye not yoked unequally together with unbelievers,' the Amish might quote. And they might continue, 'What communion hath light with darkness?' I being darkness and they being light. I had no reason to think that the Amish would compromise their four and a half centuries of separation from worldliness for me.

It's different among the English, who favor new people

and new ideas. Even with respect to basic values like family and faith. They've been toyed with, experimented with, tossed about, lionized, examined, measured, bought, sold and otherwise treated like consumables. One year, it's a great thing for a woman to get married and have babies and the next year it isn't – at least for trendsetters. I stopped trying to follow which religion was current among my friends – Eastern or Western, intellectual or passionate, mystical or pragmatic, challenging or reassuring, embracing or isolating.

Of all the standards that humans might live by, the Amish culled a few staples and succeeded in holding to them – even now, in the midst of a historical time whistling with pressures to change. I watched the Amish, admired them and finally had to try to understand how they came to have a standard of excellence gained by loving and caring, by unselfishness and humility, by humble and hard work, by commitment to community and to helping one another; whereas the English world has a standard of excellence that requires beating the other guy to the punch.

The Amish way began in the 16th century and was part of a much larger reforming tide sweeping through Europe at that time. In the opinion of the reformers, the Catholic church had disfigured the teachings of the simple carpenter of Nazareth and turned the church into a self-serving institution for the rich and powerful.

Martin Luther, in the 95 theses he nailed to the door of the castle church at Wittenberg in 1517, led the challenge. He observed that the spiritual tone of the church had been undercut by such practices as the selling of redemptions from sin. In a later document, he criticized the church's acceptance of the pronouncement by popes that they were divine; he rebelled against the idea that all messages to God should have to go through priests and popes. Luther argued that an ordinary man ought not to have to get past so many earthly brokers in order to pray to God.

On the contrary, Luther claimed, all believers were priests

and each man was directly responsible for his communion with God.

In 1523 in Switzerland, Conrad Grebel argued that if it was true that each man was responsible for his relationship with God, then it followed that infants ought not to be baptized because infants couldn't actually choose to follow God. Baptism, Grebel said, ought to be only upon profession of faith and ought, therefore, to be only for people who had reached an age of understanding. Those who followed this belief were called Anabaptists.

They refused to baptize their infants and began to follow a simple religious life. They attempted to live as Christ did. Each day, they sought to live in humility, lowliness, obedience and service. They believed that only those who truly practised Jesus's teachings of love and non-resistance deserved to be called Christians. They gathered in a brotherhood of believers.

The Roman Catholic establishment loathed the challenge to their leadership and persecuted the Anabaptists. Tortures and executions of the early Anabaptists are recorded in a book of martyrs, still found in every Amish home.

The Amish, who were one of many Anabaptist sects, were notable for emphasizing the importance of being separate from the world. They strictly interpreted standards of social avoidance, or *Meidung*. *Meidung* means that if a member of the church falls by the moral wayside, they are to be shunned; that is, members shall not eat with them, nor do business with them, nor converse with them. The standard applies to one's fallen children, one's parents, and one's spouse.

Of course, since I had not been raised Amish, I couldn't fall away and I wouldn't be shunned. But that wasn't the question; my questions were about the depth of their tolerance for my way of life. A people who are so serious about maintaining their status as 'strangers' in this world that they are willing to give up relations with their family members are a people who might be unforgiving towards those who had lived a less pure life. So I worried about whether they would be able to come comfortably to my house, have a snack by electric light, and on that inevitable day when I needed them, would they stand by me? For example, if a child were born imperfect and the parents, hurt and angry, attacked me, would the Amish keep coming to me?

'Blessed is the man that walketh not in the counsel of the ungodly.'

In the last couple of weeks before the open house and tobacco harvest party, my new English friend Helen came around to help out. Helen, a 27-year-old nurse practitioner who worked in a local clinic, talked eagerly about going out on her own, so she followed my undertaking with real enthusiasm.

Helen's ingenuous face belied her competence as a nurse. She answered calls any time of the day or night; she measured the medical circumstances with an electronic precision, made decisions, acted swiftly and kindly, asked after the entire family, faultlessly remembering whose hearts, bones, ears and bowels had last been of bother. She detected problems early on and saved lives, and she made tiresome, repetitive house calls so that her patients could be at home instead of in the hospital.

But in all things except nursing, Helen was as profound as a peppermint stick. She looked most natural when cavorting along the roadside with her puppy.

Patients loved her and she loved them back. Later, when she did go out on her own, she'd chatter endlessly about her visits to a 97-year-old Amishman. The old man, worker to the last, had been wheeling his crumbling body out to the shed every morning and working all day long on craftwork. It was wear and tear for which his old body had lost its forbearance, and he started getting sick all the time and complained of being dizzy. His family couldn't get him to slow down. Amishmen work.

Helen marched in, all five feet of her, and gave the old man the what for. She shook her finger at the cadaverous, white-haired, well-respected old man and said, 'Now you're just going to have to take care of yourself. You're not 19 anymore, are you, old man? Now let's eat ice cream and agree upon how much work you can do every day.' She gave him her swell smile and he shaped right up.

Of course, in some things, her Amish patients wouldn't do what she wanted and that bewildered her. She had an elderly woman with a bad heart. The woman was strong enough to have her own apartment in the grossdaadi house, but not so strong that a couple of her grandchildren didn't sleep right upstairs above her for protection. During the day she'd sit at a table by her window, watching the small children play in the barnyard and she'd snap beans or fold clothes, 'Eyes won't do for quilting anymore,' she said.

The old woman showed signs of having trouble with her heart and Helen urged her and the rest of the family to get her into the hospital for some tests. The old woman refused. 'We can control this,' Helen argued with exasperation. 'With the proper examinations and medications we can control this heartbeat and she can live much longer. Now come on.'

The old woman smiled and dismissed her. 'I believe I'll just leave things to go according to plan,' she said, and Helen suffered massive frustration. Helen's imagination just didn't stretch so far as old, contented and happily accepting of God's will. Neither, for that matter, did mine.

Helen helped me get things together that last couple of weeks before opening day at the office. In the evenings we got out announcements. I finished up some deliveries that I had agreed to do for Stephen. Richie hounded me until I talked to agents about office insurance (I'd long since had midwifery insurance). He painted, scraped, fixed, polished and scrubbed the entire downstairs office space; he did virtually everything but sew the curtains. Helen and I baked and froze for days, hoping to do the right thing by our Amish guests, if they came.

Everything went just fine. Our magnificent team act worked perfectly. Richie kept things in order, I worked relentlessly and Helen stayed excited.

Well, maybe not everything went fine. But so what if all the newspaper ads and telephone calls had failed to turn up used equipment, and so what if that was the case Friday afternoon before the Monday morning that my first patients were to arrive. So what if the only place I had to examine patients on was our waterbed. Actually, they could choose between the waterbed or the waiting room carpet.

So what if I was becoming – in spite of my entrepreneurial pose of confidence – thoroughly uneasy. An Amish neighbor tried to comfort me. She would say, 'If it was meant to be, it will be.' She wasn't particularly sugary about it, it's just that I could live without insipid comfort, thank you. My Amish neighbor didn't understand in the least. She didn't even guess that where I came from you made things happen and if they didn't happen right, it was your fault.

Let those who had legions of aunts, uncles, cousins and grandpas to stand in their kitchen in times of trial sing 'What will be, will be,' because it was logical when everybody in horse-and-buggy distance was prepared to drop everything and come over to start raising your barn the day after it burned down. (One Friday I was going to make a house call on a woman whose barn had burned down on Tuesday, and was planning on finding the place by using the burned-down barn as a landmark. Wrong. They'd rebuilt it by then.) One could afford the luxury of being philosophical and bending with the wind when everyone in the neighborhood has known you since you were born and when everyone takes a personal and communal interest in your welfare.

I came from the land of the lone tree.

On Saturday morning – 48 hours exactly from opening – my Amish neighbor came by. 'Call Dr Ellis's widow. She wants to talk to you.'

I did, and the widow said she'd heard that I was going into business for myself and maybe I would like to come over and look at some of the office equipment that her husband had. She'd been meaning to sell it but hadn't, and since her husband had been an advocate of midwifery she thought it would be in keeping with his memory if I could make use of some of his equipment.

I furnished my office for $150. What will be, will be.

Which left me only to get through my first attempt at a party for my Amish neighbors.

At the time, Helen didn't know many Amish. 'Oh, goody,' she said earnestly, 'a dessert party.' Dessert party, oh, dear, no. At dessert parties you serve meringue hearts to women with hollows in their cheeks. The women keep their ankles crossed the whole time.

'This, dear Helen, is not a dessert party; this is a "snack". "Snack", my dear, means mounding the table high with food.' (Our guests, remember, normally do hard physical work 12 to 14 hours a day.) 'Snack for four families means pulling out every flat surface in the house' – I was considering using the newly acquired examining table – 'spreading each one with a bed sheet and, when the guests arrive, it means making an endless parade of food to the table. That's "snack", Helen.'

I tried to remember everything I'd observed about eating in an Amish home so I would get it right.

It poured the night of the party, so Helen and Richard decided to drive out in several laps and pick up our guests. I was limp with anxiety. I figured they all would have forgotten and gone to bed. Joylessly, I waited for the cars to return empty. I tried to think of things to say to Helen and Richard so they wouldn't feel bad. But, no, pretty soon Richard came up the lane and, though I'd become accustomed to the way these people looked by now, I still stood wide-eyed and freshly charmed when I watched Rachel, my first party guest, walk into my living room in her big black bonnet, her black cape with the initials embroidered in the corner, and her baby underneath. Her face was scrubbed.

At first everyone was very quiet. They took off their bonnets or hats and then took one of the chairs that I'd put in a circle around the room. They sat there without saying too much. 'Did you get your examining table?'

'Yes, thanks, I did.'

'Good, good.'

'Did you get your pump fixed?'

'Yes, I did. Matthew helped me.'

'Good, good.'

It wasn't like I didn't know about this pace of conversation; it was the way it was always done. But I would have welcomed a sign.

The room soon filled with young women and children and young mothers in blue, brown and lavender dresses. Old Silla sat down next to old Lizzie in white wicker rocking chairs and they rocked and talked. The girls stood in groups and talked shyly, sounding like birds; the boys stood about with their hands in their pockets, grinning, asking me if I thought I had enough food. Men scooped up small children. Young women bounced them about.

Then, the last carful of people filed in the room. Helen trailed them in, glistening like a candy apple. Helen had been rendered useless. She was in love with an Amish boy. In the time it had taken to drive from his house to ours, Helen had fallen in love with young Sam. And he with her. It was done.

I brought out pumpkin custard, mincemeat pie, Helen's *New York Times Health Food Cookbook* apple crisp, pumpkin pie, Fritos. I brought out chocolate marble cake with chocolate frosting and plain chocolate cake with peanut butter frosting. I brought out pretzels and popcorn. I brought out five gallons of apple cider and, at the last minute, I set out two gallons of Cloister Dairy ice cream, cookies and pastry bars.

We sat down for a snack.

And then I asked for grace.

When I opened my eyes the beards and bright eyes were still there.

We ate. Bowls and plates filled up, layers of custard plopped flat on layers of pie, which sank into ice cream spooned over cake. Glassfuls of apple juice gurgled up to the lips of tumblers and in some cases overflowed the top, and then everything was passed from hand to hand again and they ate even more. I don't even know what they talked about; I couldn't concentrate for getting everything they needed to eat.

I knew Amish liked games. So, seeing everything was going okay, I got out my balloons and passed them out. 'Blow up your balloons,' I said. 'The person whose balloon lasts the longest wins the game.' They looked at me blankly. Surely, I thought, they get the idea. Ohmygosh. Maybe they do not believe in balloons. Maybe Anabaptists had rules about balloons. 'That is,' I went on, 'you want to break the other person's balloon and save your own.' I lunged for Richie's balloon.

They got it.

The room went bersek. With flash and gusto, old men attacked young ones, old women took out after toddlers, teenagers squealed, neighbor fell upon neighbor, husband upon wife, son upon father. They crushed each other, snuck up on each other, slid around, ganged up. Sam and Helen peeped at each other and snuck about in attacks and coun- terattacks for the duration.

We lined up for Pin the Tail on the Donkey and everyone played, starting with the little ones and working on up. It took the longest time, for the women had to remove their coverings in order to be blindfolded, and then they had to be turned carefully, once, twice, three times. Interest never flagged.

'Oh, that's just the right direction, Johnny, just right. Keep

it up and you'll be putting that pin in the side of a real donkey.'

'Okay, Reuben, maybe this one time you can keep yourself
from going round in circles.'

'Eek, eek, Rebecca, you're going to stab me.'

Everyone who lived on our road thought Richie must be
somebody very significant in the outside world – dressing up
in that uniform and flying those big planes through the sky –
so they whooped and whooped when he lost his way, nearly
stepped on baby Susie and tried to pin the donkey's tail
directly on old Silla's elbow. And Reuben filled a balloon
with water and crashed it over my head just as I put my tail
in the right place. Sam was there right in time to put his
young farmer's hand kindly on Helen's shoulders to turn her
around. She blushed the color of strawberry soda pop.

While the adults recovered themselves, the young people
wandered about, off into the kitchen and out of sight. We
thought they must be getting drinks of water or something,
but soon we heard muffled giggling.

Richard and I – having anticipated this very event – looked
at each other, melodramatically leant down in unison to untie
our shoes, got up together, and crept down the hall, in step
and on tiptoe. Neither he nor I smiled. I beckoned for the
others to follow.

Upon reaching the bedroom door, Richie turned abruptly
to his Amish platoon and dramatically signalled them to
remain silent. We cracked open the bedroom door and he
and I took the first peek at a half dozen Amish children,
bouncing, rolling about and giggling on the waterbed among
the bonnets and caps. Richie and I stepped aside and let the
others look. Finally, we threw the door open and exposed the
little vandals. They squealed appropriately and dived for the
four corners of the room.

'Why, what's this?' Reuben said, snatching his boys very
seriously from the bed. 'Now what would this bed be?' He
put his fingers to its surface and tested it.

'Stand with your back to it, Reuben,' I said, and he did and I toppled him over. He smiled wondrously. Then he rolled over to one side and back to the other.

'Where's my wife?' he said. 'Come here, wife, and see what this is like.' She climbed on, giggling like Helen would have giggled, and the two of them lay there smiling foolishly, and then Reuben sighed and said resignedly, 'I suppose you'd be needing electricity for a bed like this, now wouldn't you?'

Mothers and Fathers

They did come to me to deliver their babies. They came to me so many times to deliver their babies that by the end of my first year of private practice I was in need of major recuperation. Five babies the first month, 10 the third, increasing up to 20 a month by the time my first vacation came. I drove up to the camp at Pleasant Pond that August, walked into the lake up to my neck and stood there for two weeks, weeping with exhaustion.

It was partly the count. Just the number of hours you have to be awake to deliver 20 babies – for some reason, I won't or can't sleep when I'm out on a delivery, even if nothing's going to happen for a while. Then, in the beginning, I was applying the standards I used when I was working in the hospital; I used to arrive very early and stayed with the patient a long time after the birth so that I could protect them from unnecessary interference in their birth and in their early hours with their child. But those things are only part of it; I was most exhausted by teaching myself how to work well with the woman and her family on her own terrain.

When you go to the hospital to have your baby, they put you in a bed like all other hospital beds, they dress you in a gown like all other hospital gowns, they surround you by an entire hospital staff that guides you along a track that diminishes your individuality and its unique demands, they substitute sophisticated procedures and, relatively speaking, your having a baby is efficient and unemotional for the attendants.

When I started out in practice by myself, I didn't fully

appreciate that when I went single-handedly to deliver babies at home – one midwife in the midst of at least three genera-tions of a family – that I would be, in many respects, at their mercy. The qualities of their lives and relationships crowded in on the relatively simple act of birth, making it rich with possibilities – some beneficial, some not.

For, in spite of how uniform the Amish appear to be, in spite of their rigorous discipline over their community's behavior, not all Amish people are the same. Conventional wisdom says that no people are all the same; but when you see people who look like each other and are all quiet and say a lot of the same things when they do talk . . . it's hard to believe otherwise.

In Intercourse, at the People's Place, they have a slide show that helps tourists get some of the Amish facts straight. I usu-ally take my guests there first, partly because I never tire of the show and partly because it explains things so well.

From the show my friends have quickly grasped the idea that food is not religion, although it is an important – and loved – part of Amish life. Fairly quickly, they grasp the idea that the Amish prefer their way of life to the mainstream; they do not envy life in the cities nor do they envy 'progress'. What is hardest for my friends to grasp is that Amish people are not all the same. They are not pressed, as the slide show says, 'out of one Amish cookie cutter.'

There are lively gentle people, pious gentle people, funny ones, boring ones, mean ones, kind ones, intelligent ones, ones not so smart.

Take intelligent ones, for example.

I was still working with Stephen when Amos and Barbara King started having trouble with their fourth baby. They'd lost their third baby in the hospital one or two weeks after birth, and now the fourth was having trouble breathing and wasn't eating well. Stephen figured it was a virus but sent it to the hospital for some tests. Amos insisted it wasn't a virus. The pattern, he repeated, was the same as with the child before.

Amos was right; it wasn't a virus. The baby's metabolic system wasn't working right and though Country Hospital couldn't determine exactly why it was dysfunctional, Stephen had narrowed it down enough so that the researchers he called at Infants & Children's were ready with specific tests when the baby arrived. Thirty-six hours later, amino acid analyzer tests showed that the mother's milk was killing the fourth child, just as it probably had killed the third.

Amos King – simple Amish farmer, chicken breeder, corn picker, manure shoveller, father today of five children, two of whom are normal and three of whom have the metabolic disorder – has become an expert on this exquisitely complex and changeable condition. So educated have we all become, due to Amos's way that, in spite of the possibility of handicap in their last baby, I felt completely safe in delivering it at home. At the crucial 12th hour after birth, exactly, a local medical technician, a young man who knew the family and who was, therefore, willing to get up before dawn to make the test, appeared at the King's farmhouse door, took a blood sample from the new baby, drove it to Infants & Children's and, in a record 30 hours after birth, we found out the baby had the metabolic disorder and the special diet was begun.

Amos King found the sensitivity I had often missed in the medical system. In his gentle, self-effacing style, he succeeded at what the rest of us have often failed at: getting the specialist to adapt to an unusual circumstance. Amos King does have joy in his face and he is innocent of personal competition or self-serving motives. That's why, I guess, the hospital set aside its normal regulations and allowed Amos King to walk right alongside that second sick baby's blood as it made its way through the labyrinth of usually proud, protective, and intensely competitive researchers. He asked them about the physiology of the disease – although he wouldn't have called it that in the beginning – and explained that he needed to understand because he lived on a farm a long way from Infants & Children's and he would be needing to make as many routine tests on the baby as was possible for him to do at home, and he would be needing to figure how to adjust the baby's diet accordingly. Researchers, who don't customarily share their discoveries with each other until after publication, got chatty about the ins and outs of metabolic research with this Amish farmer.

Today Amos King probably knows more about certain metabolic disorders than most researchers in the country. He makes intricate calculations for each of the afflicted children as to what they can eat, when, and in what quantities.

The controls aren't perfect – no one knows how to do that yet – and each time a child's system goes out of balance, some brain damage is done. So in Amos and Barbara's home, a number of the children have difficulty talking and walking. It doesn't make any difference – well, yes, it does. The household seems blessed. The children are generally crawling all over each other, laughing and playing. 'We just do what we can each day,' Amos says easily and saunters off as if he were a man without responsibility or a thought in the world.

But I've said that Amish come in all kinds.

Abysmal November. A resentful dawn is ragging at the eastern sky. The phone rings.

'You gotta come here quick.'

'Who is this?'

'You don't know me.'

'Do I know your wife?'

'No.'

'What's the problem?'

'The wife, she just had a baby about an hour ago and it looks sort of funny, and the afterbirth never came yet. The wife, she still didn't want me to call you, but I didn't know what to do.'

'Who's your doctor?'

'The wife didn't want no doctor. You gotta come.'

I hated these calls. I had no choice. He'd never call the

ambulance and I couldn't leave a woman with an afterbirth still in her an hour after the baby'd come.

'All right. I'll come. You get back to that house as fast as you can. Make sure that baby is wrapped warm and you stay right next to your wife – don't you dare let her get up.'

I drove in a straight line overland through somebody's hay field, pounding my fist in fury on the steering wheel as I went, 'It's all right to put your baby's life in danger,' I screamed, 'and to put your wife's life in danger – she's probably just waiting until I get there to begin to hemorrhage. One hour, for Pete's sake – just because you're too something or other to make sure your wife gets to the doctor. So what if "she didn't want no doctor". So what!'

I marched into the kitchen. For an Amish kitchen, it was strangely disordered.

'Where's your wife?'

He looked at me dully and pointed the way.

I could see it now. The first lawsuit brought by an Amishman in four and a half centuries.

I brushed past the father and went to the bedroom.

Absolutely nothing had been prepared for this baby. I could see that. After it had come, the girl must have simply rolled over and pulled a heap of blankets over herself. She was lying with her face towards the wall, clutching the blankets, her new baby apparently hidden somewhere among them.

'How are you doing, Barbara?' I asked.

She didn't answer.

'Barbara, my name is Penny and I'm the midwife. I've come to see you and your baby. We'll have to deliver your afterbirth, otherwise you might begin to bleed heavily. And then we need to see if you and the baby are all right. It'll go better for both of you if we do this together.'

Still she didn't reply. She pulled the blankets farther up over her face, and even through the mound of them, I could see her spine stiffen.

She stayed that way. She wouldn't talk or look at me. I had to search for the child, who turned out to be fine, and delivered the afterbirth without the hemorrhage I'd expected. Apparently it had separated well enough, but she may have resisted pushing it out. Throughout these operations, she never spoke. With perfect consistency, she kept her head turned away from me, as if I were loathsome. She submitted to my taking the baby away to wash it only because her husband made her, and when I brought it back, ready for nursing, she grabbed it to her and turned her back to me again.

Her husband sat in a chair in the kitchen most of the time, his head dropped, his eyes focused on the floor.

Never had I had a delivery like this. It can't happen; even if young people aren't able to get ready for the birth themselves, even if there are mental problems, the girl's mother or a neighbor will step in and get things ready.

'Who's going to help with this baby?' I asked the father.

'She wants to do it herself,' he said helplessly.

'She can't do it herself. Surely you can see that now. That baby could have died; your wife could have died. Where's this girl's mother? Who's going to help with this baby? You make it your business to work this out and in case you think I'm not serious, I want you to know that I'm not leaving this house until I know.'

He went into the bedroom and I went out to the car to see if I could find extra boxes of diaper samples. When he came back he said his wife's younger sister would be coming.

I went back the next day. The sister and a neighbor were there. Barbara sat in a rocking chair with its back to the center of the room. The baby was in her lap and she stroked it and cooed. I asked her questions; she answered each of them in a word or two and cooed in the space between answers, successfully making the cooing a battering ram to drive me away.

On the way out, I was able to ask the neighbor how it happened that they were allowed to be so unprepared. 'We didn't know them,' she said. 'They just moved here from another county; we thought their family would be helping them. Now we found out that the girl's mother died not so long ago and we didn't realize how it was with them. But we see how they are and can help.' The father was nowhere to be seen.

A few weeks later I went back one more time. The sister was still there and the house had gained some order, but the mother hadn't changed. Again, she talked only to her baby during the visit. It was as if with the soft, beating patter she could keep all of us away and slowly herself slip inch by inch inside the baby and live within her.

This time I found the father around the back of the barn. While I talked, he looked out towards the fields and ran a leather harness nervously through his fingers. I told him that the baby was doing fine, but that I thought his wife would still need some help.

'I suppose you'll be wanting your money now then,' he said.

'Yes,' I answered, wondering if he'd heard a word I'd said about his wife. There was little I could do about it. 'I'll be sending you a bill and it will be less than I normally would charge because you didn't have the prenatal office visits, but I want you to understand that I should actually charge you more. A woman who hasn't had prenatal care is at much higher risk. Furthermore, I want to make it clear that I will never deliver another child of yours under circumstances like that. Never. Do you understand?'

'Oh,' he said, almost blithely. 'I don't believe we need to worry about that. Ever since you delivered her baby, my wife never pays me any attention.' Then he paused for a moment and his fingers stopped roaming the edge of the harness. He looked at me and only slowly did his eyes move away from mine. His defences must have abandoned him. His young body sagged and after a while he said in a low voice, 'So I believe I'll just be paying you this once.'

* * *

When I'd be hit by that reflexive fear – 'They're gonna get me' – as I was in this case, I'd calm myself by reaching back into the memory of another night that began just as this one had.

Middle of the night, didn't know the man, didn't know the woman. Then: 'We had prenatal care from Dr Blake and he's not here now and my wife and I, we haven't had a baby for seven years and would you please come?'

I went as fast as I possibly could.

When I pulled up in this farmyard, the father's Ichabod Crane body came soaring out the door to give me a hand with my suitcase. When he bent over, his face skin fell in thin, worn folds around his mouth. His sweater, with its baggy pockets and leather buttons, hung as if from a peg off his backbone. Nevertheless, he hoisted the suitcase and swung it off towards the house, leaving, I'm sure, black and blue spots on his legs for weeks.

Once inside, he rushed from drawer to cupboard; climbed, scurried, put back, folded, unfolded, shook his head in frustration, nibbled and sniffed; and soon he had something that resembled everything we needed. He stopped now and again when he heard his wife moan and stared painfully and help-lessly at her, his long fingers dragging on the hem of his sweater. Then, coming to, he'd wipe the palms of his hands on his pants and patter off to find something else.

Like the other women, this one said little. But she didn't turn her head away. 'I'm not such a young woman anymore,' she said when we began and then, seeming to fully under-stand the physiological barriers that age puts up before child-birth, she concentrated on having the baby.

All went well.

As I was leaving, the husband said, 'Thank you. We wouldn't have known what to do.' And his wife, who had remained silent even in the aftermath of the birth, called me back. 'I want to thank you,' she said. 'Every night I'll pray for you and the good work you are doing.'

At Booth in Philadelphia, Sue Yates had harped on professional responsibility. Nurses, she said at every opportunity, took orders from doctors. Certified nurse-midwives gave their own orders, made their own decisions; they and they alone had to carry the burden of responsibility for what happened at delivery. In the hospital, we had to fight for that responsibility because doctors were constantly second-guessing us.

With my home delivery practice, I had unrestricted responsibility – and thrived on it. Among other things, it allowed me to give women what I thought was the best possible care. I wanted responsibility – even when I was so tired that I didn't know if I could carry it anymore.

But I found it peculiarly difficult to know that somebody was praying for me; to have an Amishwoman asking God to look after me and my work. All of these people, all of my patients, believe in God and in prayer, and I don't care what I might have believed – I could have been an avowed atheist when I arrived – when I'm out there among them, it's different. What I believed or didn't believe was beside the point. In my patients' minds, God was in there helping or hindering my work.

It was the final responsibility. That woman said she'd pray for me and these people do what they say they will do. Every night, before she drops into bed she's saying, 'And God bless Penny and her work.' I try very hard.

Giving Yourself Up

Once you understand that Amish people are individuals, just like people in other societies, it's tempting to rush to the conclusion that Amish are like all other Americans. But that's not true either. The Amish are a disarmingly gentle people.

There's a vegetable stand over on Spring Road. I buy there whenever I can – peas in the spring, cantaloupe in summer, cauliflower in the late fall. The girl, Sara, who sells to me must be 20 by now; she mows the lawn and keeps the dirt turned between the Sweet Williams in the beds on the family farm. In the fall, she's out working in galoshes many sizes too big for her and wearing a dark sweater with holes in the elbows. She rakes the wet, leathery leaves and tends the stand – which is not a lot bigger than a phone kiosk.

The vegetable stand is my idea of an ashram or a retreat. When the IRS is niggling me, or Richie tells me one too many times not to slam the back door, or when some patient talks back to me or refuses to take her vitamins or asks me to run her errands for her – whenever my insides start clashing about, when the sharp-toothed wheels of anxiety begin whirring, I go buy vegetables at the Spring Road stand.

Sara carefully puts her rake aside when I pull up and walks over next to the stand and waits there for me to say something. She smiles. She's not outgoing, so she doesn't say anything. She just smiles, one arm folded across her waist, the other hanging loosely down her side.

'Hi, Sara. Nice day, isn't it?'

'Hi, Penny. Yes, it is.'

'Can you give me one of those cauliflowers today?' I say.

She goes to the back of her stand. Maybe she only has seven cauliflowers to sell altogether. 'What size would suit you?' she asks. I hold out my hands to make a bowl for the size I want and she nods and begins to study, one by one, the seven cauliflowers she has to choose from.

Sara is mentally retarded. For her to compare the sizes of the cauliflowers and to choose one that is the same size as I showed her with my hands is hard work. She goes deliberately, carefully and exceedingly slowly. I feel my impatience rising. My mind starts calculating on how little this young woman seems to appreciate my affairs with the IRS, my burdens as a midwife, not to mention keeping Richie happy by going to the movies with him at night when I'd rather be at home wrapped in a blanket. Sara, oblivious to the full scale of my duties or my importance, perhaps even discounting them, continues to study the cauliflowers at her implacable pace.

I don't say anything. Fortunately, I've always been able to stop myself. It's partly because I don't care to behave like a jerk; partly because I came here for the express purpose of getting things in the proper perspective again; partly because I would just bewilder Sara; but mostly because Sara is one of the most contented-looking human beings I've ever seen.

I try to subdue my internal self.

Sara concentrates. I concentrate. Tentatively she picks up one cauliflower, studies it, looks over at my hands in order to remember the size I want, then sets that head down and goes to the next one. Strangely, as she moves intently on, my irritation subsides. The third time – that's when she usually finds just what she was looking for and she knows she's gotten it right – her face is joyful. She holds the cauliflower up like an offering and looks at me expectantly.

It's about then that I come fully around myself. The young woman, patient enough to study cauliflowers, has found the exact size I was looking for. I look at Sara's hopeful face and nod. I can't remember now what I had myself agitated over. I lean back against the side of the stand and start to watch the leaves fall while Sara finds just the right size bag for my cauliflower and then begins the job of getting my money and making change.

It is the custom of the Amish to 'give themselves up' to what life delivers them because if God didn't mean it to be, they assume, it wouldn't have happened. They give themselves up to smaller events. I remember when Sadie Mae's husband was chosen to be minister. Sadie Mae confessed that she was an unlikely minister's wife – did more than her share of running around when she was young; she was the first woman in her neighborhood to start wearing black running shoes with a racing stripe instead of black oxfords. When her husband, Sam, became minister, she had to start wearing old high-buttoned black leather shoes and black stockings to church. 'I had a hard time giving myself up to that,' she said, pausing, 'but I imagine the other women had a harder time. You know, I was never the kind of girl to be a minister's wife. When I was young they had to send a team of people out to drag me back into the services; I wanted to stay outside and talk and joke. And now, you know, that I'm the minister's wife, I'm supposed to lead the women into the services. I believe there's a lot of women in my church who have a hard time with that.'

As they give themselves up, they seem to become both more gentle and more joyful.

The bedroom was more mussed than most. Katie had tossed her covering on the broad white windowsill next to a half-filled glass of juice and a Scrabble game. A throw rug, made of tags of brightly colored material and looking like a heap of oversized confetti, was jammed halfway under the bed, a toy tractor and several wooden sheep twisted among its folds.

'Well, now, where would you be wanting to put this suit-case?' said Ike, and he promptly dragged the rocking chair out of the way to make room for my equipment. He disen-tangled the toys, stuffed them under his arm, straightened the rug, and hurried off to the kitchen for fresh juice. Katie dis-appeared into the bathroom to change into her gown, calling for a box of tissues as she went, mumbling to me that she would have liked another week before the baby came so she could get her cherries put up, and I clicked my case open, got out my equipment, straightened the bed, shook the pillows, checked my radio and then all of us regathered at the bed, where it was finally quiet. We weren't going to be waiting too long for the baby, Katie and Ike's fifth.

I just thought I would let her settle, get by a couple more contractions and then examine her. The three of us sat and waited.

In the corner of the room near the bed was a door frame with a dotted swiss curtain tied back across its opening. I could see just the headboard and a few bars of crib showing. As the three of us sat, I heard a gurgling and sputtering from the room behind the curtain. Such a thing is not unusual, often older babies are in the room with us when the new ones are born – sometimes they wake and, seemingly hypnotized, stand holding onto the edge of their crib and absorbedly watch the proceedings. Sometimes when the new baby is all wrapped up, we take it over and show it to the toddler, who will poke tentatively at the arrival.

The child in the crib gurgled again and I thought, on sec-ond hearing, that it wasn't the sound of a toddler.

'Should we get Emma up?' Katie said to Ike. He nodded and without saying anything further went over to the door frame and bent over into the crib.

A farmer's forearms are powerful; his muscles wind down his arm in swirls and band his wrists with strength enough to heft 50-pound bales of hay off the back of a flatbed farm wagon and toss them 10 feet up into the upper corners of the hay barn. Ike lowered one of his forearms into the crib and lifted out a child – not a baby, but a child of 11 or 12. I stared at her. Her head, square and big, lolled on a neck that had no strength. Then came the frail carapace body. It was followed by long, spindly arms and legs. They jutted and bent across one another as she rose out of the crib; Ike tried to gather them up like sticks of firewood from a forest floor, but one arm and then another would drop and fall as he lifted her out ever so carefully from her crib. He went after them patiently. Her complexion gleamed and her eyes were radiant even in the dark humid night air of the bedroom. Ike's arms – ropy strands of iron by day – seemed to soften into a cushioned basket for the bundle of sticks of the child's body as he gathered and regathered them.

'Well now, Emma,' he said, finally having settled her in his arms, and as if returning to the middle of a chat with an old friend. 'We believe it's time now.' He stood at the foot of the bed so she could see her mother; he patted her back, stroked her arm, and looked at her affectionately. 'It's time for the baby,' he said to her. And then to me, 'We haven't many secrets from Emma.' With his great paw, he reached down and pulled a slippery stocking back up her narrow leg.

Then he sat in the rocking chair with her, talking with her and me and Katie. As her mother's contractions began to increase, Emma's face shone more, at least it seemed that way to me. Emma seemed wondrous at what was happening in the room that night. I was stunned by her presence. Honored, I suppose. She was an exaltation. When it came time for the last of the birth, Ike tucked Emma in a chair among pillows so he could help his wife.

The new baby came, squalling and yammering for attention, and as soon as we washed and wrapped him, we took him to Emma and placed him in the nest made by her long arms and legs, held together by her father's arms. Pretty soon the baby fell quiet.

It was nice for Emma, too. She would not be having children of her own, of course. She'd been a fine, tumbling child. Then, when she was three or four, she'd been stricken with a raging fever. She was sick for a week, and afterwards her parents watched her wither.

Sometime since then they had come to adore her more deeply. Not to compensate, not for the sake of pity. I think she was their special companion. I think their baby was her baby. I think her life, remnant though it seemed at first, filled and joined with theirs and made them all joyful.

Love

Helen and Sam said they were just friends and fabricated friendlike reasons for being together. Sam, for example, helped Helen train the horse she'd bought at the horse auction. I'd drive by and watch them in the afternoon – Sam with a rope, walking patiently around a corral; she beside him, asking earnest questions about the disposition of sugar cubes to pet horses. He'd explain, I suppose, and she would nod zestfully, as if it were the most intriguing thing in the universe. When their work was done, he'd hitch up his horse and buggy, and Helen would perch by his side for the ride home, enraptured; her chin would jut out a little as they drove along and so give her crispy smile a head start; her hands would be folded hard together and sunk deeply into the calico envelope of her skirt between her knees.

The attraction between them was mighty, and that was no good. If Sam and Helen felt they had to marry, then Sam, who had not yet joined the church, would be separate from his people – although not excommunicated or shunned.

Helen, after all, had not worked from sunrise to sunset, indoors and out, on a farm for her entire life; she hadn't been quilting since she was seven; she had no idea how to whip up, without sweating, a vat of silken mashed potatoes for 50 Amishmen raising a barn; she couldn't bake 20 pies on a Friday afternoon for church on Sunday, scrub her entire house from top to bottom on Saturday, serve 10 or 15 families their dinner at Sunday noon, and have everything entirely back to normal by 2.30 the same day. Helen knew no

Pennsylvania Dutch. Shirts, trousers and dresses did not stream from her sewing machine on winter evenings. Had Helen tried to put in a garden, she would have had to lay her rows out with rulers and plant her seeds in flawless straight lines as a way to know what was coming up. Helen didn't know the order in which to hang out the clothes. Her faith was an adaptation of sentiments expressed on wall posters of kittens.

Helen, not having grown up on a farm, wouldn't become Amish and live the Amish way. 'And give up nursing and my new blue Toyota?' she asked, incredulous. And even if she were willing, the chances of her succeeding weren't good. Some few have tried to adopt the Amish way; very few have succeeded.

So Sam would have to compromise his way of life; he would give up having it intertwined with that of his family. He would not be at home for dinners, harvests, sings, snacks, frolics; he would not be there for births or weddings or family celebrations. He would not be asleep on just the other side of the wall when his mother died in her sleep.

Sam's mother did not make light of the friendship; she looked straight at Helen and said, 'I suppose you'll take Sam away from us,' and later Helen would giggle and say to me, 'She's so silly to think that. I'm not going to hurt anybody,' and she'd go back to embroidering initials on a handkerchief for Sam and planning picnics for the two of them. By then they were seeing each other, with one excuse or another, almost every day of the week.

Sam's mother had put her life into raising her children Amish. Everything in Sam's upbringing, like every other child's upbringing, was designed to protect against the temptations of Helen.

From birth to five he would have lived, like every child, in his family's lap. Walk through any Amish farmyard and toddlers are underfoot as much as chickens. Should one be frightened by a sunflower that trembles like a temperamental dragon when the wind gusts, should one step barefoot on a twig, should one's eyes fill with tears, then up one is scooped into the cradle of Amish arms. One gets a soft ride then from here to there, while one's brother or sister or mother or father moves from flower bed to grape bower, from milking stool to hayloft. In the early days, you could say, a child is secured to the culture by abundant affection and belonging.

By the time they are five, children know they are not just wanted in the family; they learn they are needed and are valuable: They are depended upon to feed chickens, set the table, fold clothes and run small errands for the bigger people in the family. In that year also, like children on the outside, they arm themselves with clean clothes and lunch pails; they assemble older sisters and brothers in phalanxes about them and make the first of eight years of morning marches to the schoolhouse.

If you ever drive through Amish country, you'll pass the white one-room schoolhouses where the children get their formal education. The schoolyards are carved square out of the cornfields; they are fenced and include two outhouses, a softball field, two swings, a pump, a teeter-totter and the schoolhouse, inside which the children learn the basic skills: reading, writing, geography, spelling and arithmetic. They're not much on science, literature, politics, history or other such material. Learning is by rote, repetition is the main activity; discussion and ratiocination are left for the English. The disciplines of being Amish are once again repeated; the ways of the outside world are neglected.

Helen asked me to help her once at an inspection for lice on the heads of children at one schoolhouse.

The stragglers were just slipping in the door when we pulled into the schoolyard. We followed and were welcomed by the teacher, Anna Mae, an 18-year-old Amish girl, satisfactorily equipped for her teaching responsibility by having completed – some years ago – an eighth grade education in an Amish one-room schoolhouse.

Light poured in through double hung windows that lined either side of the classroom. The casements were pine, cleanly sanded and glossily finished. Displayed on the walls in geometric proportions was the students' work. Each student had colored in the mimeographed outline of an autumn leaf. Each child had applied the same combination of colors – brown stem, gold veins, orange palms tinged with scarlet. Each leaf had apparently drifted to the same October pond, for each one floated on the same crayoned field of blue. Some children did press hard – revealing, perhaps, a regrettable tendency to showiness – but none went out of the lines. On the far wall of the room, again symmetrically arranged, more school papers: each child's name had been drawn by the teacher in pudgy script and colored in by the student.

At the back of the room, at head height, was a pine plank with dowels set in it. Black jackets topped by flat-brimmed straw hats hung along the length of it. Two shelves, also of pine, also glossily finished, held, in military order, girls' bonnets of black and navy blue, not a ribbon dangling. Another shelf held one straight stack of identical blue binders and one straight stack of identical textbooks. Beneath the shelves were benches. On them were seated three pairs of Amish parents all looking patiently, passively ahead.

The desks, each with its hardwood fold-up top, each with its narrow pencil trench, each with its wrought-iron legs, were arranged in six neat rows, eighth-grade boys to the rear of the class, first-grade girls – in full black smocks and uncovered knots of hair – to the front. Running across the front of the room, reminding the students not so much of the superiority of the teacher as of her authority, was a low dais. On it was positioned teacher's desk, neatly kept, with sharpened pencils, small stacks of student work, a tray of accepted texts, attendance and grade books.

At the back of the room, a folding table had been erected for Helen and me to work at. We sat down – I was assigned to keep the records of who had nothing, who had nits and who had lice – and prepared to begin our inspection of heads. The three women at the back of the room stood up and came over to help. One, an older woman, smiled contentedly and patted her belly while she waited; the second, dour and drawn, scuttled restlessly back and forth behind our table. The third, a mound of womanhood built on pedestal legs, stood next to us and made wisecracks to the children as we went along. She had a toddler with her and he, with the natural arrogance of a loved child, crawled from scholar's bench to scholar's bench, assuming that each would move over and give him paper and crayon – and each one did.

Of the 36 children on the roll call, three quarters were named Stoltzfus (Stoltzfus being by far and away the most common name among the Amish); there were three Riehls and one Lantz child only. A mother asked if we could start with the girls so that the parents could leave sooner. I didn't understand the request because I didn't have the faintest idea why we had three sets of parents for helpers when we were just going to finger the children's hair.

Someone announced that the eighth-grade girls should let down their hair.

Twelve-year-old Ruth Stoltzfus raised her hands to the knot at the back of her head, pulled out a dozen pins, lifted and loosened her hair, which then billowed full and thick. As she walked to the back of the room, her head lowered and her eyes to the floor, her blond hair rippled down the slope of her back and gently stroked the inside curve of her waist. Ruth vaguely understood the power her hair had to seduce. She knew very well that the allure was not fitting for an Amish girl.

Helen took the strands of Ruth's hair and, not noticing the torment she stirred, let them fall through her fingers. A couple of the older boys sitting at the back of the room were confused by an interest they hadn't felt before. Their minds left equations and field rows and drifted vaguely towards . . .

what? They snuck glances at the falling hair. Ruth Stoltzfus blushed and kept her lashes lowered to her cheeks.

While Ruth sat with Helen, the rest of the students began work. Taking the lead, the older boys finally managed to get their math books open to the proper page, to get paper out and problems copied. Anna Mae called the first- and second-grade girls to the dais for a drill. They stood facing her and the blackboard. Anna Mae shuffled through flash cards of vowels, giving each child in turn a chance to get the answer right. A heavy redheaded girl, three times the size of her tidy, tiny peers, missed more than the others because she had to keep tugging at loose elastic in her panties with one hand and still remember to raise the other to show she knew the answer. Some horrendous conditions – loose elastic in a schoolgirl's panties, for example – cross all cultures.

While we worked, they worked. The idea was not to out-perform the other fellow. I saw no sign of gold stars or of star students. As much as possible, the students were kept even in their learning; they worked together and helped each other. They took turns. They waited. In the classroom and school-yard they learnt, as much as anything, the ways of friends they could expect to work with for the rest of their lives.

By this time, the corner of the room where the older girls were sitting was cascading with girls' hair, all of it floating with irregular freedom, all of it needing to be chased back into its own tight little bun.

The three mothers fell upon the heads with combs unsheathed – three vigilant mothers to restore symmetry and discipline. Each head was wetted down and combed flat, each had its precision part restored. Twists of hair were knit once again tightly over ears and long strands were stretched straight out in parallel lines and whipped evenly into rope. Then, each rope, now indistinguishable from that on the next head, was tightly wound, containing itself, well secured by bobby pins. Only when all the heads were smooth, slick as kitchen countertops, could the mothers relax, go to their husbands, and ask to have the buggies brought around.

By recess time, we had finished the heads of all the boys and girls. For the record, the count was four heads with lice, three with nits and the rest were clean. Helen and the parents gathered to work out prevention and treatment plans – who would tell Daniel's parents for example, and would we maybe be driving our car that way because by buggy it was a long way around? While we talked, the children made a circle about us, watching and studying. Until we drove away, the older girls hugged younger children to them, protecting them while they observed us.

The children, then, stay sequestered in their home and neighborhood schoolhouse until they are 12.

After 12 there is an apprentice adulthood. Boys start working full days in the fields with their fathers or they work out as hired boys on neighboring farms. Girls work alongside their mothers or they, too, work in the fields or they may work at cleaning house for other families, either English or Amish. Officially, their lives remain governed by their parents. They do what they are told, go where they are allowed, receive what they are given. They are silently guided by the sameness of the lives around them and by the constant reminders that they are needed, wanted, cared for, understood and protected. These conditions seem to be good ones. The young people seem strong and vital.

Then come the treacherous years: those between the time that children turn 16 and the time that they are baptized and get married. Their freedom, their being set out without tethers, is considered necessary because only then will they be able to make a genuine choice about whether they will ask to be baptized and to join the church. It's the roaming, of course, that's so hazardous. Exposure to fast cars and true love can uproot in the young even those values that are most deeply, regularly and rigorously implanted.

'Running around' the Amish call it.

I remember once, not too long after I moved to Lancaster, when I still felt that I should keep my voice down all the time because it seemed as if I was living in a massive, dirt-floored, unceilinged church. It was Sunday night, a time of special modesty and subduing of the earthly passions. It was about 3.30 am, I had just finished a delivery, and the sky was exploding with rain, charging the earth with thunder and lightning. The best of all nights of the year to be home snug in one's bed, a Bible on the bedstand.

As I drove home, I saw more buggies per square mile of road than I had ever seen in a day. One after another, buggies came towards me, their high stepping horses in flashy poses against the electric sheets that flashed across the wet, black sky. Each buggy contained a young couple totally alone, idling, for heaven's sake, way deep into the morning hours, doing who knows what. They seemed not to be paying any attention to social order then, and it was only one short hour before milking time.

I couldn't believe my eyes. These young people – the same young people who but a few years before had been hanging on the schoolyard fences waving in innocent glee at passers-by – were out carousing on a Sunday night, irrespective of all that's holy. This was a tragedy, one more in a long line of modern tragedies. Sex-indulgent, drug-distorted, authority-flaunting, punk-rock America had made its final, irreverent incursion – it had kidnapped the gentle youth of Lancaster County. I was sure I was seeing the last generation of Amish.

But no. As it turns out, they weren't following mainstream youth into garish, pointy-toed anarchy. They were merely 'running around'. 'Running around' means that on her 16th birthday, a girl makes a new dress, no different from all the others she has ever worn except for some decorative stitches on the sleeve cuffs, and on Sunday night, she joins a 'gang' at a sing in somebody's barn.

That's what I saw that night. A bunch of young people who'd been out all night singing. Singing, an activity different from say, snorting or shooting up.

I later learnt that the gangs – who call themselves things like 'Antiques', 'Sparkies' and 'Luckies' – are, in fact, worldly to different degrees. Some do stick to singing and do keep the Amish code, but others experiment more freely. Boys might wear wristwatches, drink beer and – in extreme and serious cases – find musicians with plug-in electric guitars.

It's when such musicians play in a barn just down the road from the preacher's house that the older generation – minister, bishops, and fathers in black frock coats – gather the young and remind them of the order to be kept in one's father's barn.

Girls rarely get pregnant before they are married in Lancaster County. And that's even though they take trips to the Jersey Shore, to the beaches at Sarasota and to Niagara Falls. (You can hardly get out of an Amish bedroom without gazing on a velvet painting of Niagara Falls.) So far from home the girls join the boys for bike rides along beaches and through parks at sunrise.

Some boys buy cars, which they keep in hiding in neighboring towns, available for nighttime runs. Helen's Sam had been one of these: in fact, he'd been off to the West, where he'd worked on a ranch for six months. Others, making the same exploration of the world, get ensnared in situations they understand little; they do, in fact, do drugs. The life of a church elder includes trailing off to different parts of the country to gather stray youth.

Besides those young people who wander off for adventure, some of the youth – propelled by inborn curiosity, insatiable intelligence, a desire for greater freedom, a longing for a non-Amish career or for another faith – choose to leave the community. They elect to go on to school; they elect to believe things other than what their families believe.

All in all, a little over 20 percent of the children born to Amish parents do not remain Amish.

It finally happened, of course, that Helen and Sam – prob-

ably excited from having been caught in a summer thunder-
storm – got to kissing one another during the buggy ride
back home. Helen had me believing that it started when they
were clip-clopping through a covered bridge, that there had
been snow and black-toothed trees before they entered and
pink blossomed boughs as they exited.

Apparently Sam started thinking seriously about courting
Helen, but the more he got to feeling like it, the harder it got.
He spent a lot of time with a close friend and his wife in
those days. They were getting ready to move to their own
farm in another county. Sam decided to go with them and be
their hired man for a year.

Helen insisted that the only thing in life for her was nursing. It had always been nursing, she said.

20

Home

Richie and I had been living in the rented house with the four-plant tobacco crop for two years when he began to search for land to build a house on. He studied plots in the clerk's office, on maps and from the cockpit of a small plane, and eventually found a southward-facing slope with a copse of trees. He calculated that the land would be within driving radius of my patients and determined that it could not be used for farming. Richie refused to build on land that an Amish farmer could make good use of.

Standing on the slope, we looked over a ribbon of a tossing green cornfield, to a tobacco plot dotted with fat-leafed bouquets and, beyond that, to an effervescent band of alfalfa. A pasture lay to the east. At a neighborly distance was a farmhouse, two barns, a silo and a windmill. Beyond them, more fields lapped into the distance, interrupted only by an occasional farmhouse. We could see miles across the gentle valley to the hills.

An Amishman, the one who followed his team of horses across the flow of fields below the woods, allowed us to buy this piece of his land.

Richie meant to make the basic design of the house himself. He stuffed rolls and rolls of flimsy paper under his arm and disappeared into the back room, and hours, or days, later he'd come out with pencil drawings of houses with turrets and houses with sunken bathtubs and houses with circular staircases. Timidly, I'd talk to him about them, offering praise and suggestions here and there. Richie'd go back and erase things and make more drawings. He flew out to California to see some houses he'd read about. He made more drawings. He made them into a series of blueprints.

I kept quiet.

One night, after he'd spent months and months in the back bedroom drawing and redrawing on the flimsy paper, Richie woke up, jumped out of bed, went to his drawing board and destroyed everything. The drawings were wrong, he said. He had been designing houses for someplace else. He had to go back to the beginning and make a house for Amish country.

The Amishman does not impose himself on his piece of land because, in a fundamental way, he does not really own it, not the way English own property. Instead, he considers himself its steward. It is his privilege to live on it; the land is in his trust during his lifetime. He is so serious about being a faithful steward that he nurtures his earth, he brings forth the harvest of its own disposing, he tends the land until it glows with contentment. It's just his work, his assignment, he would say, coming from Genesis. He, the Amishman, follows God's design; he is supposed to 'replenish the earth, and sub-due it: and have dominion over the fish of the sea, and over the fowl of the air, and over every living thing that moveth upon the earth.' (Genesis 1:28) And so he believes he does.

But to me, he doesn't 'have dominion'. Dominion means dominating; running the thing, being the king. Americans, crashing through the forests, tilling the plains to dust, fishing the seas empty, assumed that the earth was their dominion; that it was theirs to do with just as they pleased.

The Amishman follows the earth; it tells him when to rise and when to sleep; it tells him what he can and can't plant and when. The Amishman treats the land sensitively – he nourishes it with horse and cow manure; he treads on it light-ly – with teams of animals instead of machinery that packs it down. He works it often by hand. The Amishman's fields flourish because he pays close attention to them, because he is sensitive to the earth, because he lets it guide him.

I don't know how many times he crosses his rows in a year or in a lifetime, but each time he crosses he pays attention. When he and his horses pull a blade over the field, he bends from the waist to see the dirt being sliced. He learns from being the earth's bedfellow in all seasons. Because he is sensitive to the earth, it is abundant and beautiful.

In the same way that an Amishman discovers the best in his land and helps it produce, Richie found the house in himself, from the people who were our neighbors and from the land around us.

A crew of ten Amishmen built the passive solar, post-and-beam house Richie finally designed. The Amish contractor had built 20-odd barns or so and knew post-and-beam barns better than anyone in the county; he didn't have so much experience with houses, but he allowed he'd 'just tell the boys it's a house and not a barn.'

The roof line follows the slope of the hill and the shape of the woods around it. Looking up at it from the road below, the house seems like it belongs, like it settled in centuries ago. From Reuben's farm, it's barely noticeable – especially now, as the trees grow up in front of it. We keep our lamps turned from the windows, so that the Amish darkness is not disturbed by our show of electricity.

The living room, which takes its shape from an octagonal framework of oak beams, spreads in a low apron out towards the rows of corn and into the woods. Since the room is bounded floor to ceiling on four sides by oak-framed glass, the sun and light move almost freely in it as they do beyond its windows. At the autumn equinox, the sun rises precisely at the easternmost window and sets at the westernmost. The ceiling is webbed by the golden oak beams, which radiate out from a massive stone column. Pine planks form the ceiling proper. In the center of the house we have a two-story atrium, which gives light to the underground portions of the house and makes my indoor plants content. The house stays cool in the summer and we don't start the coal stove until late in October.

The rooms have a unique shape – shapes so distinct that I believe they are more natural to Richie than square rooms.

Each room is white, each has a pine ceiling, each has been bisected at angles with oak beams. Windows reflect in windows. Angled beams, posts, and dowels cast and pass, one over the other, triangular shadows, pentagonal shadows, square shadows and shadows of leaves. The house lets in mist and sun, dusty colors from the plowed fields; snow laces the skylights, lightning often freezes for an instant on the white walls.

The house's structure – those muscular oak beams – give me protection and distance from the demands of practice. Each time I come in, I feel like I am entering a silent cave with a broad opening facing only the fields and forests.

It's right for Richie and me here. Neither of us cares much for the city. When he gets back from a trip (Richie's now flying 727s, and I think no other man could imagine how happy he is to be doing it), he works on the house. Slowly he is completing the finishing work upstairs; this last summer he labored at a rock wall. For myself, I put in a garden, put up green tomato mincemeat and the like; I cook, sew some, decorate. I go to quiltings and Tupperware parties with my Amish neighbors. We both play with the dogs and when they have puppies I am, naturally, a wreck for weeks.

Sometimes we'll take off on short romantic interludes: once Richie kidnapped me for a day – having worked out an arrangement with my backup doctor to cover for me – and took me to New Orleans for a 'proper creole dinner'. Sometimes we'll go to Dallas to roust with Richie's old friends or we'll meet in New York for brunch. The truth is, though, for both of us, the excitement crests not when we're there, but when we see the first horse and buggy on the roads leading towards home.

I can't imagine not being married to Richie. I believe it's

the same for him. I suppose it was settled that day when I came out here to practice five years ago. I acceded not only to whatever force it was that put me here, but also, a little bit, to the idea that there are things in life that must be and that the only wise action is to accept them.

As our marriage has grown, I suppose both of us came to accept that it simply is. We are fortunate, I suppose, in that both of us have work that means so much to us; it makes it natural to respect and support the other's work.

Richie has never let me down, never complained about my work – as disruptive to our daily lives as it is. He'll have to get up at four to get a flight and, without fail, that's the night the phone will ring all night long. He doesn't say anything or show annoyance – he'll either roll over and go right back to sleep or stay semi-awake and follow the unfoldings.

He has a record of heroic efforts: for example, he's rescued me from snowbanks at three o'clock in the morning, and once, by means unknown to me yet, he found me at an obscure intersection in order to tell me that my radio had broken down and a call had come in for a delivery.

One night I was finishing one delivery when the call came in for another. Since I was near home, I decided to stop there and return the father's call. As I walked in the door – it must have been two-thirty or three in the morning – I saw Richie, standing in his pajama bottoms in the middle of the kitchen. 'Uh, gosh, Aaron,' he was saying, 'I don't know much more about these things than you do, but if you think it would help, I'd be glad to come over.'

21

Leah

Johnny, Leah's husband, called about four in the morning. He thought maybe I should come right over, so I went. Leah and Johnny were very important to me.

I met Leah the first summer I was here. Elizabeth, a new patient, had invited me to her house to make tomato soup. Shades of Nana's kitchen. I took the road through the corn rows to her yard and traipsed contentedly through her garden. I remember the pole beans were head high. Hanging from the grape arbor were bunches of dusky purple grapes. I ducked the morning laundry and turned into the wash-house-canning house.

Young Rebecca was pumping water into a slate basin piled with red and golden tomatoes. Lizzie was just coming in with bundles of yellow onions, each one tied by twine. Anna, just six and equal to errands only, was standing around with her hands on her hips waiting for a new order. Over the sink – where we would be rinsing and cutting celery, onions, green peppers and parsley – was an open window, so that as we worked the wind would blow on us and we could smell grapes all at the same time.

By the time I got there, two huge blue-and-white speckled pots were bubbling on the stove. One held the first batch of tomatoes.

Leah, probably twenty years old at the time, was there with her mother. She was the shyest thing I'd ever seen, shoulders bent down and her arms folded over her stomach. Amish women often have their arms folded over their stomachs, but Leah made it look as if she were set on sinking into her own pelvis and disappearing. She wore glasses with dark heavy rims, her skin was pale – probably from having her head sunk down into her chest all the time – and she didn't speak. Her mother spoke for her. 'Leah will help with the cutting,' she would say and push Leah in the direction of the knife. 'Leah's not really quite strong enough to put the vegetables through the grinder.' I was sorely tempted to lose respect for Leah, but I thought I should give her a chance. Pushy mothers are pushy mothers, after all. So I tried to ask her questions to bring her out, but if she did answer at all, she tended to answer inappropriately. I concluded the girl was retarded.

Only one thing was wrong with my theory and, looking back, I probably skimmed right over it.

When we really got the tomato soup operation started, every station in the summer kitchen was being worked by a girl in a bright skirt, her fingers marching smartly from tomato to tomato. I was at the slicing table with Leah. We were busily coring and cutting and dropping the sections into a massive pot when along came Anna, and quick as a green frog, she jumped up on the table, squatted down in the mushroom made by her skirt, grinned at us, stuck her arms into the pot right up to her armpits, and began to squeeze tomatoes. She squeezed a few, they burped and belched and oozed from between her fingers, and she looked up at me and Leah and grinned like she was getting away with murder. She wasn't – she was supposed to be squooshing tomatoes – but it wasn't lost on her that it was a lark, squatting on the table with everyone around her while she mashed tomatoes with her hands.

She laughed. She pulled her red-stained arms up out of the pot, turned to me, made her hands into claws, her mouth into a curl, her voice into the sound of a vicious dog and started moving across the table, as if she were the enraged beast and I the helpless lamb.

I shrieked, which made her adore me, and then back she went to squeezing tomatoes.

Leah seemed to forget herself for a moment. Her shoulders straightened, her eyes lit up, she reached down into the pot of tomato soup herself and, while Anna's back was turned, she dipped three fingers of each hand into the pot, drew them down across her face as if to look like a savage avenging a kidnapped child, tapped Anna on the shoulder. Anna turned round and Leah hissed, a dry, steamy and sharp-toothed hiss. Anna nearly jumped into the pot with fright and almost immediately begged, 'Do it again.' Leah did, and Anna batted a tomato claw at her, and I thought the two of them were going to get down on the floor and start rolling around like lion cubs. Suddenly I saw Leah's mother, her mouth looking like it had just been dusted with lye. She said, 'What's going on over there, girls?' Apparently Leah didn't hear. Her mother looked like she was headed toward us, so I reached over and tugged at Leah's apron. She looked up quickly and froze. I nodded in the direction of her mother, mimed as if to wipe my face and Leah got the idea. By the time her mother came over for her deportment inspection, Leah had sunk right back down into her doleful, ashamed way.

After that Leah disappeared back into the shadows; except when she left she looked straight at me and smiled.

I heard from Elizabeth that Leah got married that November. Hard to imagine how that happened, but, then, I don't always see these things. Maybe the fellow had seen her imitation of the savage avenger. Maybe the flicker came out when the girl was away from her mother's granite presence.

Come March, when I get my first batch of pregnancies from last year's November matches, in comes Leah. She and Johnny – having lived, like all Amish brides and grooms, at her parents' house for several months – had just moved into their own house and they were abuzz with excitement.

Leah wasn't as hunkered over as she had been and her eyes glowed even though she didn't lift her face too much, and she still couldn't fit two words together without furrowing her brow, and when I asked her questions she got the answers wrong. But she was wondrous when I confirmed for her that she was pregnant – even though now she was five months along, even though her tummy was firm and plump as a watermelon, even though the baby was bouncing around inside on a pogo stick. 'Why,' she said, mumbling, 'why, Penny, I didn't think it could happen while we were still living with Mom and Dad.'

I explained, but I wasn't sure at all that she was following. Still, she went to her baby classes. She wrote down questions and handed the list to me when she came for her checkups, and I'd answer the questions while Johnny stood there and listened and acknowledged the answers. Leah stared at me while I talked, as if fascinated, but I had no confidence at all that she understood.

She and Johnny never missed an appointment; they were never arrogant (in fact, they were properly awestruck by the whole business) and they seemed very respectful and loving of one another. They were courteous to me.

About a week before the baby was due Johnny called and said he wondered if I might stop by, that Leah seemed to be having some pains. I asked him some questions – more to get him warmed up to the real thing than anything; I was almost a hundred percent sure the baby wasn't ready to go, but I told him I'd be by.

Sure enough, all she had were warm-up cramps and they'd disappeared totally by the time I arrived. I sat for a while, trying to help them get more comforable and then pretty soon Johnny asked if I might be able to do something for Leah, as long as I was there. Leah didn't hear real well, he said, and they thought that with the baby coming it might help if she had her ears cleaned out. He'd heard of somebody who had that done and it improved his hearing quite a lot and, well, even if it only helped some, Leah would be able to hear the baby crying better.

I said sure – the afternoon was just dawdling by anyway – and cleaned out her ears, getting out a record amount of wax, and went on my way.

The next week the three of us had a good delivery. No, it was a great delivery. Under Johnny's care, Leah was blooming, and the two of them gamboled through the birth, hugging each other and kissing each other with their eyes all the time. They just oohed and aahed all over the place when little Eli was born and when he cried, Leah's eyes filled with tears. She looked at Johnny and at me and whispered, 'Listen to that sweet cry.'

We talked after the baby was born. Leah chattered about this thing and that, made jokes about her mother, acute observations about our mutual friend Elizabeth, and some thoughtful comments about a book she'd been reading on how to take care of babies.

Leah had been virtually deaf. With her ears cleaned, with Johnny's care, with a new baby, she was a transformed person. She was lively and funny. She began to thank me and they both thanked me and then they thanked me again and again.

Nothing could stop Leah and Johnny after that. He'd go off and work at a cabinetmaker's shop during the day and then come home at night and do chores on the farm where they were living. She tried to make sure the baby was awake for him to see when he did have a few minutes at home. They were forever making themselves picnics and going on rides and dancing around their kitchen.

Somewhere early on, Leah got an infection that raged like crimson fire across her breast. I had never seen such patience in a woman. The pain must have been excruciating, but she knew it was best for her baby to nurse. She stayed with it. I was with her one afternoon for about two hours while she patiently worked with her baby, talking to him, letting him sleep, waking him again, prompting him to nurse at the swollen breast, never losing patience with him, never attacking herself. It was as if nothing could harm her joy now; she had her Johnny, her hearing and her baby.

I would stop by whenever I was out their way. I would bring them small presents and they were always giving me jelly and homemade bread.

Leah had trouble getting pregnant the second time. I suggested she and Johnny move back in with Leah's mom (I think that's the night they put salt in my tea), but since they wouldn't follow that instruction I taught them about herbs and timing, and even then it took about a year and a half after they'd first started trying. I'm not sure who was more excited about the advent of the new baby – them or me. For the first time in my midwifery life, I was prepared to take up knitting again.

Johnny called at four one morning. I'd just seen Leah a week before and everything was fine, and, in fact, Richie and I had been over to their house for a snack the night before. We had been teasing them about names for the new baby; Richie kept suggesting names of old friends from Maine. 'Couldn't you name the baby "the Squire of Barker Ridge"?' he said. 'You know, I don't expect to have any children of my own and I just think the Squire ought to have somebody named after him. The Squire taught me to drink beer, you know.'

I heard fear in Johnny's voice when he telephoned. 'Is she bleeding?' I asked. 'No,' he said, 'she's having cramps. Penny,' he said, 'please come right away.'

Premature labor, I thought. 'Tell her to stay off her feet,' I said. 'It's probably just premature labor. I'll be right over.'

I sped to their house. Johnny was at the door of my car with the flashlight before I came to a halt. 'She's still having cramps,' he said, 'only they're stronger.' He put his hand on my arm, forcing me to stop before we got inside. 'We were wondering, Penny,' he said, his hand getting heavy, 'she can't feel the baby moving anymore.'

Leah was in the bedroom lying down, just as she had been

instructed. She was on her side, her head resting on the palm of one hand, her other hand clutching a pillow to her breast.

There was fear in her face. 'Penny,' she said, 'Penny, please help us. I can't feel the baby anymore.'

I use a device called a doptone for deliveries. The doptone, placed against the lower part of the mother's abdomen, picks up the sound of the placental blood rushing in and out of the cord and, over that, it drums out the sound of the fetal heart. It picks the sounds up and magnifies them, throws them against the wall in warm, reverberating, overhead arcs.

I put the doptone against Leah's tummy and the ceiling did not echo. We heard the rush and flow of the placental blood, but the baby's heart did not break in tropical waves from the room. There was no fetal heartbeat. I continued the examination, knowing already what was going on, not knowing at all what to say about it.

I keep my composure at deliveries; that's a rule. It's a necessity. Of course, things often happen that are powerfully moving, but I'm not being paid to indulge my sensitive nature.

Leah and Johnny's baby was dead. Leah was dilated to nine centimeters and contractions were coming one right after the other. I had no idea how I would keep my composure.

I cleared my throat and looked at them. 'I don't get a fetal heartbeat,' I said as simply as I possibly could. 'Your baby isn't living.' And then, without warning, for the first time in my career, I looked at my patients and, with my eye, asked them to help me. I couldn't do it alone and, what's more, I had no wish to do it alone. I needed and wanted them to be with me.

As I gave way to them, the fear left their faces. I breathed deeply and let tears fill my eyes. I went on. 'Your baby isn't living, but it's about to be born.'

Now they looked at one another. They too began to cry. In a few minutes I said, 'You can have the baby here or we can call the ambulance. What would you like to do?' I waited.

Finally Johnny spoke. 'Is it any safer one way or the other?'

'No. There's no more danger than if this were a live birth. There is no reason we can't do it here.'

We waited in the silent room for a long while. The stillness comforted us. Perhaps it made us believe that time was not passing; perhaps it made us believe that the next minutes and their sad issue would not come. Silence spreads far, it encompasses eternity. If we were part of eternity, too, then we would not really lose the baby.

After a while Leah said, 'What do you think, Johnny?'

He waited and answered, 'Whichever way you think, Leah.'

'I want Penny to give us our baby now,' she said.

Johnny went out to my car for my bag while Leah and I talked. How long had it been since she felt life? She wasn't sure. She remembered that the baby had been scrambling yesterday morning when she was baking because she'd been thinking it must be a boy it was fighting and scrapping so much inside her.

After that, she said, the baby was quiet and she just thought he'd worn himself out.

I was somewhat relieved. If the death was recent, the chances were better that the fetus might be all right to look at, but we had no assurance. When Johnny came in and we were getting Leah settled on the blue delivery sheets, I felt I had to warn them. 'The baby might be deformed, you know,'

'That's all right,' he said, 'we understand.'

By now the labor pains were coming more and more quickly. Leah flushed, perspiration gathered on her upper lip and brow; she was lost to her contractions. The labor reassured me; I knew about labor, I understood it. I slipped with relief into the coaching ritual, began to believe again that everything was all right. I abandoned myself to rhythm, began to think we were just delivering Leah and Johnny's baby, when – again and again – I'd slam up against the fact.

Needing a good push from her: knowing I would get it if I promised her something good, the way I always did, I went on to say, 'Give me a good push and then you can see . . . 'I stopped mid-sentence. I know Johnny and Leah heard the missing phrase as loudly as I did. The truth bruised us again.

Then abruptly, before we were ready at all, in one sleek movement, the silver baby whooshed out.

It came so quickly, with so little warning. I caught her from instinct. Then, still moving from instinct, I reached for my suction. I pulled my hand back. I reached for a blanket to throw over the baby to keep it warm. I pulled my hand back. Was there nothing I could do? What about all those urgent, life-ensuring necessities? I let my hands down and let the child lie, one arm tucked under her chin, her legs loosely bent at the knees; her eyes closed. She was smooth-skinned, as if very finely made. I was riveted by the look of peace on her face. And profoundly confused by the umbilical cord knotted so tightly about her neck.

'It's a baby girl,' I said. 'The cord is wrapped around her neck.'

I couldn't tell whether it was a sob or a moan from a contraction that broke out of Leah like a hand grasping for help. Anguish, perhaps, expressed by the cramp. The afterbirth came.

Birth usually feels like a steamy kitchen – similar to holiday preparations except that the smells are different. The smell of sweat is more acrid, there are some fetid odours, there is the smell and steam rising from blood. The air is thick, pungent, fertile. It is hard not to be reminded of fresh straw and night stars. There is near and heady promise.

As birth comes closer, the attendants gather around the bed. People who have never shaken hands intertwine their arms, touch their heads. Strangers breathe sympathetically for strangers, they massage, they stroke, praise, tease, cajole, whisper, wipe, instruct, hold, hug, discipline. Strangers give to strangers the best that they believe in, whole, stripped of wariness.

Because the outcome is never certain, the bond stays set until the baby is breathing, washed, wrapped and sucking at its mother's breast.

This baby came in a streak of pallid light. The light from the lantern did not mist through the room. There was no fountain of fluid, gushing out. There was no wrestling with life, no contending, no grabbing it – as babies seem to grab – holding tightly to the progress they make through the passageway. No grabbing life by the fists. Just a sleek silver-dipped baby sliding out.

It lay on the bed while I worked. I kept looking down, surprised, disbelieving. At this moment I wasn't struck so much by grief as by confusion. The baby's body was magnetic; but as I said, it wasn't her death. It was the absence of the life.

There should have been heat – I should have been working and massaging my life into her. Usually I felt as if I was helping give life, but here I was unneeded; death managed for itself.

At the moment I wasn't sad. I just felt left out. We – father, mother, and midwife – were totally and completely irrelevant. Death dismissed us; the child had been tapped by another order, one with concerns we didn't know. At first I felt genuine respect. Death was sure, uncompromising. Then, curiously, I felt peace. The death was not my fault. The death was not the parents' fault. We didn't have a chance. The force that took this baby was impossibly, imponderably vast.

For a moment, I felt an exquisite freedom; light with relief. Death does not consult us. We had nothing to say. It was not our responsibility. And if this was true, perhaps we were not consulted on other things either.

I wrapped the baby in old soft flannel. I covered her and carried her to her parents. I wanted to hold her, caress her and praise her. Maybe it was just the ritual, something in honor of what I missed or what I missed in her. I said nothing, however, not knowing what her parents would want. I carried her around the bed to them and showed her. I showed her face and body, where the cord was still around her neck. They began to stroke her ever so gently and to praise her. 'She looks just like her brother, Eli, when he was born. . . . Look at her sweet eyes and ears. . . . I am so sorry that she had to struggle.'

I offered to wash the baby up and took her to the kitchen. I meant to squeeze golden shampoo on her head to freshen her, to dip her little head underneath the water, until all the soap ran away and only new baby smell stayed. But when I touched her skin, it began to fall away. Besides, I couldn't have washed her; the old flannel clung to her skin.

I was taking instructions at something new. Each time I tried to give the baby life, death slapped me down, death reminded me that I was intruding when I had no right, no business. The affair was not mine.

The baby's skin was fragile, as if it were determinedly melting into the soft web of the cotton fibres. The baby knew better than to let go of the closeness of the cloth; it was as if it had found itself at home, as if it were single-minded about becoming part of the things, part of the earth. Again I felt reproached; I backed off, embarrassed.

I wrapped the baby in a receiving blanket and gave her to her mother. Leah was crying again and so was Johnny. She studied the baby, talking to her through her tears, talking so softly and lightly that I could not make out her words. At the same time, she talked with me and Johnny about the funeral arrangements.

After a while I left them and packed my things. When I went back into the bedroom, Johnny was sitting silently on the edge of the bed with the baby nestled on his knees. He was rocking slowly back and forth. Leah was sort of propped up against him. Johnny chanted, 'Oh, sweet little baby, little baby, oh.' I went over and kneeled by Johnny's knee and he put his arm around me, and for the longest time he rocked me, too.

* * *

I walked out of the house just as the sun was coming up and November frost was glistening on brisk green sprouts of winter rye. I walked out to my car, stopping for a minute at the barn door to watch the Amishman at his milking. Lantern light filtered across the beams on the barn roof and sifted down below. About half the cows were down, the others shifted their weight and chewed hay. The farmer moved the milking lines from one cow to the next. He shuffled pails. A four-year-old girl – her green dress pulled over her knees, a babushka tied under her chin, hands folded patiently in her lap – sat waiting while her father milked.

I drove along the hand-patted roads. A lone buggy came towards me; its young driver raised his hand and waved. The mist began to blush. I passed Ebersol's pansies, planted in September for March sales. Their lavender, white, purple, and pink blossoms tossed in the morning breeze. I couldn't tell if it was springtime or winter. Birth and death kept mixing themselves up. Death took our baby. Death gave me something. My business was life; my life was concerned with giving life. I'd had no tolerance for death; it was a vicious thing. Now what was it? How did birth and death get themselves so intertwined?

Fortunately, life had to go on. I had to call on Leah's mother. I had to get the death certificate. I had house calls to make. I had phone calls to make. I had to get some groceries.

The sun had the sky now. Children skipped like clusters of rabbits along the side of the road boys still in their summer straw-brimmed hats, girls' white coverings gleaming. Their red lunch pails bounced along beside them. I turned at the third lane on the right.

The farmhouse, an old stone Normandy, had taken on the uneven roll of the earth that it sat on. It looked as much a fit as an old man in his evening chair. The barns and outbuildings were freshly painted crisp yellow and the earth around them was gold, and even though it was November, marigolds were tumbling energetically through the front yard fence. The front door was thrown open. Leah's mother was cleaning.

She shut the door firmly after me, ordered me into the kitchen to sit down on the bench and demanded to know if I was fine. Excuse the mess, she said (there was none), she was in the middle of cleaning. Didn't I agree that it was a beautiful day? How was Richard?

I didn't know if I was going to make it through this. I'd forgotten what a bossy woman she was.

I answered her questions in order:

'Yes.'

'Don't think of it.'

'Agreed.'

'Fine.'

Then I told her that the grandchild she'd been expecting had died. She was about to make some remark that would have put whatever it was I had to say to immediate rest. But then she realized the meaning of my words and she stopped being the boss. She stood there and looked at me, and then she lowered her eyes and her whole body sobered. Then she looked at me again.

'Is Leah all right?'

'Yes.'

'When did it happen?'

I told her.

'Are you all right now?'

'Yes.'

'Well, then,' she said modestly, 'I believe I'll go tell Amos to get the buggy ready.'

'Yes.' I said.

Carrying the death certificate, I went to the funeral home. It was one of the few the Amish use. I'd passed it on the road, but had never given it any attention. Now, when I drove up, it offended me. There was the big drive with the white columns and overhanging portico. There was the massive maple, its autumn leaves a little too prettily secured onto long graceful limbs. There was the 'home' itself, a former mansion, no doubt, big and brick, with a porch that curved pretentiously around the front of the place. The porch floor was glassy with fresh gray paint and accented by a strip of just washed plastic lawn.

The last thing an Amishman does is unnecessarily to ornament or advertise himself. He does not confuse showiness with value. I could not imagine an Amishman at this funeral home; I wanted to go to a place that looked like an Amishman's cabinet shop, a place with a kitchen garden outside and linoleum inside.

Inside, of course, more funeral decor. The carpet with the spongy bounce to it, the perpetual sepulchral afternoon lighting, the heavy chandelier, the demonstration coffins with the shiny gold handles, the black glassy-faced grand piano and blue flocked wallpaper.

The owner greeted me and, of course, asked soliticitously how he might help. I told him my business. I was bringing the death certificate for Leah and Johnny's girl and finding out if there was anything else I might do for them. The owner looked like he might have been transferred from a funeral home in 1950s California. His face was cut with small wires of age and smoking; he was tan and his hair was thick and grooved from being combed back with stick-urn.

He was not cordial. On the contrary, he was contemptuous, as if I myself had slaughtered the child. I didn't know why – maybe he treated everyone like this, maybe he had medieval prejudices against midwives – but it didn't make any difference. I just knew that in the old days I would have been not cordial right back; I would have batted him with a couple of insults so quick and so final he would have dropped on his phoney rubbery carpet and bounced three times before settling.

I didn't. I didn't have the faintest desire to counterattack. I just got out the death certificate and handed it to him quietly and said I needed to ask a couple of questions to complete it.

'This death certificate won't do,' he said impatiently. Something was as wrong on the inside of the funeral parlour as it was on the outside. It made me sad to think of my Leah and Johnny having to do business with this facetious, intolerant man. Yet the people spoke so highly of him.

He pointed me towards a counter, told me to put the certificate down and he would show me how to fill one out properly. 'If you're going to do this kind of work,' he said, implying that I'd picked up midwifery in Lancaster County the way one picks up a job washing dishes in a Bronx restaurant, 'you're going to know how to fill out a death certificate.' He paused, glared at me and snarled, 'Unless you think you're God or something.'

If anything would have got me going, it would have been that, but I still didn't have the slightest urge to counterattack. What I knew best that morning was that I was not God. What I knew best was that I was a humble player in some mighty business that was so awesome and so powerful that I had abandoned all pretence of understanding it, let alone running it. That serene baby guided me.

I said I didn't think I was God.

The owner must have been caught offguard by the humbleness in my voice, because his lacerating tone softened for a moment, then he went on. He began to flick at the details of the death certificate. 'You must spell out the month, do not write it in numbers.' He lit a cigarette. 'Put the mother's full name here. You must put in the cause of death, even though the people are Amish and may not have an autopsy; the state won't have it any other way.' He puffed and paced behind the counter. Obviously the poor man had long been whipped by the state bureaucrats; he paid daily for their petty insistence on the uniformity of death, their impatience with customs any different from those they found allowable. I suddenly felt sorry for him. 'You must put in the cause of death or you'll never get rid of the certificate.'

I asked some questions that Leah and Johnny had asked me that morning before they had a chance to talk to their families. Finally I said, 'Don't they dress the baby themselves?'

The man began to change. He began to explain that with most deaths the Amish make the clothes themselves. And a woman will probably wear the white apron and cap that she was married in. 'They are very respectful and loving towards their dead.' He went on, eagerness building: 'Would you like to see the coffin and then I could tell you about how we'll care for the baby when we go get him?'

I could tell he wanted me to see the coffin. So I went. He took me back and led me to the small pine box. It was as simply made as possible – no handles, no trimming. Clean cut wood, countersunk nails, dressed only in its gray stain. He opened the lid, and with the tips of his fingers, he very carefully, very gently, unfolded the soft white batiste lining its insides.

'We'll wrap the baby in a downy covering,' he said. 'We touch stillborns as little as possible. Their skin is fragile and we don't want to cause any damage. That is the idea with one so small; touch them as little as possible.'

He talked about his craft with great integrity; he became animated, young, vigorous. The bureaucrats lost their hold on him; the cynicism that had gripped him slowly vanished. His meanness disintegrated. I began to admire him.

I realized that he tried as hard to be gentle and considerate in his work as I did in mine. He respected the Amish; no, it was something more than that – he too had been deeply influenced by them. We began to understand one another. We talked.

'How long have you been a midwife?' he said.

'Five years.'

'How many babies have you delivered?'

'About a thousand.'

'Have you lost many?' he asked.

'One,' I answered. 'This one.'

He was pulled up short. 'Then I guess I won't be telling you anything about your work,' he said deferentially. 'Let me know any time I can do something for you.

It wasn't until I got back to Leah and Johnny's that day that I'd figured out why the funeral director had been so rude to me in the first place. I think he was just like me. Actively, fervently, and feverishly does he loathe the quacks who – driven out of hospitals – peddle themselves to the non-litigating Amish and casually take their money and their lives. He had no reason to think that I was not one of them, bouncing into his shop to toss him my careless errors. I was guilty until proven innocent in his eyes. And in this case, his was, I believe, the proper attitude.

I couldn't go directly home that night. I was too restless, too ungrounded. As if something wasn't finished. As if there was something waiting for me still. I passed the time by driving along the fields and by the streams, waiting to understand, waiting for whatever it was inside me to finish its groping and shifting.

I came inevitably to the cemetery where we would bury the baby Susan the next day.

Amish cemeteries have no formal entrance. Laid out behind a whitewashed post-and-slat fence – little more set out than a pasture or a cornfield – the cemetery takes its turn like any other piece of earth along the road, its rows of head-stones continuing the rows of corn stubble next to it.

It was warm for a November night. The sky was clear and the moon gleamed, but there was no wind. I pulled the car over to the side of the road, got out, and walked into the small cemetery. The grass inside, less well tended than an Amish woman keeps her lawn, lay comfortably rumpled under the headstones. No flowers, no debris from dried bouquets, no loose ribbons from flower arrangements chattered or flapped in the wind. It was safe here from pretence and I could consider the baby's death.

As each Amish person wears the same hat or bonnet as his or her neighbor, each Amish person's headstone is like the one next to it. Each has the same shape – rounded at the top – and of the same height and width. Each is unadorned except by time and the weather. One planted in this yard fifty years ago had darkened with age and, during the same years, moss, the color of goldenrod, had spilled ever so slowly down its face and into the crevices made by the letters. Another, next to it and brand-new, flashed back to the moon its bright white marble face. Next to these two was a series of stones of slate, their faces smooth or fissured or broken off. The rows lined up, not precisely, because the ground had not been rolled by heavy machinery, but in good order. Down the path between them, at irregular intervals, were footstones. There is no unnecessary space left between one grave and the next.

The inscriptions are no more individual than the stones. It is enough to enter a man's name, the date of his birth and the date of his death; also the number of days he had lived altogether. For a woman, her husband's name is also given.

I made sure to see that no one was coming up the road, and then, for a moment, I lay down to see if I would fit between a headstone and a footstone. It hadn't seemed quite long enough or wide enough, but it sufficed.

The Amish are born, do their work – as directed by their abilities – and die. Each one of them has value because each one is part of the life of the earth. For them, to be part of the earth is to be part of God's work. That is enough of an awesome thing. No one life counts more than another; each life is necessary to the whole. During his time on earth, each man is responsible for being a steward of the earth, of his own life, of his inheritance, and of his brotherhood. During, his time on earth, each person works to maintain well the portion of life they have received. Others follow and do the same. Each tries to be good and kind as they do so.

I leant on fence slats and watched for a while across the road at a cow barn, silo, tobacco barn and farmhouse with porch, dressed with its wiry strands of grapevines. A farmer, carrying a lantern and followed by his dog, strolled to his barn.

I had believed that I was alone, that I created all my weakness and all my failures; I believed that I had created all my successes. I thought I had to be invulnerable, that I would have to survive in the universe on the strength of my personality and my will. I advertised myself and I made myself tough – hoping, I think, that the universe would admit that for the first time in its history, some Penny had come along who could outsmart it.

But I was no contestant against death. This baby's death so disregarded me that I no longer considered myself self-sufficient. That would be absurd. Other forces – forces far too mighty for me to comprehend – held sway. I had been silly.

Neither was I a contestant against gentleness. The Amish people live decently and kindly. They love what is. I've watched them keep their gardens and their farms with delicacy and respect. I've seen them adore the weak equally with the strong. I've known them to give themselves away completely when the brotherhood needed it. I've come to love their way – soft, clean and so often joyful. I've discovered the strength they have that comes from depending on one another. I've discovered the peace they gain in knowing that none of us is alone. I've discovered the freedom that comes in taking a smaller place in the order of things. I shrink now before their understanding of time, generations, life, death, and, yes, God.

The next afternoon I watched black carriages arrive at the cemetery. Nothing is more sombre than that uninterrupted line, paced by a walking horse.

In the morning, some of Leah and Johnny's family and friends had come and dug the small grave.

I shivered and waited as the buggies pulled in. There weren't many, as big funerals are not the custom for stillbirths. The buggies were arranged at the fence, rows of headstones were arranged at my feet, and now at the graveside a row of Amish men and Amish women stood wearing their black hats and capes. The coffin, looking like an abandoned cradle, sat separate and independent on a small table. The baby was white, pure white – finished in porcelain.

Her tiny lips were blue. The woman next to me turned and whispered. 'It makes you want to put a blanket over her, doesn't it?'

I stood with my arms clamped around me for warmth. Still I shook from the cold.

The Amish began to pray and so did I. I did not pray in their way, but I prayed. As we stood in silence with our eyes closed and our heads dropped, a huge dark and warm wing folded round me. Johnny's father pulled me inside his cape to keep me warm.

also by **Penny Armstrong** & **Sheryl Feldman**

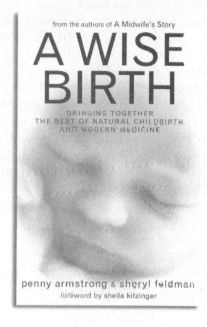

from the authors of A Midwife's Story

A WISE BIRTH

BRINGING TOGETHER
THE BEST OF NATURAL CHILDBIRTH
AND MODERN MEDICINE

penny armstrong & sheryl feldman
foreword by sheila kitzinger

A Wise Birth
ISBN 978-1-905177-03-5
£8.99 – US$17.95

What is the best way to give birth to your baby? Is it a hi-tech delivery in a hospital? Or is it more naturally, at home or in a birth center? Is it possible to combine the best of modern medicine with the non-intervention of natural childbirth?

Penny Armstrong and Sheryl Feldman, authors of the wonderful *A Midwife's Story*, explore the many issues that influence the way women give birth today: culture and history, technology and psychology. They demonstrate, in a warm and convincing fashion, how to find a setting that will help make your child's birth a healthy and powerful experience.

Informative and provocative, moving and thought-provoking, *A Wise Birth* is based on Penny Armstrong's years of experience as a midwife. It is essential reading for mothers, fathers and childbirth professionals – in fact, anyone interested in the politics of birth.

DIABETES MELLITUS

Una Guía Práctica

Sue K. Milchovich, RN, BSN, CDE

Barbara Dunn-Long, RD

Bull Publishing
Boulder, Colorado

El uso de nombres de marcas es para identificar un producto y no significa que las autoras recomiendan o promocionan estos productos.

El concepto de utilizar IDEAS (IDEAS—Una Manera de Entender Su Azúcar en la Sangre, página 25) para representar insulina, dieta, emociones, actividades y sentirse enfermo se acredita a Sally Myres, R.N., M.S. del artículo, "Diabetes Management by the Patient and the Nurse Practitioner", *Nursing Clinics of North America,* Vol. 12, No. 3, septiembre 1977.

Casa editorial James Bull
Composición y Diseño de Interior: Publication Services, Inc.
Diseño de Portada: Lightbourne Images
Ilustraciones: Publication Services, Inc., basado en caricaturas por Terry Syndergaard y Kevin Opstedal

Library of Congress Cataloging-in-Publication Data

Milchovich, Sue K.
    [Diabetes mellitus. Spanish]
    Diabetes mellitus : una guía práctica / Sue K. Milchovich,
    Barbara Dunn-Long. — 10th ed.
      p. cm.
    Includes bibliographical references and index.
    ISBN: 978-1-933503-64-6
    1. Diabetes—Handbooks, manuals, etc. I. Dunn-Long, Barbara.
    II. Title.
    RC660.5.M5418 2011
    616.4'62—dc22

                            2010040184

Derechos del autor © 2011 S.K. Milchovich y B. Dunn-Long
Bull Publishing Company
P.O. Box 1377
Boulder, Colorado 80306
(800) 676-2855
www.bullpub.com

ISBN 978-1-933503-64-6

Contenido

Reconocimientos

Nosotras especialmente deseamos reconocer y expresar nuestro agradecimiento a Herbert I. Rettinger, M.D., editor de las ediciones pasadas de este libro; a Saundra J. Emerson, R.N., por su contribución a la escritura original de este libro y a Andrea D. Manes, Charlotte L. Penington, Beverly Worcester, R.N., Beatrice Edquist, R.N. y Susan Magrann, M.S., R.D., por sus valiosas contribuciones.

S.K.M. y B.D.L.

Algunas veces es muy difícil el poner pensamientos en palabras, pero en este momento yo deseo expresar mis más profundas y sinceras gracias a mi esposo, Dan, y a mi amiga Sue Bermond-Perry. Si no hubiese sido por su constante estímulo y entendimiento y la revisión crítica del manuscrito, yo me hubiese rendido hace tiempo en este proyecto. Yo les quiero agradecer desde el fondo de mi corazón.

—Sue

Prefacio

Diabetes. ¿Usted recuerda su reacción inmediata a esta palabra cuando alguien se la dijo por primera vez? Lo más probable es que usted estaba en shock o deprimido. Tal vez usted negó que tal cosa pudiera sucederle a usted. "¿Por qué a mí?" fue probablemente algo que usted continuaba repitiendo hasta que comenzó a aceptar la realidad. Desde ese momento en adelante puede que usted haya realizado incontables, algunas veces drásticos, cambios en su estilo de vida. El tener diabetes no es fácil. Tampoco es acostumbrarse a ella si la falta de conocimiento y miedo son sus únicas herramientas.

DIABETES MELLITUS: Una Guía Práctica debe ser leído. Éste explica la diabetes en un lenguaje sencillo y con diagramas. Con un conocimiento propio de la diabetes se hace más fácil el vivir con ella y controlarla. El conocimiento y guías presentadas en este libro son esenciales para todos aquellos que quieren ayudarse a ellos mismos o alguien que ellos conocen y quieren.

S.K.M. y B.D.L.

Acerca de las Autoras

Suellyn K. Milchovich, R.N., B.S.N., C.D.E. es una Educadora y Enfermera de Diabetes Certificada para HealthCare Partners Medical Group, un miembro de la Asociación Americana de la Diabetes y miembro de la Asociación Americana de Educadores de Diabetes.

Barbara Dunn-Long, R.D., está en la práctica privada y es miembro de la Asociación Americana de la Diabetes y miembro de la Asociación Americana de Dietistas.

Destrezas de Supervivencia

Ciertos pasajes en este libro son particularmente importantes. Éstos son lo que nosotras llamamos destrezas de supervivencia—la información que las personas con diabetes deben saber. Éstos pasajes estarán en cajas sombreadas, como este aviso.

Vea la página 196 para centros de recursos donde usted puede comprar los libros mencionados en este libro.

EL CÍRCULO DEL BUEN CONTROL DE LA DIABETES

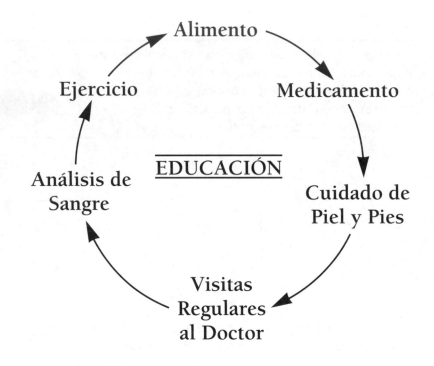

Alimento

Ejercicio

Medicamento

EDUCACIÓN

Análisis de Sangre

Cuidado de Piel y Pies

Visitas Regulares al Doctor

Diabetes Mellitus

El ser humano tiene conocimiento de la diabetes mellitus desde los años 2000–3000 A.C. Los griegos y los romanos le dieron a la diabetes su nombre:

DIABETES = SIFÓN (orinar frecuentemente)

MELLITUS = MIEL (azúcar en la orina)

En el presente, la diabetes afecta alrededor de 21 millones de americanos. A medida que hay más y más personas con sobrepeso y a medida que vivimos por más tiempo, continuaremos observando un aumento en el número de personas con diabetes. Se estima que por cada persona que se *conoce* que tiene diabetes, hay un diabético DESCONOCIDO, que tiene síntomas mínimos.

HERENCIA

La diabetes no es una enfermedad contagiosa. Usted no puede contraerla de alguien, ni puede transmitirla a otros. La herencia juega un papel muy importante en su ocurrencia. Se cree que la susceptibilidad a la diabetes es pasada de generación en generación a través de los genes, pero no en un patrón específico. La herencia juega un papel más importante en la diabetes Tipo 2 (no insulinodependiente) que en la diabetes Tipo 1 (insulinodependiente) (vea las páginas 4–5), pero la naturaleza de estos factores genéticos y cómo éstos son heredados aún no es comprendida. Usted puede que conozca o no de otros familiares que padecen de diabetes.

VIRUS Y EL SISTEMA INMUNE

El entendimiento de la forma en que el sistema inmune del cuerpo humano funciona podría contestar muchas preguntas acerca de la causa de la diabetes Tipo 1 (insulinodependiente). Normalmente, el sistema inmune funciona para proteger el cuerpo de bacterias y virus dañinos, pero por razones no completamente entendidas, en algunas personas este sistema de protección falla. Entonces comienza a destruir las células del páncreas que producen la insulina, de manera que el cuerpo no puede producir su propia insulina.

También hay un factor de temporada en la diabetes Tipo 1—un número mayor de personas son diagnosticadas con este tipo de diabetes durante la temporada de la influenza y de virus.

NUTRICIÓN Y OBESIDAD

Existe una conexión directa entre tener sobrepeso y tener diabetes Tipo 2 (no insulinodependiente). El páncreas de una persona con diabetes Tipo 2 produce insulina, pero el exceso de peso previene que sea utilizada por las células o tejidos del cuerpo. A esto le llamamos RESISTENCIA A LA INSULINA. Muchas veces una persona también padece de alta presión sanguínea y colesterol alto, creando lo que se llama "Síndrome de Resistencia a la Insulina". El perder peso y el hacer ejercicio puede hacer que las células y tejidos del cuerpo puedan utilizar nuevamente la insulina producida por el páncreas. Entonces, el azúcar en la sangre, la presión sanguínea y el colesterol todos regresarán a niveles saludables.

Actualmente hay un aumento acelerado en el número de personas en los Estados Unidos con diabetes Tipo 2, incluyendo adolescentes y niños. Este tipo de diabetes ocurre con más frecuencia en personas que

- Tienen familiares con diabetes
- Tienen sobrepeso
- Tienen la presión sanguínea alta
- Tienen niveles altos de colesterol, especialmente los triglicéridos altos y el nivel de HDL bajo (vea la página 187)
- Son hispanoamericanos
- Son afroamericanos
- Son nativos americanos
- Son asiático-americanos/de las Islas del Pacífico
- Han tenido diabetes durante el embarazo (diabetes gestacional)
- Han tenido bebés grandes (más de nueve libras)

Éstos son conocidos como los *factores de riesgo* para la diabetes. ¿Cuántos tiene usted? ¿Cuántos tienen sus familiares?

TIPOS DE DIABETES

Diabetes Tipo 1 (Insulinodependiente)

- Antiguamente llamada diabetes juvenil
- Usualmente ocurre antes de los 20 años, pero puede ocurrir a cualquier edad
- Afecta un 10% del total de la población con diabetes
- No hay producción de insulina en el páncreas
- Tiene cierta conexión hereditaria
- Afecta hombres y mujeres por igual
- Rápida pérdida de peso
- Muchos síntomas, más cetonas
- Temporal: diagnosticada más frecuentemente durante la temporada de influenza
- Tratamiento:

  Insulina: aprendiendo a ajustar la insulina por cambios en la alimentación, ejercicio, enfermedad o embarazo

  Plan personal de comidas y bocadillos para permitir comidas "usuales" o étnicas

  Buena nutrición para ayudar al crecimiento o embarazo (y lactancia)

  Ejercicio

  Educación

Diabetes Tipo 2 (No Insulinodependiente)

- Antiguamente llamada diabetes del adulto
- Ocurre en adultos y en niños
- Afecta un 90% del total de la población con diabetes
- Insulina es generada en el páncreas, pero no es suficiente o el cuerpo no la puede usar correctamente
- Tiene una fuerte conexión hereditaria y con estar con sobrepeso
- Se desarrolla lentamente
- La mayoría tienen sobrepeso, pocos están en su peso normal
- No tiene conexión con temporadas
- Tratamiento: Pérdida de peso (si tiene sobrepeso)

  Mantener su peso (si su peso es bueno)

  Plan personal de comidas y bocadillos para:

  - Incluir comidas "usuales" o étnicas
  - Cambios en el trabajo, la escuela, y las actividades
  - Trabajar para alcanzar el nivel ideal de azúcar en la sangre
  - Trabajar para alcanzar niveles normales de grasa en la sangre (colesterol y triglicéridos)
  - Trabajar para alcanzar una presión sanguínea normal

  Ejercicio

  Medicamento oral y/o insulina si es necesario

  Educación

Intolerancia a la Glucosa

- También se conoce como Diabetes de Ayuno Alterada o Tolerancia Alterada de Glucosa
- Antiguamente llamada diabetes fronteriza o química
- Tienen los niveles de azúcar de la sangre en ayuno sobre 100 mg/dl pero debajo de 126 mg/dl
- En una prueba de tolerancia oral a la glucosa tienen niveles de azúcar en la sangre entre 140 y 199 mg/dl
- Tienen resultados de Hemoglobina A1c de 5.7%–6.4%
- Normalmente tienen sobrepeso
- Tienen resistencia a la insulina
- Tratamiento: Comer saludablemente para
    - perder peso
    - lograr un nivel normal de azúcar en la sangre
    - lograr un nivel normal de grasa en la sangre (colesterol y triglicéridos)
    - lograr una presión sanguínea normal
  - Ejercicio
  - Educación

Diabetes Gestacional

- Ocurre durante el embarazo, en el último trimestre
- Tiene resistencia a la insulina
- Se hacen análisis para detectarla entre las semanas 24 y 28 del embarazo en muchas mujeres embarazadas
- Tratamiento: dieta y en algunas ocasiones insulina
- Buen control del azúcar en la sangre es absolutamente necesario para proteger al bebé
- Los niveles de azúcar usualmente vuelven a la normalidad una vez que el bebé nace
- Muchas mujeres desarrollan diabetes más tarde
- Es importante el mantener un peso normal

GLUCOSA E INSULINA

Para mantener el control del azúcar en la sangre, debe entender las definiciones de *glucosa e insulina*.

- Glucosa o azúcar → viene de alimentos que usted ingiere
  sube el nivel de azúcar en la sangre
- Insulina → es creada por el páncreas

  ayuda al hígado, a los músculos y a las células de grasa a utilizar la glucosa

  debe haber suficiente de ella y ésta debe funcionar correctamente

Vamos a Comenzar con la GLUCOSA

Todos los alimentos que comemos consisten de CARBO-HIDRATOS, PROTEÍNAS y GRASAS.

- CARBOHIDRATOS (vea las páginas 43–56) incluyen:

  Alimentos altos en azúcar—"dulces", miel, almíbar, azúcar, etc.

  Almidones—cereales, pan, papas, arroz, pasta, maíz, guisantes, frijoles, etc.

  Frutas

  Leche, yogur
- PROTEÍNAS (vea las páginas 58–63) incluyen:

  Carne—aves, carne de res, pescado, etc.

  Huevos

  Queso, requesón

  Mantequilla de cacahuate

  Tofu

■ GRASAS (vea las páginas 63–65) incluyen:

   Aceites

   Margarina y mantequilla

   Aderezo para ensalada

   Mayonesa

   Tocino

   Aguacate

   Frutos secos y semillas

El estómago y los intestinos transforman el 100% de todos los CARBOHIDRATOS que usted ingiere en glucosa. Esa glucosa entra a la sangre, causando que aumente su azúcar en la sangre. Esté consciente de la CANTIDAD TOTAL de alimentos con carbohidratos que ingiere en cualquier momento de una sola vez.

Si ingiere una cantidad grande de alimentos con carbohidratos. → El azúcar en la sangre puede subir muy alto.

Si ingiere poco o ningun alimento con carbohidratos. → El azúcar en la sangre puede bajar mucho.

El azúcar en la sangre se mantendrá más estable si mantiene la CANTIDAD TOTAL de carbohidratos ingeridos entre una comida y otra constantes y las balancea con algunas proteínas, grasas y vegetales. No se enfoque en el contenido de azúcar en los alimentos—mire la cantidad TOTAL DE CARBOHIDRATOS (vea la etiqueta de nutrición en la página 83).

Los vegetales contienen carbohidratos, pero porque éstos tienen tan pocas calorías y pocos carbohidratos, no afectan el azúcar en la sangre a menos que sean consumidos en grandes cantidades.

La PROTEÍNA no afecta el azúcar en la sangre. El tipo de proteína y la cantidad de alimentos con proteína que usted elija depende de qué necesita hacer acerca de su peso (perder, ganar o mantener) y si su colesterol está alto o normal.

INCLUYA UNA PEQUEÑA CANTIDAD DE PROTEÍNA CON CADA COMIDA para ayudarle a controlar el aumento de azúcar en la sangre que ocurre después de comer y para ayudarle a mantenerse de 4 a 5 horas entre comidas.

La GRASA no causa que el azúcar en la sangre aumente. El tipo y la cantidad de alimentos con grasa que usted ingiera va a depender de lo que usted necesite hacer con su peso (perder, ganar o mantenerlo) y de si su colesterol está alto o normal. Una comida que contiene mucha grasa (por ejemplo, pizza) mantendrá su azúcar en la sangre *alto por más tiempo*.

La "comida perfecta" está compuesta por pequeñas cantidades de alimentos de *todos los grupos*.

¡LA CANTIDAD ES LA CLAVE![1]

Insulina

La INSULINA es una hormona creada por el páncreas, el cuál esta localizado detrás y debajo del estómago.

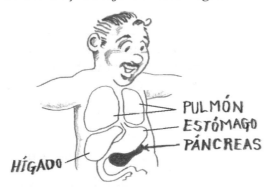

Cuando el azúcar en la sangre aumenta, la insulina es liberada en la sangre. Tanto la insulina como la glucosa viajan por todo el cuerpo a través de la sangre.

---

[1]Éste es el primer pasaje de "Destrezas de Supervivencia". Éstos estarán sombreados como éste a través del libro.

En los MÚSCULOS, la glucosa es transformada en ENERGÍA.

El HÍGADO almacena la glucosa para usarla en el futuro (especialmente si el azúcar en la sangre baja demasiado).

Las células de GRASA toman y almacenan todo el exceso de glucosa como grasa.

Para que la glucosa entre a una célula y haga su trabajo, debe haber INSULINA presente para actuar como transportador. Imagínese que la glucosa viene a una puerta cerrada y la insulina es la llave que abre esa puerta.

Cuando tiene diabetes, hay un problema con la insulina:

■ Diabetes Tipo 1 → No se produce insulina.

Las células en el páncreas que hacen la insulina han sido destruidas por el cuerpo, por lo tanto no se produce insulina.

■ Diabetes Tipo 2 → Muy poca insulina es producida

o

Se produce insulina, pero no trabaja muy bien

Diabetes Tipo 2

En alguien que es delgado o tiene peso normal, las células del páncreas no producen suficiente insulina.

En los que tienen sobrepeso, se produce mucha insulina al principio pero ésta disminuye con el tiempo. La insulina tampoco trabaja correctamente. La insulina no puede entrar en las células de grasa o de los músculos para hacer su trabajo. Esto se llama *resistencia a la insulina.*

Hay dos maneras de romper la resistencia a la insulina y conseguir que el cuerpo use la insulina:

- PERDIENDO PESO—10 a 20 libras es la cantidad "clave".
- EJERCICIO: Vea los ejercicios en las páginas 147–158.

Hoy en día, la causa exacta de la diabetes (Tipo 1 y Tipo 2) es desconocida y no tiene cura. Una vez usted tiene diabetes la tendrá por el resto de su vida.

Usted aprenderá a mantener su azúcar en la sangre tan cerca como sea posible al nivel normal balanceando los alimentos, peso, medicamentos y ejercicio. La mejor manera de hacer esto es trabajando con varias personas (una sola persona no puede enseñarle todo lo que necesita saber) conocidas como su "equipo de diabetes".

Usted debe ser el centro de su equipo. Los otros miembros pueden incluir algunas o todas estas personas:

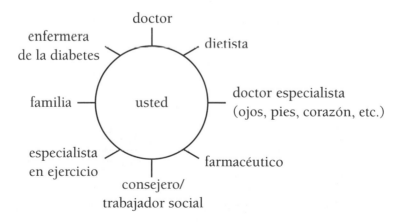

Con un buen plan y buenos hábitos, usted será capaz de sentirse mejor y tener el control de su diabetes, en vez de tener la diabetes controlándolo a usted.

Hiperglucemia

Un problema que usted puede tener es si el balance de sus alimentos, medicamentos y actividades es perturbado y hay demasiado azúcar en la sangre. Esto se llama **HIPERGLUCEMIA**.

HIPER = mucho
GLUC = azúcar
EMIA = sangre

}   *HIPERGLUCEMIA*

HIPERGLUCEMIA puede ocurrir

- Si olvida o reduce la insulina o medicamento oral
- Si come mucho, especialmente alimentos altos en carbohidratos y comidas altas en grasas
- Si tiene fiebre, resfriado, influenza, infección, cirugía u otra enfermedad o estrés emocional
- Por "mala" medicación—medicamentos que están vencidos o ya no trabajan, o insulina que ha sido congelada o guardada a temperaturas demasiado altas
- Por inactividad

Los síntomas clásicos de hiperglucemia son

- Sed mayor a la normal
- Orinar frecuentemente
- Fatiga, cansancio extremo
- Infecciones persistentes

La hiperglucemia puede ocurrir lentamente, y su nivel de azúcar puede subir a niveles bastante altos (alrededor de 300 mg/dl) antes de que pueda sentir estos síntomas. Siga con atención el azúcar en su sangre a través de análisis de sangre y orina.

Para aquellos que tienen diabetes Tipo 1, a medida que su azúcar en la sangre aumenta usted puede que forme cetonas, las cuales aparecerán en su sangre y orina (explicaciones de cetonas, acidosis y coma diabética se hallan en las páginas 115–117).

Cuando se forman las cetonas puede que sienta síntomas como

- Pérdida de peso
- Nauseas y vómitos
- Retortijones
- Respiración rápida y profunda
- Aliento a "con sabor a frutas"

Otros nombres que puede haber escuchado para hiperglucemia o azúcar en la sangre alto son CETOACIDOSIS DIABÉTICA y COMA DIABÉTICO.

CAPÍTULO 3

Hipoglucemia

Los alimentos, medicamentos y ejercicios deben estar balanceados para mantener la cantidad de azúcar en la sangre tan cerca de lo normal como sea posible. Si el balance no se mantiene, usted podría tener demasiada o muy poca azúcar en la sangre, lo cual puede llevar a problemas serios.

HIPOGLUCEMIA, REACCIÓN A LA INSULINA y SHOCK DE INSULINA son todos nombres para poca azúcar en el torrente sanguíneo. Esto ocurre cuando el azúcar en la sangre baja por debajo de los 70 mg/dl o baja rápidamente de un nivel más alto a un nivel más bajo. (Cómo medir el azúcar en la sangre se explica en las páginas 107–114).

HIPO = muy poco
GLUC = azúcar
EMIA = sangre
} *HIPOGLUCEMIA*

HIPOGLUCEMIA puede ocurrir

■ Si usa demasiada insulina o demasiados medicamentos orales

■ Si come muy poco o brinca o retrasa sus comidas y bocadillos

■ Por ejercicio extremo o ejercicio sin planificación o el horario de ejercicio

La hipoglucemia puede ocurrir durante la noche mientras se duerme, especialmente si utiliza insulina. Usted puede dormir con ella y no despertar.

Indicios de hipoglucemia en la noche son

■ La ropa de cama mojada por el sudor

■ Dolor de cabeza al despertar

■ Pesadillas y no descansa bien

■ Fatiga extrema al despertar

■ Niveles de azúcar altos en la mañana (en ayuno)

La hipoglucemia puede ocurrir en personas que usan insulina o medicamentos orales. Aquellos que controlan su diabetes con dieta solamente usualmente no desarrollan hipoglucemia.

Cuando usted tiene reacción a la insulina o se vuelve hipoglucémico, los síntomas empezarán DE REPENTE. Algunos de los primeros síntomas son

■ Sudores fríos, sensación de humedad

■ Sacudidas, mareos o debilidad

■ Irritabilidad, mal humor, impaciencia

■ Corazón latiendo fuerte y rápido

- Nerviosismo

- Hambre

Cuando el cerebro siente que su azúcar en la sangre está muy bajo, usted puede sentir

- Dolor de cabeza

- Adormecimiento u hormigueo en la yema de los dedos o labios

- Visión borrosa o doble

- Pensamiento confuso

- Mala pronunciación al hablar

- Cambio de personalidad

- Convulsiones

- Pérdida de conocimiento

Si usted es hipoglucémico, usualmente tendrá 2, 3 ó 4 de estos síntomas. Uno solo a la vez probablemente no significa azúcar bajo en la sangre. Si es posible, analice su azúcar en la sangre inmediatamente, tan pronto sienta cualquiera de estos síntomas, y vea si su azúcar está bajo. No importa cuán fuertes o numerosos sean los síntomas,

TOME ACCIÓN FRENTE A LAS ADVERTENCIAS TEMPRANAS

y no espere a ver si los síntomas desaparecen.

Llame a su doctor cuando tenga reacciones fuertes de hipoglucemia repetidamente.

Cuando tenga el azúcar en la sangre bajo, haga lo siguiente:

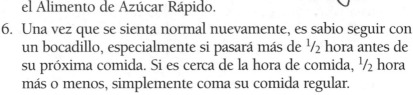

1. Examine su azúcar en la sangre, inmediatamente.

2. Tome alguna clase de "Alimento de Azúcar Rápido" inmediatamente. Usted necesita de 10 a 15 gramos de glucosa o carbohidratos para poner azúcar rápidamente en su torrente sanguíneo.

3. Limite las actividades inmediatamente. Siéntese o acuéstese.

4. Si es posible, dígaselo a alguien.

5. Una vez que haya comido un Alimento de Azúcar Rápido, los síntomas deben empezar a perder intensidad (en los próximos 10 ó 15 minutos). Si no comienza a sentirse mejor repita el Alimento de Azúcar Rápido.

6. Una vez que se sienta normal nuevamente, es sabio seguir con un bocadillo, especialmente si pasará más de $^1/_2$ hora antes de su próxima comida. Si es cerca de la hora de comida, $^1/_2$ hora más o menos, simplemente coma su comida regular.

Ejemplos de Bocadillos[*]

1 carne o proteína	(vea las páginas 57–63)	1 onza de carne	2 cdas. mantequilla de cacahuate
+	=	+	Ó +
1 almidón	(vea las páginas 43–47)	1 rebanada de pan	5–6 galletas de soda

[*]Si no tiene que perder peso usted puede aumentar la cantidad sugerida.

Algunos ejemplos de Comidas Rápidas de Azúcar que tienen de 10–15 gramos de glucosa o carbohidratos son

5–7 Lifesavers

4–6 onzas de jugo de naranja o manzana

2 onzas de jugo de uva

4–6 onzas de soda regular (*no de dieta*)

6 caramelos de gelatina azucarada

10 pastillas de goma

2 trozos (o cucharaditas) de azúcar

2 cucharaditas de miel o jarabe de arce

8 onzas de leche libre de grasa

Además hay algunas pastillas de glucosa y gel que usted puede utilizar:

Gel para decorar pasteles	disponible en el supermercado 1 tubo = 10 gramos de glucosa
Insta Glucose	disponible en farmacias 1 tubo = 30 gramos de glucosa
Glutose	disponible en farmacias 1 tubo = 15 gramos de glucosa 1 tubo para múltiples dosis = 45 gramos de glucosa
Glucosa en pastillas	disponible en farmacias 1 pastilla = 4 gramos de glucosa 10 pastillas por tubo

GlucoBurst Gel

disponible en farmacias
1 bolsa = 15 gramos de glucosa
3 bolsas por caja

Dex Glucose Gel

disponible en farmacias
1 tubo = 17 gramos de glucosa
3 tubos/caja

Liquid Shot

disponible en farmacias
1 botella = 15 gramos de glucosa

Glucose Rapid Spray

disonible en farmacias
5–10 sprays
100 sprays/botella

¡SIEMPRE lleve COMIDAS RÁPIDAS DE AZÚCAR consigo!
¿QUÉ LLEVARÁ PARA SU COMIDA RÁPIDA DE AZÚCAR?

_____

¿DÓNDE LO LLEVARÁ?

_____

¿QUÉ LLEVARÁ PARA BOCADILLO?

_____

INYECCIÓN DE GLUCAGÓN

GLUCAGÓN es una hormona que es inyectada debajo de la piel o en un músculo y aumenta los niveles de azúcar rápidamente. Si usted es encontrado inconsciente por un miembro de su familia o un amigo y usted no puede ingerir azúcar por la boca por el peligro de que se pueda ahogar, la persona que lo está cuidando puede ponerle una inyección de glucagón en el músculo o área donde usted se pondría la inyección de insulina (página 140). Después de haber recibido la inyección de glucagón usted debe responder en los próximos 5 a 15 minutos. Cuando usted responda, es necesario que coma—pan y carne o leche—porque los efectos de glucagón duran sólo una hora más o menos. Si tiene diabetes Tipo 1, usted puede necesitar tener glucagón en su casa y llevarlo cuando viaje. Verifique la fecha de expiración en la botella y reemplácela si es necesario. Si glucagón es utilizado para tratar una reacción hipoglucémica, usted debe informar a su doctor tan pronto como sea posible.

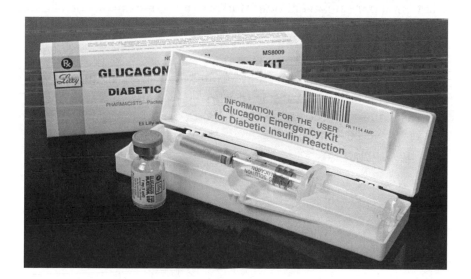

POR FAVOR LEA ESTA HISTORIA

Precisamente como cualquier otra mañana, Jake Summer se inyectó su dosis normal de insulina, comió lo que normalmente come en el desayuno y manejó hasta su trabajo. Jake Summer es un maestro de matemáticas de escuela superior (secundaria). Debido a la reunión obligatoria de maestros, Jake no tuvo suficiente tiempo para comer su almuerzo y dejó como la mitad de él. En la tarde después de la escuela, algunos amigos de Jake decidieron ir a jugar nueve hoyos de golf y Jake se unió a ellos. Cerca del hoyo número cuatro, Jake se sintió muy irritado con el juego y sus compañeros de juego. Unos minutos más tarde él empezó a ponerse tembloroso y nervioso y empezó a sudar frío. Inmediatamente se acordó de su medio almuerzo, la dosis normal de insulina y el ejercicio adicional que estaba haciendo. "Reacción a la insulina", él pensó mientras buscaba en sus bolsillos los Lifesavers que normalmente llevaba. ¡No tengo Lifesavers! Además, ninguno de sus amigos tenían Alimentos de Azúcar Rápido con ellos. Así que Jake envió uno de sus amigos a la tienda por Lifesavers mientras otro amigo se quedó con él. Por suerte, la tienda estaba muy cerca y tenían alimentos de azúcar rápido. Jake lo comió rápidamente y a los 10 minutos se sentía mucho mejor. En lugar de continuar jugando, él se excusó y se fue a su casa. Jake sabía que si seguía jugando él tendría otra reacción. Además, para prevenir otra reacción a la insulina, Jake comió un bocadillo de galletas y queso, porque no podría cenar por una hora más. Debido a la reacción, Jake Summer se recordó de cuatro aspectos de la diabetes muy importantes:

- Debe comerse la porción de alimentos completa en cada comida.

- Debe llevar consigo alguna forma de Alimento de Azúcar Rápido todo el tiempo.

- El ejercicio ayuda a que la insulina que está utilizando trabaje más efectivamente, permitiendo que la glucosa entre a las células.

- Si no puede comer comida en los próximos 30 minutos, debe comer un bocadillo que incluya una porción del grupo de pan y de carne.

P R U E B A

Hiperglucemia e Hipoglucemia

Aquí tiene una prueba en hiperglucemia e hipoglucemia. Vea si puede responder a las preguntas sin mirar sus notas. Podrá encontrar las respuestas en la página 201.

1. Escriba HIPER o HIPO o AMBAS en el espacio que sigue cada artículo.

    a. Somnolencia o apatía _____

    b. Ocurre repentinamente _____

    c. Dolor de cabeza _____

    ch. Sed _____

    d. Nauseas, vómitos _____

    e. Infección _____

    f. Respiración profunda, rápida _____

    g. Muy poca comida _____

    h. Olvidó la insulina _____

    i. Fiebre, resfriado _____

    j. Impaciente, irritable _____

    k. Exceso de ejercicio _____

    l. Visión borrosa _____

    ll. Corazón palpitando rápidamente _____

2. Circule las letras que son síntomas de reacción a la insulina o azúcar bajo en la sangre.

    a. Orinar más de lo usual

    b. Sacudidas, nerviosismo

    c. Irritabilidad

    ch. Retortijones

    d. Sudor frío y húmedo

    e. Visión borrosa

IDEAS

Entender Su Azúcar en la Sangre

Todo lo que usted hace y todo lo que le ocurre afecta el azúcar en su sangre. Recuerde que la palabra clave IDEAS le ayudará a entender por qué su azúcar en la sangre es muy alto, muy bajo o aceptable (dentro del rango de azúcar en la sangre que su doctor y usted han acordado que es el mejor).

I para *Insulina* y/o medicamentos orales

D para *Dieta* o alimentos

E para *Emociones*

A para *Actividades* o ejercicio

S para *Sentirse* enfermo

ALIMENTOS, MEDICAMENTOS y EJERCICIO pueden ser herramientas que se pueden usar para "balancear" o controlar el azúcar en la sangre. Imagínese un subibaja:

ALIMENTOS   MEDICAMENTOS   EJERCICIO

Usted quiere mantener estos tres balanceados para que el azúcar en la sangre se mantenga en un rango aceptable. Los análisis caseros de glucosa en la sangre dirán si el azúcar en la sangre está en un rango aceptable o si está fuera de balance.

Cuando algo perturba sus alimentos, medicamentos o ejercicios o usted se enferma o sufre de estrés emocional, el subibaja se inclina y el azúcar en la sangre sube mucho o baja mucho.

La siguiente tabla le ayudará a entender qué altera el subibaja, dejando el azúcar en la sangre sin balance. Las *IDEAS* están enumeradas abajo en el centro de la página. En la izquierda están esos eventos que aumentan el azúcar en la sangre y en la derecha aquellos que la bajan. En más de un caso usted encontrará más de un evento que inclina su subibaja y afecta el balance de azúcar en la sangre.

Eventos que **Aumentan** *el Azúcar en la Sangre*	*Eventos que* **Bajan** *el Azúcar en la Sangre*
Insulina o Medicamento Oral	
Olvidar tomar su medicamento	Toma mucho medicamento
No tiene suficiente medicamento[*]	Dosis muy alta de medicamento[*]
Medicamento "malo" (vencido, insulina mantenida sobre 80° F o congelada)	Horario

[*]La cantidad de medicamento que su doctor le ha recetado es demasiado o muy poco para usted.

Eventos que **Aumentan** *el Azúcar en la Sangre*	*Eventos que* **Bajan** *el Azúcar en la Sangre*
Los medicamentos ya no están haciendo efecto	
Horario	

Dieta/Alimentos

Comer demasiado	Comer muy poco
Comer comidas con azúcar solas (incluye frutas)	Saltar comidas/bocadillos
Comidas altas en grasa	Retraso de comidas/ bocadillos
Comidas que no están bien balanceadas	Comidas que no están bien balanceadas
Comidas/bocadillos muy cerca uno del otro	Comidas/bocadillos muy separados uno del otro

Emociones

Emociones traumáticas, como la pérdida de un ser querido, accidentes, cirugías o enfermedades graves	Ninguna

Actividades

Inactividad	Demasiado ejercicio o sin planificación
	Ejercicio justo antes de la comida
	Ejercicio al mismo tiempo que la insulina es mayor

Eventos que Aumentan el Azúcar en la Sangre	*Eventos que Bajan el Azúcar en la Sangre*
Sentirse enfermo	
Resfriado, influenza, fiebre, dolor, infecciones, enfermedades graves, cirugía, algún trabajo dental	Ningún
IDEAS en balance ➔	el azúcar en la sangre está en su rango aceptable.
IDEAS fuera de balance ➔	el azúcar en la sangre está muy alto o muy bajo.

Mantenga esta lista a la mano para que pueda verla cuando esté tratando de entender sus niveles particulares de azúcar en la sangre y su patrón.

RANGOS IDEALES O ACEPTABLES PARA EL AZÚCAR EN LA SANGRE

Usted debe hablar con su doctor y decidir cuál es el RANGO IDEAL DE AZÚCAR EN LA SANGRE para usted. Puede usar lo siguiente como una guía:

En ayuno o antes de las comidas	70–130
2 horas después de comer o a la hora de dormir	Menos de 160
Promedio estimado de Glucosa (eAG) (Hemoglobina A1c) (vea las páginas 150–151)	Menos de 154 (7%)

CAPÍTULO 5

La Dieta

LA DIETA ES LA PIEDRA ANGULAR PARA EL CONTROL DEL AZÚCAR EN LA SANGRE.

El tener diabetes no significa que usted debe dejar todos los alimentos que le gustan, pero sí significa que debe prestar más atención a los tipos de alimentos que come y cuándo los come.

En la mayoría de los casos le darán un plan de comida para seguir y para ayudarlo a mantener el elquilibrio del azúcar en la sangre. El tipo de diabetes que usted tenga (Tipo 1 o Tipo 2) ayuda a determinar este plan de comida. ¡No piense en su plan de comida como si fuese una dieta sino como UNA GUÍA PARA COMER SALUDABLEMENTE!

La Guía Dietética para Americanos (escrita por los Departamentos de Agricultura y Salud y Servicios Humanos de los Estados Unidos) recomienda una buena nutrición básica para TODAS LAS PERSONAS con el propósito de mejorar la salud y prevenir enfermedades a largo plazo (tales como enfermedades cardíacas, alta presión sanguínea y algunos cánceres).

Cuando usted tiene diabetes, seguir estas guías es el primer paso importante para bajar su azúcar en la sangre y aprender a elegir OPCIONES DE ALIMENTOS SALUDABLES. La ventaja más grande es que toda su familia puede comer saludablemente junto con usted. **Al elegir opciones de alimentos saludables**, usted podrá:

- Mantener su peso normal
- Mantener normal su glucosa en la sangre
- Mantener niveles normales de grasa en la sangre

Cuando esté planeando sus comidas, va a ayudar a su diabetes si usted:

- Come la cantidad correcta de alimentos en los momentos correctos y no salta comidas. Mantiene la cantidad de alimentos con carbohidratos constantes de comida a comida.
- Come una variedad de alimentos y elige OPCIONES DE ALIMENTOS SALUDABLES. Incluya suficientes productos de granos, vegetales y frutas y una cantidad moderada de proteína.
- Sustituye los productos lácteos con mucha grasa por productos sin grasa.
- Come menos grasa, especialmente grasa saturada y colesterol (vea la página 95). Esto ayudará a mantener niveles bajos de grasa en la sangre.
- Evita los ácidos grasos trans (grasas trans).
- Utiliza menos azúcar. Limita las deleites especiales, dulces y postres dulces. Estos alimentos no tienen valor nutricional, tienen grasas añadidas y proveen calorías vacías y pocas vitaminas y minerales.

DIABETES TIPO 1

Si usted tiene diabetes Tipo 1, necesita trabajar con su dietista para crear un plan de comida que le permita hacer ajustes en su dieta durante el ejercicio, la enfermedad, el embarazo y en ocasiones especiales. Los adolescentes con diabetes Tipo 1 necesitan tener sus comidas planificadas para satisfacer sus necesidades especiales de crecimiento.

Usted también debe colaborar muy bien con su doctor y enfermera educadora de diabetes para aprender cómo trabaja su insulina. Una vez que entienda esto, puede aprender a hacer ajustes en su insulina para manejar los cambios en el azúcar en la sangre durante el ejercicio, los cambios en las comidas, las ocasiones especiales, la enfermedad, el embarazo y los períodos de crecimiento en los adolescentes.

El saber hacer estos ajustes en su insulina y alimentos le permite mantener un mejor control de su azúcar en la sangre. Recuerde:

- Mantenga su peso constante. Si eres un niño o adolescente, tu peso debe estar en un buen rango para tu edad.
- Una buena nutrición conduce a una buena salud.
- Siga con el plan personal para comidas y bocadillos, el cual corresponde con las horas y la acción de su insulina.

DIABETES TIPO 2 Y EL SOBREPESO

Si usted tiene diabetes Tipo 2 y tiene sobrepeso, ¡es muy importante adelgazar y mantener un peso adecuado! Usted no tiene que perder peso hasta llegar al peso ideal para su cuerpo, pero perder tanto como 10 a 20 libras bajará su azúcar en la sangre. Muchas personas que tienen diabetes también tienen alta presión sanguínea y altos niveles de grasa en la sangre (colesterol y triglicéridos). La pérdida de peso no sólo bajará su azúcar en la sangre sino también trabajará para bajar su presión sanguínea y los niveles de grasa en la sangre.

Para ayudarse a sí mismo a adelgazar y a comer saludable-mente:

■ Baje la cantidad total de grasa que come.

■ Coma porciones más pequeñas.

■ Coma bocadillos reducidos en grasa y en calorías (verifique las etiquetas).

■ Aumente la fibra en su dieta.

■ Sea más activo. Salga y disfrute de la vida—camine, nade, baile o haga cualquier cosa que usted disfrute.

Si tiene la presión sanguínea alta le van a pedir que coma alimentos bajos en sodio (sal).

EL HORARIO

El HORARIO de sus comidas y bocadillos es importante para equilibrar los alimentos que come y los medicamentos que está tomando. Trate de comer sus comidas y bocadillos casi a la misma hora todos los días. No salte comidas o guarde porciones de una comida para otra comida más tarde. Trate de comer casi la misma cantidad de comida cada día.

Ejemplo

Desayuno	7:00–9:00 A.M.
Almuerzo	11:30 A.M.–1:30 P.M.
Cena	5:00–7:00 P.M.
Bocadillo	9:30–10:30 P.M.

CANTIDADES DE ALIMENTOS/CALORÍAS

Las CANTIDADES de los diferentes alimentos que usted va a comer van a depender de su EDAD, PESO y ACTIVIDAD. Todos los adultos necesitan consumir el número correcto de calorías para mantener un peso normal y tener la diabetes bien controlada. Esto incluye las calorías adicionales durante el embarazo y cuando se está lactando. Los niños y adolescentes necesitan consumir la cantidad correcta de calorías para un crecimiento y desarrollo normal.

Su doctor o dietista determinará el número de calorías que usted necesitará cada día. El dietista usa esas CALORÍAS para hacerle a usted un plan de comida a su medida, el cual normalmente está dividido en tres comidas y en los bocadillos que usted necesite. Él le dirá el número de porciones que usted necesita de cada lista de intercambios o de opciones para cada comida y bocadillo.

Medir los Alimentos

Al comienzo usted debe medir todos los alimentos para estar seguro de las cantidades. Utilice una taza de medir estándar de 8 onzas, una cucharadita de medir y una cucharada de medir. La mayoría de los alimentos son medidos después de cocidos. Luego, cuando esté más familiarizado con su plan de comida, usted será capaz de estimar los tamaños de sus porciones sin tener que medir. Aun así, no siempre podemos confiar en nuestros ojos y los tamaños de las porciones que usted está midiendo a ojo de buen cubero pueden aumentar o disminuir con el paso del tiempo. Para controlarse usted mismo, trate de medir su tamaño de porción cada seis meses.

Equivalentes de Medidas Comunes

3 cdtas. = 1 cda.

4 cdas. = $^1/_4$ taza

$5^1/_2$ cdas. = $^1/_3$ taza

4 onzas = $^1/_2$ taza

8 onzas = 1 taza

Las etiquetas de nutrición y los libros de cocina de dieta miden los ingredientes en gramos. Una manera simple de entender es que 28.4 gramos iguala 1 onza de alimento. Por ejemplo, si 100 gramos es lo que pide, esto iguala más o menos 4 onzas.

¿QUÉ ES UN PESO SALUDABLE?

Su doctor o dietista puede usar una herramienta útil llamada IMC (índice de masa corporal o BMI, por sus siglas en inglés) para determinar si usted tiene un peso saludable. Un exceso de grasa corporal puede causar resistencia a la insulina. Perder peso y aumentar la cantidad de músculo que usted tiene a la vez que disminuye su grasa corporal le ayuda a su cuerpo a usar mejor la insulina.

Índice de Masa Corporal

IMC	Normal							Sobrepeso				Obeso										Obesidad Extrema														
	19	20	21	22	23	24	25	26	27	28	29	30	31	32	33	34	35	36	37	38	39	40	41	42	43	44	45	46	47	48	49	50	51	52	53	54
Altura (Pulgadas)												**Peso (libras)**																								
58	91	96	100	105	110	115	119	124	129	134	138	143	148	153	158	162	167	172	177	181	185	191	196	201	205	210	215	220	224	229	234	239	244	248	253	258
59	94	99	104	109	114	119	124	128	133	138	143	148	153	158	163	168	173	178	183	188	193	198	203	208	212	217	222	227	232	237	242	247	252	257	262	267
60	97	102	107	112	118	123	128	133	138	143	148	153	158	163	168	174	179	184	189	194	199	204	209	215	220	225	230	235	240	245	250	255	261	266	271	276
61	100	106	111	116	122	127	132	137	143	148	153	158	164	169	174	180	185	190	195	201	206	211	217	222	227	232	238	243	248	254	259	264	269	275	280	285
62	104	109	115	120	126	131	136	142	147	153	158	164	169	175	180	186	191	196	202	207	213	218	224	229	235	240	246	251	256	262	267	273	278	284	289	295
63	107	113	118	124	130	135	141	146	152	158	163	169	175	180	186	191	197	203	208	214	220	225	231	237	242	248	254	259	265	270	278	282	287	293	299	304
64	110	116	122	128	134	140	145	151	157	163	169	174	180	186	192	197	204	209	215	221	227	232	238	244	250	256	262	267	273	279	285	291	296	302	308	314
65	114	120	126	132	138	144	150	156	162	168	174	180	186	192	198	204	210	216	222	228	234	240	246	252	258	264	270	276	282	288	294	300	306	312	318	324
66	116	124	130	136	142	148	155	161	167	173	179	186	192	198	204	210	216	223	229	235	241	247	253	260	266	272	278	284	291	297	303	309	315	322	328	334
67	121	127	134	140	146	153	159	166	172	178	185	191	198	204	211	217	223	230	236	242	249	255	261	268	274	280	287	293	299	306	312	319	325	331	338	344
68	125	131	138	144	151	158	164	171	177	184	190	197	203	210	216	223	230	236	243	249	256	262	269	276	282	289	295	302	308	315	322	328	335	341	348	354
69	128	135	142	149	155	162	169	176	182	189	196	203	209	216	223	230	236	243	250	257	263	270	277	284	291	297	304	311	318	324	331	338	345	351	358	365
70	132	139	146	153	160	167	174	181	188	195	202	209	216	222	229	236	243	250	257	264	271	278	285	292	299	306	313	320	327	334	341	348	355	362	369	376
71	136	143	150	157	165	172	179	186	193	200	208	215	222	229	236	243	250	257	265	272	279	286	293	301	308	315	322	329	338	343	351	358	365	372	379	386
72	140	147	154	162	169	177	184	191	199	206	213	221	228	235	242	250	258	265	272	279	287	294	302	309	316	324	331	338	346	353	361	368	375	383	390	397
73	144	151	159	166	174	182	189	197	204	212	219	227	235	242	250	257	265	272	280	288	295	302	310	318	325	333	340	348	355	363	371	378	386	393	401	408
74	148	155	163	171	179	186	194	202	210	218	225	233	241	249	256	264	272	280	287	295	303	311	319	326	334	342	350	358	365	373	381	389	396	404	412	420
75	152	160	168	176	184	192	200	208	216	224	232	240	248	256	264	272	279	287	295	303	311	319	327	335	343	351	359	367	375	383	391	399	407	415	423	431
76	156	164	172	180	189	197	205	213	221	230	238	246	254	263	271	279	287	295	304	312	320	328	336	344	353	361	369	377	385	394	402	410	418	426	435	443

Fuente: Adaptado de Clinical Guidelines on the Identification, Evaluation, and Treatment of Overweight and Obesity in Adults: The Evidence Reports.

Cómo Determinar su Índice de Masa Corporal (IMC)

El IMC mide su peso y lo compara con su altura.

Su IMC debe estar en el rango saludable de 19 a 25.

Si usted está en la parte alta de este rango o más de 25, su proveedor de atención médica puede sugerirle perder suficiente peso para bajar su IMC uno o dos números. Un IMC de más de 26 se considera sobrepeso. Un IMC de 30 se considera obesidad. Las investigaciones demuestran que a medida que su nivel de IMC aumenta, los niveles de la presión sanguínea y colesterol aumentan y la lipoproteína de alta densidad (HDL) o niveles de colesterol bueno disminuyen.

Cómo se Calcula el IMC

1. Multiplique su peso en libras por 704.
    (Ejemplo: 704×123 libras = 86,592)
    Su respuesta: _____

2. Multiplique su altura en pulgadas por su altura en pulgadas.
    (Ejemplo: 60 pulgadas $\times$ 60 pulgadas = 3,600)
    Su respuesta: _____

3. Para obtener su IMC, divida su respuesta en el paso 1 por su respuesta en el paso 2.
    (Ejemplo: $86,592 \div 3,600 = 24$)
    Su IMC: _____

PLANIFICAR LAS COMIDAS

Los tres grupos de alimentos en los cuales usted debe pensar son:

CARBOHIDRATOS

PROTEÍNAS

GRASAS

Explicaremos cada uno de éstos en detalles.

Carbohidratos

Los carbohidratos son la fuente principal de energía para su cuerpo, mantienen a su corazón latiendo y le proveen energía para subir escaleras. Ellos son una parte importante de un plan de alimentación saludable y afectan sus niveles de glucosa en la sangre más que ningún otro alimento. El almidón y el azúcar en los alimentos que usted come son carbohidratos. El almidón se encuentra en los panes, la pasta, los cereales, las papas, los guisantes, los frijoles y las lentejas. El azúcar está naturalmente presente en las frutas, la leche y en algunos vegetales. Los azúcares añadidos se encuentran en los postres, los dulces, las mermeladas y los almíbares. Estudios han encontrado que el número total de gramos de carbohidratos en una comida es más importante que si algunos de los carbohidratos provienen o no del azúcar. El azúcar y los alimentos que contienen azúcar deben ser intercambiados por otros carbohidratos y alimentos, y no solamente añadidos al plan de comida.

En 1995 las Asociaciones Americanas de Diabetes y Dietéticas cambiaron las opciones viejas de intercambio de pan/almidón, frutas, vegetales y leche en un grupo llamado Grupo de

Carbohidratos. La mayoría de los carbohidratos que comemos vienen de tres grupos de alimentos: almidón, fruta y leche. Cada uno de estos grupos contiene alrededor de 15 gramos de carbohidratos por porción. La leche tiene 12 gramos de carbohidratos por porción, pero puede redondear el valor a 15 para hacer la planificación de sus comidas más fácil. Usted puede intercambiar las opciones de almidón, fruta y leche en su plan de comida. Los vegetales están en el grupo de los carbohidratos pero solamente contienen alrededor de 5 gramos de carbohidratos por porción, así que tres porciones de vegetales contienen 15 gramos de carbohidratos. (No es necesario contar una o dos porciones de vegetales).

Cada uno de los siguientes es un ejemplo de 1 carbohidrato:

1 almidón = 1 papa pequeña *o* $^{1}/_{2}$ taza de frijoles

1 fruta = $^{1}/_{2}$ banana *o* 1 manzana pequeña

1 leche = 1 taza de leche *o* 1 taza de yogur

¿Cuántos carbohidratos debe comer y qué es contar carbohidratos?

Un plan de comida saludable normalmente incluye de 3 a 4 opciones de carbohidratos en cada comida y 1 ó 2 opciones de carbohidratos para sus bocadillos.

El contar los carbohidratos es una manera de calcular cuántos carbohidratos comer en las comidas y bocadillos. La razón por la que se presta más atención a contar los gramos de carbohidratos es porque los carbohidratos tienden a tener el mayor efecto en su azúcar en la sangre. A medida que los carbohidratos se degradan en glucosa y son absorbidos, la cantidad de glucosa en su sangre aumenta. En el conteo de carbohidratos, una porción de cualquier grupo de carbohidratos (almidón, fruta y leche) es igual a 1 porción o 15 gramos. Esto significa que si su plan de comida requiere

2 almidones, 1 fruta y 1 leche en el almuerzo, usted tiene un total de 4 opciones de carbohidratos (60 gramos).

**2 almidones + 1 fruta + 1 leche =
4 opciones de carbohidratos (60 gramos)**

La tabla de abajo muestra la manera de contar el número de gramos de carbohidratos en una etiqueta de comida en su plan de comida.

Carbohidratos Totales (gramos en una porción)	Cómo Contar
0–5 gramos	no contar
6–10 gramos	1/2 opción de carbohidratos
11–20 gramos	1 opción de carbohidratos
21–25 gramos	1 1/2 opciones de carbohidratos
26–35 gramos	2 opciones de carbohidratos

Carbohidratos y la Glucosa en la Sangre

Cuanto más carbohidratos usted coma, más aumentará su glucosa en la sangre. Algunos alimentos contienen más carbohidratos que otros, aunque el tamaño de porción sea el mismo. Diferentes tipos de carbohidratos varían en el tiempo que le toma a su cuerpo degradarlos. Los alimentos cocidos se digieren más rápido que los crudos. Los alimentos mezclados con líquidos se digieren más rápido que los secos. Los alimentos combinados, carbohidratos mezclados con grasas, pueden tomar más tiempo en ser digeridos y su glucosa en la sangre podría aumentar más lentamente.

Discuta con su dietista, educador de la diabetes o médico acerca de lo que funciona mejor para usted.

RECUERDE: Usted puede analizar su nivel de azúcar en la sangre dos horas después de una comida para ver cómo los carbohidratos han afectado a su azúcar en la sangre. Vea la página 28 para el rango ideal de azúcar en la sangre después de una comida.

Proteínas

Su cuerpo usa las proteínas para crecer y mantener los tejidos. Las proteínas se encuentran tanto en fuentes vegetales como animales, incluyendo la carne, las aves, el pescado, la leche y otros productos lácteos, los huevos, los frijoles, los guisantes y los frutos secos. Los almidones y los vegetales también tienen una pequeña cantidad de proteína. El cuerpo necesita insulina para utilizar la proteína que se come.

Grasas

La cantidad de calorías que usted debe obtener de la grasa depende de sus propias necesidades especiales—su nivel de colesterol y su peso. Las grasas son importantes porque éstas transportan las vitaminas y los ácidos grasos en el cuerpo. Para mantener saludables su corazón y sus vasos sanguíneos, escoja grasas que son poliinsaturadas o monoinsaturadas y evite las grasas saturadas y las grasas trans. (Vea "Grasa Saturada y Colesterol", páginas 95–97).

Use Éstos:

Grasas Moninsaturadas:
Aguacates
Aceite de oliva
Aceite de canola
Frutos secos: almendras,
  cacahuates, anacardos,
  avellanas, mantequilla
  (crema) de cacahuate

Grasas Poliinsaturadas
Aceite de maíz
Aceite de soja
Aceite de girasol
Margarina blanda
Aceite de cártamo
Aceite de semilla de
  algodón
Linaza
Nueces

Evite Éstos:

Grasas Saturadas
Aceite de coco
Grasa de carnes
Tocineta
Mantequilla de cacao
  (Chocolate)
Queso crema
Manteca solidificada
Crema agria
Aceite de palma

Grasas Trans
Productos que contengan
  aceites hidrogenados
Productos horneados pro-
  cesados (panecillos,
  galletas)
Bocadillos procesados
  (galletas saladas,
  papas fritas)
Manteca
Aceites de palma
Papas fritas de comidas
  rápidas
Margarina sólida en barra

RECUERDE: Todas las grasas tienen muchas calorías. Limite los tamaños de porción cuando elija las **opciones de alimentos saludables.**

LISTAS DE INTERCAMBIO PARA LA PLANIFICACIÓN DE COMIDAS

Para facilitarle la planificación de comidas, los alimentos con carbohidratos, proteína y grasa se han clasificado en grupos llamados de SISTEMA DE INTERCAMBIO o DE OPCIONES. El intercambio u opción es una cantidad medida de un alimento seleccionado de un grupo de alimentos. La lista le provee una variedad amplia de alimentos para escoger. Una vez que se haya familiarizado con estas listas, la planificación de su comida se le hará más fácil.

Hay tres grupos principales en este sistema:

- Grupo de carbohidratos que incluye

    almidones

    frutas

    leche

    otros carbohidratos

    vegetales
- Grupo de carne y sustitutos de carne
- Grupo de grasas

Carbohidratos

Opciones de almidones

En la siguiente lista, una opción de almidón contiene 15 gramos de carbohidratos, 3 gramos de proteína y 80 calorías. Los alimentos integrales contienen alrededor de 2 gramos de fibra por porción (aquellos que tienen 3 o más gramos de fibra por porción están marcados con un símbolo *).

En esta lista los panes y cereales integrales y enriquecidos, los productos de germen de trigo y de salvado y los frijoles y guisantes secos son buenas fuentes de hierro y entre las mejores fuentes de tiamina. Los productos integrales, de salvado y de germen de trigo tienen más fibra que los productos hechos con harinas refinadas. Los frijoles y guisantes secos también son buenas fuentes de fibra. El germen de trigo, el salvado, los frijoles secos, las papas, las habas de lima, la chirivía, la calabaza y la calabaza de invierno son buenas fuentes de potasio.

Los vegetales almidonados están incluidos en esta lista porque contienen la misma cantidad de carbohidratos y proteína que una rebanada de pan.

Una opción de almidón es igual a cualquiera de los siguientes. Si usted desea comer un alimento con almidón que no está en la lista, la regla general para una opción de almidón es:

$1/2$ taza de un cereal, grano, pastas o vegetal almidonado

1 onza de un alimento de pan, como 1 rebanada de pan

$3/4$ a 1 onza de la mayoría de los bocadillos (Algunos bocadillos pueden contener grasa añadida así que verifique la etiqueta).

Pan

pan, blanco, trigo integral, centeno,
centeno integral, de pasas (no azucarado) . . . . 1 rebanada (1 oz.)

pan, bajo en calorías. . . . . 2 rebanadas ($1^1/2$ oz.)

bagel (rosca de pan), pequeño (4 oz.) . . . . $1/4$ (1 oz.)

panecillo inglés, pequeño . . . . $1/2$ (1 oz.)

Pan (cont.)

rodillo de pan simple . . . . 1 (1 oz.)

pan de perro caliente . . . . $^1/_2$ (1 oz.)

pan de hamburguesa . . . . $^1/_2$ (1 oz.)

migas de pan secas . . . . 2 cdas.

tortilla, maíz o harina, 6" 1

tortilla, harina, 10" de diámetro . . . . $^1/_3$

palitos de pan (8" de largo,
$^1/_2$" de diámetro) . . . . 1 palito

crutones, sin grasa añadida . . . . 1 taza

pan pita, 6" de diámetro . . . . $^1/_2$

Cereal

*cereales de salvado, hojuelas (All Bran,
Bran Buds) . . . .$^1/_2$ taza

otros cereales sin azúcar, listos para comer . . .$^3/_4$ taza

avena . . . .$^1/_2$ taza

Grapenuts . . . .$^1/_4$ taza

cereal soplado (no azucarado) . . . .$1^1/_2$ tazas

cereal (cocido) . . . .$^1/_2$ taza

maíz a medio moler (cocido) . . . .$^1/_2$ taza

trigo desmenuzado . . . .$^1/_2$ taza

Kasha (trigo serraceno) . . . .$^1/_2$ taza

Muesli . . . .$^1/_4$ taza

Granos/Pastas

arroz, blanco o integral (cocido) . . . .$^1/_3$ taza

pasta (cocida): espagueti, fideos, macarrones . .$^1/_3$ taza

harina de maíz (seca) . . . . .2 cdas.

pan de maíz (2" × 2" × 1") . . . . .1 normal (2 oz.)

harina . . . .$2^1/_2$ cdas.

*germen de trigo . . . . .3 cdas.

———————

*3 gramos o más de fibra por porción

Granos/Pastas (cont.)

maicena . . . . .2 cdas.

bulgur (cocido) . . . .$^1/_2$ taza

cuscús . . . .$^1/_2$ taza

Galletas/Bocadillos

galleta de animalitos .8

galletas graham, cuadrado de $2^1/_2$ " 3

tostada melba, rectángulo . . . . .4 rebanadas

pan sin levadura (matzo) . . . .$^3/_4$ oz.

galletas oyster 24

palomitas de maíz (hecha, sin grasa
añadida) . . . . .3 tazas

palitos de pretzel, $3^1/_3$" largo, $^1/_8$" diámetro . . . .25 ($^3/_4$ oz.)

Rye Crisp, 2" × $3^1/_2$" 4

galleta salada 6

galleta de soda, cuadrada $2^1/_2$" 4

Galletas/Bocadillos de Poca Grasa—Trate de consumir galletas que contienen menos de 3 gramos de grasa por porción. ¡Recuerde verificar las etiquetas!

galletas de queso bajas en grasa,
3 gramos de grasa . . . . .12 pequeñas

galletas bajas en grasa (50%),
1.5 gramos de grasa .15 pequeñas

galletas de trigo entero horneadas,
de grasa reducida, 1.5 gramos de grasa . . . . . .5 galletitas finas

panes crujientes de trigo entero
(como Kavli, Wasa), sin grasa añadida . . . . . . .2–4 rebanadas ($^3/_4$ oz.)

nachos, sin aceite añadido, horneados,
0 gramos de grasa 7

pretzels, sin grasa, 0 gramos de grasa 12

pan horneado dos veces (zweibach) . . . . .3 ($^3/_4$ oz.)

tortas de arroz, 4" de diámetro 2

Frijoles Secos, Guisantes y Lentejas

frijoles y guisantes (cocidos) como
judías, arvejas, frijoles blancos y pintos,
guisantes ojinegros y garbanzos . . . . $^1/_2$ taza

habas . . . . $^2/_3$ taza

*lentejas (cocidas) . . . . $^1/_2$ taza

miso . . . . .3 cdas.

Vegetales Almidonados

frijoles horneados (sin cerdo, enlatados) . . . . . $^1/_3$ taza

*maíz . . . . $^1/_2$ taza

*maíz en la mazorca, grande . . . . $^1/_2$ mazorca (5 oz.)

guisantes, verdes . . . . $^1/_2$ taza

chirivía . . . . $^2/_3$ taza

*guisantes, verdes (enlatados o congelados) . . . . $^1/_2$ taza

papas (blancas), hervidas . . . . $^1/_2$ taza o
$^1/_2$ mediana (3 oz.)

papas (majadas) . . . . $^1/_2$ taza

papas, horneadas (con piel) . . . . $^1/_4$ grande (3 oz.)

jícama (cocida) . . . . $^3/_4$ taza

*habas blancas y maíz, cocido (succotash) . . . $^1/_3$ taza

batata, ñame, simple . . . . $^1/_2$ taza

calabaza de invierno (bellota, sidra,
calabaza) . . . . $^1/_2$ taza

*plátano . . . . $^1/_2$ taza

Alimentos con Almidón Preparados con Grasa—Cuente lo siguiente como 1 opción de almidón/pan + 1 opción de grasa:

crutones . . . . .1 taza

panecillo, $2^1/_2$" de diámetro 1

mollete (popover) . . . . .1 normal

frijoles refritos . . . . $^1/_2$ taza

---

*3 gramos o más de fibra por porción

Alimentos con Almidón Preparados con Grasa (cont.)

torta para taco, 5" de diámetro 2

fideos chow mein . . . .$^{1}/_{2}$ taza

galletas, redondas de mantequilla 6

papas fritas, 2" a $3^{1}/_{2}$" de largo . . . . .10 ($1^{1}/_{2}$ oz.)

arroz frito . . . .$^{1}/_{3}$

mollete, simple, pequeño 1

panqueque, 4" de diámetro 2

relleno, de pan (preparado) . . . .$^{1}/_{3}$ taza

wafle 4" cuadrado 1

galletas de trigo entero,
con grasa añadida (como Triscuits) 4–6 (1oz.)

paté de garbanzos (hummus) . . . .$^{1}/_{3}$ taza

galletas de emparedados, con relleno
de queso o mantequilla de cacahuate 3

chips de bocadillo (papas, tortilla) . . . .   9–13 ($^{3}/_{4}$ oz.)

Opciones de frutas

Una opción de fruta contiene 15 gramos de carbohidratos y 60 calorías (pesos incluyen piel, hueso, semillas y cáscara).

Las frutas son una fuente valiosa de vitaminas, minerales y fibra. Las frutas frescas, congeladas o secas tienen alrededor de 2 gramos de fibra por porción. Las frutas que tienen 3 o más gramos de fibra por porción están marcadas con el símbolo * en la lista. Los jugos de frutas contienen muy poca fibra.

La vitamina C es abundante en los jugos y frutas cítricas y se encuentra en las frambuesas, las fresas, los mangos, el melón cantalupo, el melón dulce y las papayas. La mejor fuente de vitamina A entre estas frutas son los albaricoques frescos o secos, los mangos, el melón cantalupo, los nectarinas, los duraznos amarillos y el caquis. Muchas frutas son fuentes valiosas de potasio—los albaricoques, las bananas, varios tipos de bayas, la toronja, el jugo de toronja, los mangos, el melón cantalupo, el melón dulce, los nectarinas, las naranjas, el jugo de naranjas y los duraznos.

Las frutas de la lista pueden ser frescas, secas, enlatadas, congeladas, cocidas o crudas, siempre y cuando no tengan azúcar añadida. Frutas completas son más saciantes que jugos de frutas por lo cual son una mejor opción para aquellos que están tratando de perder peso. Es mejor tomar el jugo junto con una comida.

Una opción es igual a:

$^1/_2$ taza de fruta fresca o jugo de frutas

$^1/_4$ taza de fruta seca

1 fruta fresca pequeña o mediana

Fruta

manzana, fresca . . . . .1 pequeña ó
$^1/_2$ mediana (4 oz.)

manzanas, secas . . . . .4 anillos

manzana en rebanadas, sazonadas . . . .$^1/_2$ taza

compota de manzana . . . .$^1/_2$ taza

albaricoques, frescos . . . . .4 enteros (5$^1/_2$ oz.)

albaricoques, enlatados . . . .$^1/_2$ taza

*albaricoques, secos . . . . .8 mitades

banana, pequeña .1 (4oz.)

Bayas:

*zarzamora, cruda . . . .$^3/_4$ taza

zarzamora, cocida o enlatada . . . .$^3/_4$ taza

*arándanos azules . . . .$^3/_4$ taza

bayas de Boysen (boysenberries) . . . .$^3/_4$ taza

frambuesas americanas . . . .$^3/_4$ taza

frambuesas, crudas, cocidas
o enlatadas . . . . .1 taza

*fresas, crudas, enteras . . . . .1$^1/_4$ taza

fresas, cocidas o enlatadas . . . . .1$^1/_4$ taza

melón cantalupo, pequeño . . . . .1 taza en cubos (11 oz.)

---

*3 gramos o más de fibra por porción

Fruta (cont.)

melón chino o de indias	$^1/_{10}$
cerezas, dulces, frescas	12 (3 oz.)
cerezas, dulces, enlatadas	$^1/_2$ taza
secciones cítricas	$^3/_4$ taza
dátiles	3
*higos, frescos o secos	$1^1/_2$ grande
cóctel de fruta	$^1/_2$ taza
toronja, enlatada, en secciones	$^3/_4$ taza
toronja, fresca	$^1/_2$ pequeña (11 oz.)
uvas, frescas, pequeñas	17 (3 oz.)
guayaba	1 pequeña
melón dulce, en cubos	1 taza
kiwi	1 ($3^1/_2$ oz.)
naranja china	3–4 medianas
naranja mandarina, enlatada	$^3/_4$ taza
mango	$^1/_2$ pequeño ($5^1/_2$ oz.)
mezcla de frutas frescas	$^1/_2$ taza
*nectarina, pequeña	1 (5 oz.)
naranja, enlatada, en secciones	$^1/_2$ taza
naranja, fresca	1 pequeña ($6^1/_2$ oz.)
papaya, picada	1 taza
melocotones, enlatados	$^1/_2$ taza
melocotón, fresco	1 mediano (4 oz.)
peras, enlatadas	$^1/_2$ taza
pera, fresca, grande	$^1/_2$ (4 oz.)
caquis	2 medianos
piña, enlatada	$^1/_2$ taza
piña, fresca, picada	$^3/_4$ taza
ensalada de piña	$^1/_2$ taza

---

*3 gramos o más de fibra por porción

Fruta (cont.)

ciruelas, frescas 2" de diámetro . . . . .2 pequeñas

*granada . . . . .1 pequeña

*ciruelas pasas, cocidas o secas . . . . .3 medianas

pasas . . . . .2 cdas.

tangelos . . . . .1 mediano

naranjas tangerinas, pequeñas . . . . .2 (8 oz.)

ensalada de frutas tropicales . . . .$^{1}/_{4}$ taza

sandía . . . .$1^{1}/_{4}$ taza, 1 rebanada
                                                     ($13^{1}/_{2}$ oz.)

Jugo de Fruta, sin endulzar

jugo de manzana/sidra . . . .$^{1}/_{2}$ taza

cóctel de jugo de arándano agrio . . . .$^{1}/_{3}$ taza

cóctel de jugo de arándano agrio, ...1 taza
reducido en calorías

mezcla de jugo de fruta, 100% jugo . . . .$^{1}/_{3}$ taza

jugo de uva . . . .$^{1}/_{3}$ taza

jugo de toronja . . . .$^{1}/_{2}$ taza

jugo de limón . . . .$^{3}/_{4}$ taza

jugo de lima . . . .$^{1}/_{2}$ taza

jugo de naranja . . . .$^{1}/_{2}$ taza

jugo de piña . . . .$^{1}/_{2}$ taza

jugo de ciruelas pasas . . . .$^{1}/_{3}$ taza

jugos bajos en carbohidratos . . . . .1 taza
(sin azúcar, tipo "light")

---

*3 gramos o más de fibra por porción

Opciones de leche

Una opción de leche contiene 12 gramos de carbohidratos y 8 gramos de proteína.

Esta lista tiene diferentes tipos de leche y productos lácteos. Los quesos están en las listas de la carne, y la crema y otros productos lácteos grasos están en la lista de opciones de grasa.

La cantidad de grasa en la leche se mide según el porcentaje (%) de nata de la leche. Las calorías en los productos lácteos varían dependiendo de la clase de leche de la que están hechos.

La leche es una fuente rica de proteína, calcio y riboflavina (una vitamina B). Usted puede usar la leche permitida en su plan ya sea para beber, en cereal o para cocinar. Busque la leche con chocolate, la leche de arroz, el yogur helado y el helado en las otras listas de opciones de carbohidratos.

Una porción de cada uno de estos tres tipos de leche (sin grasa, grasa reducida, y entera) incluye lo siguiente:

	Carbohidratos (gramos)	Proteína (gramos)	Grasa (gramos)	Calorías
sin grasa o con poca grasa ($^1/_2$% ó 1%)	12	8	0–3	90
grasa reducida (2%)	12	8	5	120
entera	12	8	8	150

Una opción de leche iguala:

1 taza de leche

$^3/_4$ taza de yogur

Leche sin Grasa (0–3 gramos de grasa por porción)

leche sin grasa . . . . .1 taza
leche ¹/₂% . . . . .1 taza
leche 1% . . . . .1 taza
suero de leche, sin grasa o con poca grasa . .1 taza
leche evaporada, sin grasa . . . . .¹/₂ taza
leche en polvo, sin grasa . . . . .¹/₃ taza
Lactaid 100, sin grasa . . . . .1 taza
leche de soja, sin grasa o con poca grasa . . .1 taza
yogur natural, sin grasa . . . . .³/₄ taza (6 oz.)
yogur, sin grasa, con sabor,
endulzado con un endulzador no
nutritivo y fructosa . . . . .³/₄ taza (6 oz.)

Leche con Grasa Reducida (5 gramos de grasa por porción)

leche con grasa reducida (2%) . . . . .1 taza
yogur, natural de poca grasa . . . . .³/₄ taza (6 oz.)
leche dulce acidophilus . . . . .1 taza
Lactaid 100, grasa reducida . . . . .1 taza
leche de soja . . . . .1 taza

Leche Entera (8 gramos de grasa por porción)

leche entera . . . . .1 taza
leche evaporada entera . . . . .¹/₂ taza
leche de cabra . . . . .1 taza
leche agria (kefir) . . . . .1 taza
yogur, natural (hecho de leche entera) . . . .1 taza (8 oz.)

Otras opciones de carbohidratos

Usted puede usar las opciones de alimentos de la lista de la próxima página como una opción de almidón, fruta o leche en su plan de comida. Algunas opciones también contarán como una o más opciones de grasa. Cantidades moderadas de estos alimentos pueden usarse en su plan de comida aún si contienen azúcar y grasa, siempre y cuando usted mantenga controlada su azúcar en la sangre. Verifique con su dietista para ver con qué frecuencia usted puede planear estos alimentos en su dieta. Recuerde siempre verificar la información nutricional en las etiquetas de alimentos, las cuales serán su mejor fuente de información.

Una opción iguala 15 gramos de carbohidratos, o 1 almidón, 1 fruta o 1 leche.

Alimento	Tamaño de Porción	Opciones por Porción
aderezo para ensalada, libre de grasa	$^1/_4$ taza	1 carbohidrato
almíbar, liviano	2 cdas.	1 carbohidrato
almíbar, regular	1 cda.	1 carbohidrato
almíbar, regular	$^1/_4$ taza	4 carbohidratos
arándanos agrios secos	$^1/_2$ onza	1 carbohidrato
barquillos de vainilla	5	1 carbohidrato, 1 grasa
barras de energía, deportivas o de desayuno	1 barra ($1^1/_2$ oz.)	$1^1/_2$ carbohidratos, 0–1 grasa
barras de jugo de frutas, congeladas, 100% jugo	1 barra (3 oz.)	1 carbohidrato
bebidas deportivas	8 oz. (1 taza)	1 carbohidrato
bizcocho de chocolate y nueces, no azucarado	cuadrado de 2"	1 carbohidrato, 1 grasa

Alimento	Tamaño de Porción	Opciones por Porción
bocadillos de frutas, gomoso (puré concentrado de fruta)	1 rollo ($^3/_4$ oz.)	1 carbohidrato
Croissant (cruasán)	1 pequeño	1 carbohidrato, 2 grasa
galleta, libre de grasa	2 pequeñas	1 carbohidrato
galleta o galleta sándwich con relleno de crema	2 pequeñas	1 carbohidrato, 1 grasa
galletita con sabor a jengibre	3	1 carbohidrato
gelatina, regular	$^1/_2$ taza	1 carbohidrato
helado	$^1/_2$ taza	1 carbohidrato, 1 grasa
helado, de poca grasa	$^1/_2$ taza	$1^1/_2$ carbohidratos
helado, ligero	$^1/_2$ taza	$1^1/_2$ carbohidratos, 1 grasa
helado, sin grasa, sin azúcar añadida	$^1/_2$ taza	1 carbohidrato
leche de arroz, de poca en grasa, con sabor	1 taza	$1^1/_2$ carbohidratos
leche de arroz, sin grasa o con poca grasa, sencilla	1 taza	1 carbohidrato
leche entera con chocolate	1 taza	2 carbohidratos,
magdalena, con azucarado	1 pequeña	2 carbohidratos, 1 grasa
mermelada o jalea, regular	1 cda.	1 carbohidrato
nachos	6–12 (1 oz.)	1 carbohidrato, 2 grasas
panecillo dulce o pastelillo con fruta	1 ($2^1/_2$ oz.)	$2^1/_2$ carbohidratos, 2 grasas

Alimento	Tamaño de Porción	Opciones por Porción
papas "chips"	12–18 (1 oz.)	1 carbohidrato, 2 grasas
pastel, con azucarado	cuadrado de 2"	2 carbohidratos, 1 grasa
pastel de ángel, no azucarado	$1/_{12}$ del pastel completo	2 carbohidratos
pastel, no azucarado	cuadrado de 2"	1 carbohidrato, 1 grasa
paté de fruta, 100% fruta	$1^1/_2$ cda.	1 carbohidrato
pudín, regular (hecho con leche baja en grasa)	$^1/_2$ taza	2 carbohidratos
pudín, sin azúcar (hecho con leche libre de grasa)	$^1/_2$ taza	1 carbohidrato
reemplazo de comida de calorías reducidas (batida)	1 lata (10–11 oz.)	$1^1/_2$ carbohidratos 0–1 grasa
rosquilla, azucarada	$3^3/_4$" de diámetro (2 oz.)	2 carbohidratos, 2 grasas
rosquilla, tipo pastel, simple	1 mediana ($1^1/_2$ oz.)	$1^1/_2$ carbohidratos, 2 grasas
salsa de arándano, gelatinada	$^1/_4$ taza	2 carbohidratos
salsa para espagueti o pasta, enlatada	$^1/_2$ taza	1 carbohidrato, 1 grasa
sorbete	$^1/_2$ taza	2 carbohidratos
tarta, de calabaza o de flan (preparado comercialmente)	$^1/_8$ tarta	2 carbohidratos, 2 grasas
tarta, de frutas, 2 cortezas	$^1/_6$ tarta	3 carbohidratos, 2 grasas

Alimento	Tamaño de Porción	Opciones por Porción
yogur, de poca grasa, con fruta	1 taza	3 carbohidratos, 0–1 grasa
yogur, helado	½ taza	1 carbohidrato 0–1 grasa
yogur, helado, sin grasa	⅓ taza	1 carbohidrato

Siempre verifique la etiqueta. Los productos pueden variar.

Opciones de vegetales

Una opción de vegetal tiene 5 gramos de carbohidratos, 2 gramos de proteína, 0 gramos de grasa, 2 ó 3 gramos de fibra y 25 calorías.

Los vegetales que tienen pequeñas cantidades de carbohidratos y calorías están en esta lista. Los vegetales tienen muchos nutrientes muy importantes. Incluya dos o tres opciones en su plan de comida cada día. Los vegetales almidonados como maíz, guisantes, papas y calabaza de invierno los cuales tienen grandes cantidades de carbohidratos y calorías están en la lista de opciones de almidón.

Los vegetales de color verde oscuro y amarillo intenso son las fuentes principales de vitamina A. Muchos de los vegetales en el grupo de almidones son buenas fuentes de vitamina C—espárragos, brécol, col, repollo, coliflor, col rizada, diente de león, mostaza, berza, rutabaga, espinacas, tomates y nabo.

Cantidades moderadas de vitamina B_6 son suministradas del brécol, col, coliflor, col rizada, chucrut, espinaca, tomates y jugo de tomates.

Buenas fuentes de potasio incluyen brécol, col, remolacha y acelga, tomates, jugo de tomates y cóctel de jugo de vegetales.

Si grasa es añadida para cocinar estos vegetales, debe ser contada junto con la cantidad permitida de opciones de grasa.

Cuando use vegetales cocidos, tenga en cuenta que una libra de vegetales crudos rinde alrededor de $4\frac{1}{2}$ tazas. Una libra de espinacas o berza rinde entre 8 y $12\frac{1}{2}$ porciones.

Una opción de vegetal iguala:

$^1/_2$ taza de vegetales cocidos o jugo de vegetales

1 taza de vegetales crudos

Si usted come una o dos opciones de vegetal en la comida o bocadillo, no tiene que contarlos, porque éstos contienen solamente pequeñas cantidades de calorías y carbohidratos.

alcachofa común

alcachofa, corazones

apio

berenjena

berro

bok choy

brécol

brotes de bambú

brotes de fríjol

calabacín

calabaza de verano

castañas de agua

cebollas

cebollinos

chayote

chucrut

col de Bruselas

coliflor

colinabo

espárragos

hojas verdes (todas—de remolacha, acelga, diente de león, berza, mostaza, espinaca, nabo)

jícama

judías (verdes, italianas, amarillas)

jugo de tomate/vegetales

nabo

pasta de tomate

pepino

pimentón

pimiento

pimientos (todas las variedades)

pimiento verde

puerro

puré de tomate

quingombú

rábano

remolacha

repollo (rojo/verde)

ruibarbo

rutabaga

salsa de tomate

setas/champiñones

tomates (enteros frescos)

tomates, enlatados

vaina de guisantes (incluyendo las chinas)

vegetales mixtos (sin maíz, guisantes ni pasta)

verduras de ensalada (endivia, escarola, lechuga, lechuga romana, espinaca)

zanahoria

Opciones de Carne o de Sustitutos de Carne

Una opción normal de carne tiene 7 gramos de proteína.

Todos los alimentos en la lista de carne son buenas fuentes de proteínas, y muchos son también buenas fuentes de hierro, zinc, vitamina B12 (presente solamente en alimentos de origen animal) y otras vitaminas B.

Las carnes toman la mayor parte del presupuesto de alimento, pero lo más importante es que éstas tienen muchas calorías, grasa saturada y colesterol. El uso de carne magra y muy magra, ave y pescado en su comida puede ayudarle a reducir su riesgo de enfermedades cardíacas. Las carnes en el grupo con mucha grasa deben limitarse a sólo 3 porciones por semana.

Compre solamente lo que planifique comer. Como guía, permita una cuarta parte de pérdida de peso cuando cocina la carne—para 1 libra de carne cruda permita una pérdida de 4 onzas, dejando 12 onzas de carne cocida (vea la página 86).

Esté seguro de quitar toda la grasa visible de las carnes. Use un rociador para que no se peguen sus alimentos al sartén o un sartén con un revestimiento antiadhesivo para saltear y dorar sus alimentos. Si usted le añade harina o pan a sus carnes, cuente esa porción de almidón en su plan de comida. Los jugos de las carnes con la grasa removida pueden usarse con sus carnes o vegetales para añadir sabor sin tener que contarlos como una porción adicional.

La siguiente lista está dividida en cuatro secciones: muy magra, magra, de grasa moderada y de mucha grasa. Éstas están basadas en la cantidad de grasa y calorías en una porción, o una onza de carne.

	Carbohidratos	*Proteína*	*Grasa*	*Calorías*
muy magra	0 gramos	7 gramos	0–1 gramo	35
magra	0 gramos	7 gramos	3 gramos	55
moderada grasa	0 gramos	7 gramos	5 gramos	75
mucha grasa	0 gramos	7 gramos	8 gramos	100

Una opción de carne iguala:

1 oz. de carne, pescado, ave o queso

$1/_2$ taza de frijoles secos

Carne muy magra y sustitutos

Una opción iguala 0 gramos de carbohidratos, 7 gramos de proteína, entre 0 y 1 gramo de grasa y 35 calorías. Una opción de carne muy magra es igual a cualquiera de los siguientes:

Aves

pollo o pavo (carne blanca, sin piel), ...1 oz.
gallina de Cornualles (sin piel)

Pescado

bacalao fresco o congelado, platija, abadejo, mero, ...1 oz.
trucha, salmón ahumado o curado, atún fresco o
enlatado en agua

Mariscos

almejas, cangrejo, langosta, escalope, ...1 oz.
camarones, imitación de mariscos

Caza

pato o faisán (sin piel), venado, búfalo, avestruz . . . . .1 oz.

Queso con 1 Gramo o Menos de Grasa por Onza

requesón sin grasa o de poca grasa . . . .$1/_4$ taza
queso sin grasa . . . . .1 onza

Otros

carnes procesadas para sándwich con 1 gramo o menos . . . .1 oz.
de grasa por onza, como fiambrera delgada, carnes en
tiras finas, carne de res picada, jamón de pavo
claras de huevo 2

Otros (cont.)

sustitutos de huevo, simples . . . .$^1/_4$ taza

perros calientes con 1 gramo o menos de grasa por onza . . . .1 oz.

riñón (alto en colesterol) . . . . .1 oz.

salchicha con 1 gramo o menos de grasa por onza . . . . .1 oz.

Cuente como una opción de carne muy magra y una de almidón:

frijoles secos, guisantes, lentejas (cocidas) . . . .$^1/_2$ taza

Carne magra y sustitutos

Una opción iguala 0 gramos de carbohidratos, 7 gramos de proteína, 3 gramos de grasa y 55 calorías. Una opción de carne magra iguala cualquiera de los siguientes:

Carne de res

grado USDA selecto (select) o selección (choice) . . . .1 oz.
de carne de res magra sin la grasa visible, como
masa redonda, lomo, bistec de costado; filete;
carne para asar (costilla, paletilla, grupa); bistec
(grueso con hueso en forma de T, filete,
machacado), masa redonda molida

Cerdo

cerdo magro, como jamón fresco; jamón . . . . .1 oz
enlatado, curado o hervido; tocino
canadiense; chuleta de filete de centro

Cordero

asado, chuleta, pierna . . . . .1 oz.

Ternera

filete de chuleta, asado . . . . .1 oz.

Aves

pollo, pavo (carne oscura, sin piel), pollo . . . . .1 oz.
(carne blanca, con piel), pato o ganso
doméstico (bien escurrido, sin piel)

Pescado

arenque (ahumado, sin crema) . . . . .1 oz.

ostras . . . . .6 medianas

salmón (fresco o enlatado), bagre . . . . .1 oz.

sardinas (enlatadas) . . . . .2 medianas

atún (enlatado en aceite, escurrido) . . . . .1 oz.

Caza

ganso (sin piel), conejo . . . .   1 oz.

Queso

requesón con 4.5% de grasa . . . .$^1/_4$ taza

queso parmesano rallado .2 cdas.

quesos con 3 gramos o menos de grasa por onza . . . .1 oz.

Otros

perros calientes con 3 gramos o menos . . . .$1^1/_2$ oz.
de grasa por onza

carne procesada para sándwich con . . . . .1 oz.
3 gramos o menos de grasa por onza,
como pastrami o salchicha polaca de pavo

hígado, corazón (alto en colesterol) . . . . .1 oz.

Carne media en grasa y sustitutos

Una opción iguala 0 gramos de carbohidratos, 7 gramos de proteína, 5 gramos de grasa y 75 calorías. Una opción de carne media en grasa iguala cualquiera de los siguientes:

Carne de res

la mayoría de los productos de carne de res . . . . .1 oz.
(res molida, barra de carne, res en salmuera,
costillas cortas, carne grado de primera sin la grasa,
como costillas de primera)

Cerdo

lomo, chuleta, cabeza de lomo, croqueta . . . . .1 oz.

Cordero

costillas para asar, molido . . . . .1 oz.

Ternera

chuleta (molida o machacada, sin empanar) . . . . .1 oz.

Aves

carne oscura del pollo (con piel), molida . . . . .1 oz.
de pollo o pavo, pollo frito (con piel)
tocino (panceta) de pavo . . . . .2 rebanadas

Pescado

cualquier pescado frito . . . . .1 oz.

Queso con 5 Gramos o Menos de Grasa por Onza

feta . . . . .1 oz.
mozzarella . . . . .1 oz.
requesón . . . .$^1/_4$ taza (2 oz.)

Otros

huevo (alto en colesterol, límite 3 por semana) 1
salchicha con 5 gramos o menos de grasa por onza . . .1 oz.
soja fermentada y frita . . . .$^1/_4$ taza
tofu . . . . .4 oz. o $^1/_2$ taza
edamame (porotos de soja) . . . .$^1/_2$ taza

Carnes de mucha grasa y sustitutos

Una opción iguala 0 gramos de carbohidratos, 7 gramos de proteína, 8 gramos de grasa y 100 calorías.

Recuerde que todos estos artículos contienen mucha grasa saturada, colesterol y calorías, y pueden subir los niveles de colesterol si se comen regularmente. Una opción de carne con mucha grasa iguala cualquiera de los siguientes:

Cerdo

costillas, molido, salchicha . . . . .1 oz.

Queso

todos los quesos regulares, como . . . . .1 oz.
americano, cheddar, Monterrey Jack, suizo

Otros

carne procesada para sándwich con . . . . .1 oz.
8 gramos o menos de grasa por onza,
como Boloña, barra de pimiento, salame

salchichas, como bratwurst, Italiana, ...1 oz.
knockwurst, Polaca, ahumada

perro caliente (pavo o pollo) 1 (10/lb.)

tocino . . . . .3 lonjas (20
lonjas/lb.)

mantequilla de cacahuate (contiene . . . . .1 cda.
grasa insaturada)

Cuente como una carne alta en grasa más un intercambio de grasa:

perro caliente (de res, cerdo o combinado) 1 (10/lb.)

Opciones de grasa

Una opción de grasa contiene 5 gramos de grasa y 45 calorías.

Las grasas provienen de fuentes animales y vegetales y varían entre aceites líquidos y grasas duras. Los aceites son grasas que se mantienen líquidas a temperatura ambiente y normalmente provienen de una fuente vegetal. Los aceites vegetales comunes son el de oliva, de cacahuate, de maíz, de soja, canola y girasol. Las grasas comunes de animales son la mantequilla, la crema y la grasa de tocino. Todas las grasas tienen muchas calorías, así que los alimentos en esta lista deben medirse cuidadosamente para controlar su peso. Trate de incluir más grasa monoinsaturada y poliinsaturada en su dieta—éstas son buenas para su salud. Las grasas saturadas en su dieta pueden subir su nivel de colesterol en la sangre (vea la sección "Grasa Saturada y Colesterol", páginas 95–96).

Una opción de grasa iguala:

1 cdta. de margarina regular o aceite vegetal

1 cda. de aderezo para ensalada regular

La siguiente es una lista de alimentos para usar para una opción de grasa.

Grasas monoinsaturadas (use éstas)

aguacate, mediano . . . . .2 cdas
                                                        (1 oz.)
aceite (canola, oliva, cacahuate) . . . . .1 cdta.
aceitunas:
    maduras negras . . . . .8 grandes
    verdes rellenas . . . . .10 grandes
frutos secos:
    almendras, anacardos . . . . .6 frutos secos
    mixtas (50% cacahuate) . . . . .6 frutos secos
    cacahuate . . . . .10 frutos secos
    nuez lisa . . . . .4 mitades
mantequilla de cacahuate, suave o crujiente . . . .$^{1}/_{2}$ cda.
semillas de sésamo . . . . .1 cda.
pasta de sésamo . . . . .2 cdtas.

Grasas poliinsaturadas (use éstas)

margarina:
    en barra, tubo o de apretar . . . . .1 cdta.
    baja en grasa (30% a 50% de aceite vegetal) . . . . .1 cda.
mayonesa:
    regular . . . . .1 cdta.
    grasa reducida . . . . .1 cda.
aceite (maíz, cártamo, soja) . . . . .1 cda.
nueces: nueces inglesas . . . . .4 mitades
aderezo para ensalada:
    regular . . . . .1 cda.
    grasa reducida . . . . .2 cdas.

aderezo para ensalada Miracle Whip:

    regular . . . . .2 cdtas.

    grasa reducida . . . . .1 cda.

semillas: calabaza, girasol, piñones . . . . .1 cda.

Grasas saturadas (evite éstas)

tocino . . . . .1 lonja
                                             (20 lonjas/lb.)

grasa de tocino . . . . .1 cdta.

mantequilla:

    barra . . . . .1 cdta.

    batida . . . . .2 cdtas.

    grasa reducida . . . . .1 cda.

mondongo, hervido . . . . .2 cdas.

chocolate, sin azúcar . . . . .2 cdtas.

coco, endulzado, rallado . . . . .2 cdas.

leche de coco . . . . .1 cda.

crema, mitad y mitad . . . . .2 cdas.

queso crema:

    regular . . . . .1 cda. ($^{1}/_{2}$ oz.)

    grasa reducida . . . . .1$^{1}/_{2}$ cdas. ($^{3}/_{4}$ oz.)

crema: pesada, batida . . . . .1 cda.

crema agria:

    regular . . . . .2 cdas.

    grasa reducida . . . . .3 cdas.

cerdo salado . . . . .1 oz.

manteca vegetal o de cerdo . . . . .1 cdta.

Nota: Los productos no lácteos como cremas, en polvo o líquidas, no están incluidos en esta lista de alimentos (vea los alimentos sin cargo en la lista de la página 68). Estos productos varían en valor nutricional, pero normalmente 1 cucharada tiene alrededor de 20 calorías (mayormente en la forma de carbohidratos). En la forma en polvo, 2 cucharaditas tienen de 20–25 calorías, incluyendo 2 gramos de carbohidratos y menos de 1 gramo de grasa. Trate de usar 1 cucharadita de leche sin grasa en polvo en su café. Le costará menos y tiene solamente 10 calorías por cucharadita.

Combinación de Alimentos

La mayoría de las comidas que comemos contienen diferentes clases de alimentos mezclados. Es difícil acomodar esto en cualquiera de nuestras listas, por lo que los agrupamos todos juntos. Muchas veces es difícil saber qué hay en una cacerola o en un alimento preparado. Con el conteo de carbohidratos es fácil acomodar estas combinaciones de alimentos como sopas y comidas congeladas en su plan de comida. Recuerde mirar los gramos de carbohidratos, proteína y grasa en la etiqueta de información nutricional del empaque. Pregúntele a su dietista acerca de comidas favoritas que usted desea incluir en su plan de comida.

Alimento	*Medida*	*Opciones de Alimento*
Plato principal		
cacerola, hecha en casa	1 taza (8 oz.)	$2^1/_2$ carbohidratos 2 carnes media en grasa
pizza de queso, masa fina	$^1/_4$ de 15 oz. ó $^1/_4$ de 10"	2 carbohidratos 2 carnes media en grasa 1 grasa
chili con frijoles	1 taza (8 oz.)	2 carbohidratos 2 carnes media en grasa
lasaña	3" × 4"	2 carbohidratos 2 carnes media en grasa
chow mein, sin arroz o fideos	2 tazas (16 oz.)	1 carbohidrato 2 carne magra
Sopas		
instantánea de frijoles/lentejas	1 taza (8 oz.)	$2^1/_2$ carbohidratos 1 carne muy magra

Alimento	Medida	Opciones de Alimento
de crema (preparada con agua)	1 taza (8 oz.)	1 carbohidrato 1 grasa
de arvejas (preparada con agua)	¹/₂ taza (4 oz.)	1 carbohidratos
de tomate (preparada con agua)	1 taza (8 oz.)	1 carbohidrato
de vegetales y carne de res, de pollo y fideos u de otro tipo de caldo	1 taza (8 oz.)	1 carbohidrato

Platos Principales Congelados (*estos tienen pocas calorías*)

crema de ajo camarones en	1 paquete 11.5 onzas 270 calorías	2 almidones 2 carnes muy magras 1 vegetal
pollo Teriyaki	1 paquete 11 onzas 260 calorías	2 almindones 2 carnes muy magras 1 vegetal
pollo con glaseado dulce	1 paquete 8.5 onzas 230 calorias	2 almidones 2 carnes muy magras
pollo con glaseado de queso	1 paquete 9.5 onzas 260 calorías	2 almidones 2 carnes muy magras
pechuga de pavo y papas majadas	1 paquete 8.5 onzas 210 calorías	1¹/₂ almidones 2 carnes magras
manicotti	1 paquete 11 onzas 290 calorías	2¹/₂ almidones 1 carne magra 1 vegetal
ziti marinara con tres quesos	1 paquete 9 onzas 290 calorías	3 almidones 2 carnes media en grasa 1 grasa

Alimentos Sin Cargo

Algunos alimentos se llaman *alimentos sin cargo*. Éstos son alimentos o bebidas que contienen menos de 20 calorías por porción y contienen menos de 5 gramos de carbohidratos por porción. Limite estos "alimentos sin cargo" a 3 porciones al día divididas entre comidas y bocadillos. Cuando un alimento o bebida contiene más de 5 gramos de carbohidratos, siempre cuéntelos en su plan de comida.

Cuando use los siguientes alimentos sin cargo, use sólo la cantidad señalada.

salsa A-1 . . . . .1 cda.

ketchup . . . . .1 cda.

salsa de chili . . . . .1 cda.

cacao (seco, sin edulcorante en polvo) . . .1 cda.

arándano . . . .$^1/_3$ taza cocida sin azúcar

queso crema, libre de grasa . . . . .1 cda.

crema, liviana no láctea, líquida . . . . .2 cdas.

crema, no láctea, líquida . . . . .1 cda.

crema, no láctea, en polvo . . . . .2 cdtas.

bombón, sin azúcar . . . . .1 pieza

jalea o mermelada, de poca azúcar . . . . . .2 cdtas.

margarina, sin grasa . . . . .4 cdas.

margarina, grasa reducida . . . . .1 cdta.

mayonesa, sin grasa . . . . .1 cda.

mayonesa, grasa reducida . . . . .1 cdta.

Miracle Whip, sin grasa . . . . .1 cda.

Miracle Whip, grasa reducida . . . . .1 cdta.

Nestlé Quik, sin azúcar . . . . .1 cda. hasta el tope

pepinillos . . . .$1^1/_2$ grande

picadillo de pepinillos (relish) . . . . .1 cda.

pepinillos, dulces (en rebanada) . . . . . . .2 rebanadas

pepinillos, dulces (en vinagre) . . . .$^3/_4$ oz.

aderezo para ensalada, sin grasa . . . . . . .1 cda.

aderezo para ensalada, sin grasa . . . . . . .2 cdas.
Italiano

aderezos para ensaladas en aerosol . . . . . . .10 rocíos

salsa . . . .$^1/_4$ taza

jugo de chucrut .1 taza

crema agria, libre de grasa, ...1 cda.
grasa reducida

salsa soja . . . . .1 cda.

almíbar, sin azúcar . . . . .2 cdas.

salsa picante para tacos . . . . .1 cda.

cubierta batida, regular o liviano . . . . .2 cdas.

salsa Worcestershire . . . . .1 cda.

levadura (de cerveza) . . . . .2 cdtas.

yogur (natural) . . . . .2 cdas.

Cuando utilice pastas de productos 100% fruta que lucen como mermeladas, límite su porción a 1 cucharadita.

La siguiente lista incluye artículos que no tienen azúcar y tienen pocas calorías. Se pueden usar en su plan de comida tanto como desee:

Bebidas

agua de Seltz

agua tónica, sin azúcar

caldo

gaseosas, sin azúcar

mezclas de bebidas, sin azúcar

té o café

Condimentos

jugo de lima

jugo de limón

mostaza

rábano picante

rociador vegetal PAM

vinagre

Artículos sin azúcar

edulcorantes alternativos

gaseosas

gelatina (sin sabor)

gelatina de postre

goma de mascar

Los condimentos también son alimentos sin cargo. Usted puede usar cualquier cantidad de los siguientes en su plan de comida:

ablandador de carne

achiote

ajo

albahaca

alcaravea

anís

apio

canela

cardamomo

cebollín

clavos de olor

comino

condimento para ave

corteza de angostura

curry

eneldo

extractos (vainilla, etc.)

glutamato monosódico

jengibre

laurel

macia

mejorana

menta

mostaza, seca

nuez moscada

orégano

perejil

perifolio

pimentón dulce

pimienta

pimienta inglesa

polvo de chili

romero

salvia

semillas de adormidera

semillas de ajonjolí

tomillo

Alimentos Dietéticos

Tenga cuidado con todo tipo de alimento dietético. Aunque tienen poca azúcar, los alimentos dietéticos frecuentemente contienen otros alimentos que se descomponen en azúcar. Sea extremadamente cauteloso con productos dietéticos como los helados, las galletas, las barras de dulce, las tortas y cosas así, porque muchos de estos productos contienen más calorías que los alimentos que están reemplazando.

Aprenda a leer las etiquetas de Información Nutricional (vea las páginas 80–83) y conozca la naturaleza del producto que está comprando. Un producto marcado como "dietético" puede que no sea adecuado para los que tienen diabetes. Éste podría contener menos azúcar, menos sal, menos grasa o menos colesterol que un producto regular.

Usted necesita leer la etiqueta para saber por qué afirma ser dietético, y entonces usted puede decidir si realmente lo necesita. Por ejemplo, las galletas dietéticas puede que no contengan azúcar pero siguen teniendo harina, grasas y calorías de edulcorantes alternativos que deben ser contadas en su plan de comida diario.

Comidas y Bocadillos Alternativos

Hay suplementos disponibles que pueden ser usados por cualquier persona con diabetes. Éstos están disponibles como batidas líquidas y barras y pueden usarse como reemplazo de comidas, como un bocadillo o durante una enfermedad siempre y cuando formen parte de su plan de comida. Hay varios productos disponibles. Siempre verifique las etiquetas.

Ejemplo:

Bebida Glucerna
Vainilla, 8 onzas
220 calorías
1 almidón
1 leche baja en grasa
1 grasa

Barra Glucerna
Limón crujiente
1 barra 140 calorías
$1^1/_2$ almidón
$^1/_2$ grasa

Bebida Choice
Vainilla, 8 onzas
220 calorías
1 almidón
1 leche baja en grasa
2 grasas

Barra Choice
Fudge Brownie
1 barra 140 calorías
1 almidón
1 grasa

EJEMPLOS DE PLANES DE COMIDA

Los siguientes son ejemplos de planes de comida para niveles de 1,500 a 2,000 calorías. Úselos solamente como una guía temporal, pregúntele a su doctor o dietista para un plan completo de comida, preparado basándose en sus necesidades especiales (horario, bocadillos y medicamentos) y gustos.

El plan de comida en la página 74 está en blanco. (Formularios adicionales están incluidos en la parte de atrás del libro.) Éste puede ser usado por su dietista cuando planifique su plan personal de comida. Ella o él determinará el total de opciones de carbohidratos, carne y grasa para un día basado en sus necesidades de calorías.

Usando el mismo formulario, planifique varios de sus propios menús. Se han provisto ejemplos para que los use como guías. Primero, regrese atrás a las listas de opciones en las páginas 43–67 y marque todos los alimentos que le gustaría comer para su desayuno, almuerzo, cena y bocadillos. Tenga en cuenta la cantidad de esos alimentos que equivalen a una opción. Después, planifique sus comidas para acomodar su plan de comida.

Ejemplo: Si usted está en un plan de comida de 1,500 calorías y el desayuno le permite 3 opciones de carbohidratos, un día usted puede escoger:

$^1/_2$ taza de cereal
$^1/_2$ banana
1 taza de leche libre de grasa

o

1 bagel pequeño
$^1/_2$ toronja

Cuando escoja otros alimentos, puede escoger dentro del mismo grupo de alimento, pero no cambie un alimento almidón por una carne. También puede incluir alimentos sin cargo, siempre y cuando se mantenga dentro de las guías para su plan de comida.

Guías para Bocadillos

Aquí tiene algunas reglas fáciles de seguir a la hora de prepararse un bocadillo.

A la hora de dormir o más de 4–5 horas entre comidas:

1 almidón	5 galletas o 1 rebanada de tostada de trigo (15 gramos de carbohidratos)
1 proteína	1 onza de queso bajo en grasa o 1 onza de carne baja en grasa

Menos de 4–5 horas entre comidas:

1 porción cada uno	cualquier cantidad de lo siguiente
pudín sin grasa	gelatina sin azúcar
vegetales	paleta helada sin azúcar
frutos secos o semillas	bebidas sin azúcar
galletas sin azúcar	
dulces sin azúcar	

Plan de Comida Personalizado

Número de Calorías _____
Carbohidratos :_____ gramos Proteína:_____ gramos
Grasa: _____ gramos

Hora del Desayuno: _____

_____ Opciones de Carbohidratos
_____ almidón
_____ fruta
_____ leche
_____ Opciones de Carne
_____ Opciones de Grasa

Hora para el Bocadillo de la Mañana: _____
_____

Hora de Almuerzo: _____

_____ Opciones de Carbohidratos
_____ almidón
_____ fruta
_____ leche
_____ Vegetales
_____ Opciones de Carne
_____ Opciones de Grasa

Hora para el Bocadillo de la Tarde: _____
_____

Hora de la Cena: _____

_____ Opciones de Carbohidratos
_____ almidón
_____ fruta
_____ leche
_____ Vegetales
_____ Opciones de Carne
_____ Opciones de Grasa

Hora para el Bocadillo de la Noche: _____
_____

Ejemplo para un Plan de Comida
1,500 Calorías

Menú de Ejemplo

Desayuno

3 opciones de carbohidratos:
I almidón	$^1/_2$ taza de cereal de salvado
I fruta	$^1/_2$ banana
I leche libre de grasa	I taza de leche libre de grasa
I opción de carne muy magra	$^1/_4$ taza de requesón de grasa reducida

Almuerzo

4 opciones de carbohidratos:
2 almidones	2 rebanadas de pan de trigo
I fruta	I manzana pequeña
I leche libre de grasa	I taza de leche libre de grasa
vegetal	palitos de zanahoria, lechuga y tomate
2 opciones de carne muy magra	2 oz. de pavo en lonjas (carne blanca)
I opción de grasa	I cda. de mayonesa de grasa reducida

Cena

4 opciones de carbohidratos:
3 almidones	I taza de arroz salvaje
I fruta	$^1/_2$ taza de fruta fresca
vegetal	$^1/_2$ taza habichuelas tiernas
	ensalada de lechuga y tomate
2 opciones de carne magra	2 oz. de pollo horneado (sin piel)
2 opciones de grasas	I cdta. margarina
	2 cdas. aderezo de grasa reducida
	té helado (sin azúcar)

Bocadillo antes de Dormir:

I almidón	I rebanada de tostada de trigo
I opción de carne magra	I onza de queso bajo en grasa

Ejemplo para un Plan de Comida
2,000 Calorías

Desayuno

4 opciones de carbohidratos:
  2 almidones   I panecillo inglés
  I fruta $^1/_2$ toronja
  I leche libre de grasa   I taza de leche libre de grasa
I opción de grasa   I cdta. margarina
I opción de carne magra   I huevo escalfado

Bocadillo de la Mañana

I opción de carbohidrato $^3/_4$ taza yogur sin azúcar

Almuerzo

4 opciones de carbohidratos:
  3 almidones   I taza de sopa de vegetales y carne de res
                           2 rebanadas de pan de trigo
  I fruta   17 uvas frescas pequeñas
vegetal   lechuga y tomate
2 opciones de carne magra   2 oz. de pavo en lonjas (carne blanca)
I opción de grasa   I cda. de mayonesa de grasa reducida
                           gaseosa sin azúcar

Bocadillo de la Tarde

I opción de almidón   6 galletas saladas
I opción de carne magra   I oz. de queso en tiras

Cena

5 opciones de carbohidratos:
  3 almidones   I taza de papas majadas
                           I panecillo pequeño
  I fruta $1^1/_4$ taza de fresas enteras
  I vegetal almidonado $^1/_2$ taza de arvejas
vegetal   ensalada de lechuga

3 opciones de carne magra	3 oz. de salmón a la parrilla
2 opciones de grasas	2 cdas. aderezo de grasa reducida
	1 cdta. margarina
1 bebida sin cargo	té helado (sin azúcar)

Bocadillo antes de Dormir:

1 almidón	$^1/_2$ bagel, pequeño
1 proteína	1 cda. de mantequilla de cacahuate

ALTERNATIVAS PARA EDULCORANTES

Hay tres tipos de edulcorantes: calóricos, no-calóricos y aquellos que son mitad y mitad. Los edulcorantes calóricos, tales como la sacarosa (azúcar de mesa) contiene alrededor de 16 calorías por cucharadita. Los edulcorantes etiquetados como bajos en calorías o "lite" son mitad azúcar y mitad edulcorante no-calórico y contienen 8 calorías por cucharadita. Actualmente hay cinco edulcorantes no-calóricos en el mercado. Éstos contienen una cantidad muy pequeña de carbohidratos, azúcar o calorías y le darán el sabor dulce de la azúcar pero no aumentarán su nivel de azúcar en la sangre. Usted hallará estos edulcorantes en gaseosas de dieta, gelatina de dieta, goma de mascar, jugos de frutas y mezclas en polvo para jugos. Siempre y cuando la porción tenga menos de 20 calorías y menos de 5 gramos de carbohidratos por porción, usted puede usarlos como alimentos sin cargo. Cuando usa los edulcorantes no-calóricos, 1 paquete generalmente equivale a 2 cdas. de azúcar.

En la siguiente tabla, se comparan los edulcorantes no-calóricos.

Aspartame – (NutraSweet, Equal) se usa para endulzar muchos alimentos y bebidas. No se recomienda para hornear porque la exposición prolongada al calor causa pérdida de dulzura.

Sucralosa – (Splenda) es el edulcorante no-calórico más dulce disponible. Puede usarse al cocinar y al hornear y también se usa para endulzar muchos alimentos y bebidas.

Sacarina – (Sweet'n Low, Sugar Twin) ha sido usada por muchos años. Puede usarse al cocinar, hornear, enlatar (hacer conservas) o puede rociarse sobre frutas o cereales. La sacarina puede dejarle un sabor amargo a algunas personas.

Acesulfame-K – (Sweet One, Sunett) también puede dejarle un sabor amargo a ciertas personas. Éste puede usarse en el café y en el té y en el cereal y las frutas. También en combinación con otros edulcorantes no calóricos en muchos alimentos bajos en calorías, libres de azúcar y sin azúcar añadida.

Stevia (Truvia) proviene de la hoja de una planta y se usa en otros alimentos y bebidas.

Alcoholes de Azúcar

Algunos alimentos bajos en calorías o sin azúcar añadida reemplazan la sacarosa con alcoholes de azúcar. Éstos son carbohidratos que tienen un nivel calórico menor que otros carbohidratos. Ellos proveen 2 calorías por gramo por porción comparado con 4 calorías por gramo. Los alcoholes de azúcar son absorbidos más lentamente que la sacarosa y causan un menor aumento en el nivel de azúcar en la sangre.

Los alcoholes de azúcar estarán listados en la etiqueta de Información Nutricional y se suman como parte de los carbohidratos totales. Si el total de carbohidratos en el alimento proviene de alcoholes de azúcar y hay menos de 5 gramos por porción, entonces éste puede contarse como un alimento sin cargo. Si un alimento contiene más que 5 gramos de azúcar alcohólico (polialcohol), divida los gramos de azúcar alcohólico por dos y reste esta cantidad de los gramos de carbohidratos para obtener los gramos de carbohidratos disponibles. Los carbohidratos restantes deben incluirse en su plan de comida. Los productos que pueden usar alcoholes de azúcar son los dulces, las galletas, la goma de mascar, las bebidas y el pudín bajos en calorías al igual que las pastillas contra la tos sin azúcar.

Alcoholes de Azúcar
Se usan en lo alimentos para reemplazar azúcar o grasa.

CÓMO ENTENDER LAS ETIQUETAS DE ALIMENTOS

En 1993, la Administración de Drogas y Alimentos de los Estados Unidos (ADA o FDA, por sus siglas en inglés) creó las etiquetas de Información Nutricional. Estas etiquetas pueden ser útiles para elegir sus OPCIONES DE ALIMENTOS SALUDABLES. Para ayudarle a entender las etiquetas de alimentos, la ADA ha elaborado una explicación de los términos utilizados en dichos marbetes, por ejemplo *liviano, sin calorías, bajo en grasa, alto en fibra y bajo en colesterol.*

La siguiente información le ayudará a entender estos términos y le servirá como una guía que usted puede usar cuando esté seleccionando los alimentos.

Término	*Significado*
Sin calorías	Menos de 5 calorías por porción.
Caloría reducida	Tiene al menos 25% menos calorías que el alimento regular pero es igual en valor alimenticio.
Bajo en caloría	Alimentos que tienen no más de 40 calorías por porción.
De dieta, dietético	Término utilizado para los alimentos bajos en calorías y de caloría reducida. También puede ser usado en alimentos bajos en sodio pero no bajos en caloría.
Endulzado artificialmente	Igual que bajo en caloría o caloría reducida, excepto que la sacarosa (azúcar de mesa) ha sido removida y un edulcorante alternativo ha sido añadido.
Liviano, ligero, light	$1/3$ menos calorías ó 50% menos grasa por porción que el alimento regular.
Libre de grasa	Menos de $1/2$ gramo de grasa por porción.
Bajo en grasa	3 gramos o menos de grasa por porción.
Grasa reducida	Al menos 25% menos grasa que el alimento regular.

Término	Significado
Alto en fibra	5 gramos por porción
Más fibra o fibra añadida	2.5 gramos o más por porción que los alimentos regulares.
Bajo en grasa saturada	1 gramo o menos de grasa saturada por porción. No más de 15% de las calorías provienen de grasa saturada.
Libre de colesterol	Menos de 2 miligramos de colesterol por porción.
Bajo en colesterol	Menos de 20 miligramos de colesterol y menos de 2 gramos de grasa saturada por porción.
Libre de sodio, libre de sal	Menos de 5 miligramos de sodio por porción.
Bajo en sodio	Menos de 140 miligramos de sodio por porción.
Enriquecido, fortificado	Alimentos deben contener 10% o más del Valor Diario para proteína, vitaminas, minerales, fibra dietética o potasio por porción.
Sin azúcar añadida	Permitido si no se usan azúcares u otros ingredientes sustitutos del azúcar y no contiene ningún concentrado de jugo de fruta ni jalea.

Cómo Leer una Etiqueta de Alimento

La Información Nutricional en una etiqueta de alimento puede ayudarle con la selección de alimentos.

Los *tamaños por porción* están basados en lo que las personas normalmente comen. Examine su plan de comida para ver si la cantidad equivale a sus opciones de alimento.

Las *calorías* por porción y las *calorías* por porción *de grasa* están indicadas.

El % del *valor diario* puede ser usado para comparar alimentos y ver cómo la cantidad de un nutriente en una porción de alimento encaja en una dieta de 2,000 calorías diarias.

La lista de nutrientes cubre la información importante para ayudarle a elegir sus OPCIONES DE ALIMENTOS SALUDABLES.

- *Grasa total* muestra la cantidad en una porción. Una opción de grasa tiene 5 gramos de grasa. Si la etiqueta indica 10 gramos de grasa, una porción contará como 2 grasas en su plan de comida. Las cantidades de grasa saturada y grasa trans están indicadas.

- *Colesterol* muestra cómo una porción de este alimento se compara con la recomendación de 300 miligramos de colesterol por día.

- *Sodio* muestra cómo una porción de este alimento se compara con la recomendación de 2,400 miligramos de sodio por día.

- *Carbohidratos totales:* son más importantes mirarlos que el contenido de azúcar solamente. Un almidón, fruta, leche u otro carbohidrato tiene alrededor de 15 gramos de carbohidratos. Si la etiqueta indica 30 gramos, una porción contará como 2 opciones de almidón. La fibra dietética se encuentra bajo carbohidratos totales.

- *Proteína* le dice el número de opciones de carne en una porción. Una opción de carne tiene 7 gramos de proteína. Si la etiqueta indica 14 gramos de proteína, una porción contará como 2 opciones de carne.

Vitaminas y minerales: Los manufactureros sólo tienen que indicar las vitaminas A y C y los minerales, calcio y hierro. Las cantidades son un porcentaje de las raciones diarias recomendadas (USRDA, por sus siglas en inglés).

Fibra muestra cómo este alimento se compara con la recomendación de 25 gramos de fibra por día.

El **Tamaño Por Porción** está dado tanto en unidades caseras y métricas y refleja las cantidades que las personas normalmente comen.

Las **Calorías de Grasa** ahora son mostradas en la etiqueta para ayudar a los consumidores a seguir las guías dietéticas que recomiendan que las personas no deben obtener más de 30 por ciento de sus calorías de grasa.

La **Lista de Nutrientes** cubre aquellos más importantes para la salud de los consumidores actuales, la mayoría de los cuales necesitan preocuparse por no obtener *demasiado* de ciertos elementos (grasa por ejemplo) en lugar de muy pocas vitaminas y minerales como en el pasado.

Recuerde: Es más importante mirar el contenido *total* de *carbohidratos* en una etiqueta de un alimento que la cantidad de azúcar.

% del Valor Diario le da una idea general de cuanta grasa, sodio, carbohidratos o fibras dietéticas cada porción le provee a su dieta diaria. Utilícelo para encontrar alimentos bajos en grasa y altos en fibra.

Las **Calorías por gramo** le da el número de calorías en un gramo de grasa, carbohidratos y proteína, respectivamente.

Información Nutricional

Tamaño de Porción ½ taza (114g)
Porciones Por Envase 4

Cantidad Por Porción

Calorías 90   Calorías de Grasa 30

	% Valor Diario*
Grasa Total 3g	5%
Grasa Saturada 0g	0%
Grasa Trans 0g	
Colesterol 0mg	0%
Sodio 300 mg	13%
Carbohidratos Totales 13g	4%
Fibra Dietética 3g	12%
Azúcares 3g	
Proteína 3g	

Vitamina A	80%	• Vitamina C	60%
Calcio	4%	• Hierro	4%

* Los porcentajes del Valor Diario están basados en una dieta de 2,000 calorías. Sus Valores Diarios pueden ser más altos o bajos dependiendo de sus necesidades calóricas:

	Calorías:	2,000	2,500
Grasa Total	Menos de	65g	80g
Grasa Saturada	Menos de	20g	25g
Colesterol	Menos de	300mg	300mg
Sodio	Menos de	2,400mg	2,400mg
Carbohidratos Totales		300g	375g
Fibra Dietética		25g	30g

Calorías por gramo:
Grasa 9   •   Carbohidratos 4   •   Proteína 4

ALCOHOL

En muchas ocasiones uno se hace la pregunta, "¿Qué hacer con el alcohol—puedo beber un trago de vez en cuando?" No hay una respuesta determinada a esta pregunta. Depende mucho del control de su azúcar en la sangre, peso y niveles de grasa en la sangre. Por eso, **discuta el consumo de alcohol con su doctor.** Si usted decide ingerir alcohol, debe entender completamente cómo hacerlo correctamente en su plan de comida. Para ayudarlo, aquí tiene algunos factores que necesita saber.

- El alcohol es absorbido rápidamente y tiene 7 calorías por gramo.
- El alcohol no tiene valor como alimento.
- El alcohol es quemado diferente que los alimentos por su cuerpo y NO requiere insulina para ser utilizado.
- El alcohol puede causar hipoglucemia (azúcar en la sangre bajo), especialmente si usted toma píldoras para diabetes o insulina y las comidas se omiten o se retrasan (éste impide que el cuerpo tome glucosa o azúcar de lugares en los que se encuentra almacenado en el hígado y los coloque en la sangre).
- Si es tomado por alguien que toma Diabinese (vea las páginas 120–121), el alcohol puede causar reacciones como enrojecimiento, sudor, dolor de cabeza, náusea o una sensación de atragantamiento.
- Evite el alcohol si sus triglicéridos están altos o si está tomando Glucophage-Metformin.
- Evite el alcohol si debe perder peso—el alcohol tiene calorías y puede estimular el apetito.

Sugerencias para el Consumo de Alcohol

- Si decide beber alcohol, el consumo diario debe ser limitado a una copa para una mujer adulta y dos copas para un hombre adulto. Un trago es definido como 12 oz. de cerveza, 5 oz. de vino o 1.5 oz. de licor fuerte (un tiro).

- El alcohol puede bajar su azúcar en la sangre, así que consúmalo solamente con comidas y bocadillos. Tomar alcohol con comidas retrasa la absorción en el torrente sanguíneo y "suaviza" el efecto en el cuerpo.

- Evite vinos dulces, licores y mezclas dulces de bebidas porque estas tienen un contenido alto de azúcar. Acompañantes para mezclas tales como jugo de naranja, deben ser contados en el conteo total de calorías.

Cómo Planificar el Alcohol en Su Dieta

El alcohol corre a través del cuerpo como GRASA por lo tanto debe ser contado como una opción de GRASA. Una opción de grasa debe ser removida por cada 45 calorías en la bebida alcohólica. Consulte la tabla de abajo para el contenido de calorías:

licor	ginebra, vodka, ron, whisky 1 oz. = 70 calorías
vino seco	chablis, chianti, champaña 3 oz. = 60 calorías
cerveza (baja en caloría)	12 oz. = aproximadamente de 70 a 100 calorías
cerveza (regular)	12 oz. = 171 calorías

COCINAR con alcohol: El alcohol se evapora alrededor de los 172° F, lo cual es por debajo de la temperatura a la cual hierve. El sabor de la bebida se queda, pero las calorías y el alcohol se pierden.

RECUERDE: Discuta el consumo de alcohol con su doctor.

CONSEJOS PARA COMPRAS

Planifique sus menús para una semana a la vez, tomando ventaja de las ofertas especiales en el supermercado. Haga la lista de los artículos que necesita de acuerdo a cómo están localizados en la tienda. Busque los productos lácteos, fríos y congelados al final. También, para evitar comer de más, estime la cantidad de alimentos que necesita comprar.

Ejemplo: Para una familia de dos adultos y dos niños menores de 12 años (si es 12 años o más, trátelo como un adulto):

Para cada niño: 3 oz. (antes de cocinar) de carne × 2 = 6 oz.

Para cada adulto: 4 oz. (antes de cocinar) de carne × 2 = 8 oz.

Cantidad de carne que necesita para una comida = 14 oz.

Si, en el ejemplo de arriba, usted cocina 2 libras de pollo, debe tener alrededor de una libra de carne que le sobró para usarse en otra comida (sándwiches, tacos, cocidos, etc.).

COMER FUERA EN RESTAURANTES

Para hacer más fácil el mantenerse con su plan de comida, utilice las siguientes sugerencias en los alimentos que debe y que no debe ordenar en un restaurante.

Ordene

Aperitivos	Sopas y jugos de vegetales; jugos sin edulcorantes y de fruta fresca; cócteles de fruta fresca; caldo claro; vegetales frescos, ensalada, apio, rábano, eneldo, lechuga o tomate (todos sin el aderezo añadido). Pida aceite y vinagre, aderezo Francés o Italiano aparte.
Carne, pescado, ave	Asada, cocida en el horno, hervida o asada a la parilla. Quite toda la grasa. Ordene pescado, pollo o pavo en vez de carne de res o cerdo.
Papas	Majadas, horneadas, hervidas o al vapor, tortillas simples, arroz al vapor o fideos simples. Cuando son servidas con mantequilla, cuéntelo como una opción de grasa.
Vegetales	Cocidos, al vapor o hervidos. Cuando son servidos con mantequilla, cuéntelo como una opción de grasa.
Panes	Cualquier clase de pan de un grueso promedio. Ordene panecillos duros o suaves. Un mollete, "biscuit" o pan de maíz puede ser usado pero debe ser contado como 1 opción de almidón y 1 opción de grasa.
Grasas	Margarina, mayonesa, aderezo para ensalada o aguacate. Utilice solamente las cantidades permitidas en su plan de comida.
Postres	Frutas frescas; pastel esponjoso, pastel de ángel o pastel de mantequilla (pound cake); helado de vainilla natural. Recuerde contar todos los artículos en su plan de comida.
Bebidas	Café, té, leche libre de grasa o de grasa reducida, jugos de vegetales o gaseosas sin de azúcar.

No Ordene

Aperitivos	Sopas cremosas, jugos endulzados, cóctel de frutas enlatado, ensaladas con aderezos ya añadidos (excepto en ensalada de col o papas o ensalada de pasta).
Carne, pescado, ave	Frito, salteado, cocido, estofado, empanado o a la caserola. Alimentos servidos con jugos de la carne o en salsa.
Papas	Fritas en casa, papas fritas, doradas, en crema, escalopes. Tortillas fritas.
Vegetales	En crema, escalopes, al gratén, fritos o salteados.
Panes	Panes dulces, torta para café, escarchado o panes endulzados.
Grasas	Jugo de las carnes, alimentos fritos, alimentos con salsas cremosas como pollo con crema.
Postres	Postres ricos, tartas o pasteles.
Bebidas	Gaseosas regulares, leche con chocolate, cacao, bebidas con leche como batido de leche.

Sugerencias para Ayudarle a Hacer las Comidas en Restaurantes Fáciles para Usted

- Memorice su plan de comida para que pueda sustituir alimentos con sólo ojear el menú.

- Mida los alimentos en casa para que pueda juzgar los tamaños de las porciones en los restaurantes.

- Cuando vea alimentos con nombres especiales en el menú (por ejemplo, Pollo Supremo), pregunte al mesero que hay en el plato o de qué está hecho.

- Limite el número de restaurantes a los que usted va tanto como sea posible—usted se familiarizará con sus menús y los meseros pueden recordar cómo usted quiere que le preparen sus comidas.

- No tenga el hábito de comer todo lo de su plato. Si el tamaño de la porción es muy grande, lleve a casa lo que le sobró en una bolsa para llevar.

- Esté pendiente de las grasas. Si planifica en forma anticipada, usted puede reservar sus opciones de grasa de más temprano en el día para poder usarlas en la comida que va a comer fuera.

- Pida las salsas, los jugos de la carne y aderezo aparte para que pueda usar menos de lo que es normalmente servido en un plato.

- Piense en el horario de sus comidas. Si usted está tomando medicamentos para su diabetes, el tener las comidas a tiempo es crítico para prevenir hipoglucemia. Cuando su comida es retrasada más de una hora, tenga una opción de carbohidratos (almidón, fruta, leche) mientras espera. Si necesita tomar la insulina antes de su comida, llévela con usted.

¿Qué hacer acerca de las Comidas Rápidas?

Contrario a la creencia popular, las comidas rápidas pueden ser nutritivas. Si se toman decisiones sabias, las comidas rápidas pueden tener cabida en su plan de comida de vez en cuando.

Evite órdenes grandes de alimentos altos en grasa como hamburguesas dobles con queso y papas fritas. Esté consciente de las salsas altas en grasa añadidas a los sándwiches y de las grasas escondidas en alimentos fritos (aros de cebollas, calabacines fritos, etc.). Cuando ordene una papa horneada, evite muchas grasas y calorías poniendo en su papa vegetales, cebollín o especias en vez de salsa de queso, tocino y crema agria.

La mayoría de las cadenas de comidas rápidas ofrecen una variedad de ensaladas. Utilice aderezos bajos en calorías, livianos (light) o de grasa reducida. Evite ensaladas preparadas como las de papas o pasta. Nunca ordene alimentos altos en azúcar como tortas de frutas, galletas, helado, helado con frutas y almíbar y batidos de leche. Ordene gaseosas de dieta en vez de las que no son de dieta. Esté consciente que alimentos como sándwiches de pescado, pollo en pedazos frito y sándwiches a la barbacoa o fritos pueden parecer saludables pero pueden ser altos en calorías, grasa y sodio.

Aquí tiene algunos consejos que le ayudarán a escoger bien cuando ordene, para acomodar las opciones de alimento en su plan de comida:

- Sepa que la comida promedio de las comidas rápidas tiene alrededor de 685 calorías. Esto no es muy alto para una comida, pero es muy alto en calorías para un bocadillo.

- Si come comida rápida para una comida, tenga sus otras comidas del día con un contenido de más alimentos saludables, como frutas y vegetales.

- Escoja sándwiches asados a la parilla con carnes, como carne de res magra asada, pavo o pechuga de pollo o jamón. Ordene sus comidas sin nada añadido o con mostaza y lechuga.

- Evite los croissants. Coma sus sándwiches en panecillos o pan de trigo para consumir menos calorías y grasa.

- Ordene tacos, tostadas, burritos de frijoles, tacos suaves y otras comidas sin freír cuando coma en lugares de comidas rápidas Mexicanos. Escoja pollo en vez de res. Evite los frijoles refritos en manteca de cerdo. Utilice lechuga, tomate y salsa adicional en lugar de queso, crema agria o guacamole.

- La pizza es una buena opción para comida rápida. Ordénela de masa fina y con vegetales.

- Cuando ordene sándwiches, su mejor opción es uno de tamaño regular o pequeño ("junior") en lugar del tamaño con todo ("deluxe").

- Utilice mostaza en lugar de mayonesa o aderezos con base de mayonesa. Esto le permitirá consumir alrededor de 100 calorías menos por cucharada.

- Si el desayuno lo tiene en un restaurant de comidas rápidas, escoja un bagel sencillo, tostada, un mollete libre de grasa o un panecillo inglés. Ordene huevos revueltos sencillos o panqueques sin mantequilla.

Opciones de Comida Rápida para Su Plan de Comida

Alimento	Tamaño por Porción	Calorías	Opciones
Burger King			
Hamburguesa	1	330	2 almidones 2 carnes medias en grasa
Chicken Tenders	5 piezas	220	1 almidón 2 carnes medias en grasa 1 grasa
Pollo a la Parilla Salad Red. Cal. Lt. Italian	1	200	2 vegetales 3 carnes muy magras 1 grasa

Opciones de Comida Rápida para Su Plan de Comida

Alimento	Tamaño por Porción	Calorías	Opciones
McDonald's			
Hamburguesa	1	260	2 almidones 2 carnes medias en grasa
Ensalada Bacon Ranch con Pollo a la Parrilla	1	260	4 carnes magras 1 almidón
Sándwich de Pollo Clásico a la Parrilla	1	420	2 almidones 4 carnes magras
In-n-Out Burger			
Hamburguesa *con mostaza y ketchup en lugar de aderezo	1	390	2$^1/_2$ almidones 2 carnes medias en grasa 2 grasas
Wendy's			
Hamburguesa Junior	1	280	2 almidones 1 carne alta en grasa
Sándwich de Pollo a la Parilla	1	370	3 almidones 3 carnes magras
Papa horneada con Brécol y Queso	1	340	4 almidones 1 vegetal
Jack in the Box			
Pita con Fajita de Pollo	1	290	2 almidones 3 carnes medias en grasa
Ensalada de Pollo Asiática	1	140	1 almidón 2 carnes medias en grasa
Hamburguesa	1	310	2 almidones 2 carnes medias en grasa 3 grasas

Opciones de Comida Rápida para Su Plan de Comida

Alimento	Tamaño por Porción	Calorías	Opciones
Taco Bell			
Taco	1	170	$1^1/_2$ almidón 1 carne media en grasa
Tostado	1	250	2 almidones 1 carne media en grasa
Taco Suave de Pollo	1	190	1 almidón 1 carne magra
Baja Fresh			
Taco Estilo Baja con Pollo	1	190	$1^1/_2$ almidón 1 carne magra
Ensalada de camarones	1	180	$^1/_2$ almidón 2 vegetales 2 carnes magras 1 grasa
Taco Estilo Baja con Bistec	1	220	$1^1/_2$ almidón 1 carne magra 1 grasa
Rubio's			
Taco de Pollo Health Mex	1	170	$1^1/_2$ almidón 2 carnes magras
Ensalada de Pollo Health Mex	1	260	2 almidones 3 carnes magras
Subway			
Sándwich Veggie Delight	1 pequeño	230	$2^1/_2$ almidones 1 carne magra 1 vegetal
Sándwich de Pechuga de Pavo	1 pequeño	280	$2^1/_2$ almidones 2 carnes magras 1 vegetal

Alimento	Tamaño por Porción	Calorías	Opciones
Opciones de Comida Rápida para Su Plan de Comida			
Subway			
Sándwich de Pavo	6", pequeño	280	3 almidones 2 carnes magras 1 vegetal
Pizza Hut			
Pizza de Queso en Masa Fina	2 rebanadas	400	3 almidones 2 carnes medias en grasa 2 grasas
Starbucks			
Café Latte (libre de grasa)	12 oz.	120	1 leche libre de grasa
Cappuccino (libre de grasa)	12 oz.	80	1 leche libre de grasa
Frappuccino de Café	12 oz.	200	$2^1/_2$ almidones $^1/_2$ grasa

RECUERDE: Cuando decida comer comidas rápidas, esté seguro de que balancea su plan de comida comiendo vegetales, frutas, leche sin grasa y alimentos de granos enteros en sus otras comidas.

Para más información acerca de las comidas rápidas, puede escribir a o verificar los sitios web de los siguientes restaurantes:

Burger King Corporation
   Consumer Information M/S 1441
   P.O. Box 520783
   General Mail Facility
   Miami, FL 33152
   www.burgerking.com

McDonald's Corporation
   Consumer Affairs
   2111 McDonald's Drive
   Oak Brook, IL 60523
   www.mcdonalds.com

Carl's Jr.
Carl Karcher Enterprises
1200 N. Harbor Blvd.
Anaheim, CA 92803
www.carlsjr.com

El Pollo Loco (Denny's)
3333 Michelson
Irvine, CA 92612
www.elpolloloco.com

In-n-Out Burger
4199 Campus
Irvine, CA 92612
(800) 786-1000
www.in-n-out.com

Jack In The Box
9330 Balboa Ave.
San Diego, CA 92123
www.jackinthebox.com

KFC
Consumer Affairs Dept.
P.O.Box 32070
Louisville, KY 40232
www.kfc.com

Pizza Hut, Inc.
Consumer Affairs Dept.
P.O. Box 428
Witchita, KS 67201
www.pizzahut.com

Rubio's
Corporate Office
1902 Wright Place
Carlsbad, CA 92008
www.rubios.com

Subway
325 Bic Drive
Medford, CT 06460
www.subway.com

Taco Bell
17901 Von Karman
Irvine, CA 92714
(800) TACO BELL
www.tacobell.com

Wendy's International, Inc.
Consumer Affairs Dept.
P.O. Box 256
Dublin, OH 43017
www.wendys.com

GRASA SATURADA Y COLESTEROL

Se recomienda que las personas con diabetes reduzcan su consumo de grasas saturadas a menos de 10 por ciento de las calorías y que eliminen las grasas trans de su dieta. El colesterol en la dieta debería limitarse a 300 miligramos de colesterol por día. Si su colesterol LDL es demasiado alto, se le puede decir a los individuos que reduzcan el consumo de grasas a un 7% de las calorías y que limiten su consumo de colesterol a 200 miligramos por día.

Diabetes y las Metas de Grasa Sanguínea

Colesterol HDL ("bueno")	Más de 40 mg/dl para hombres, Más de 50 mg/dl para mujeres
Colesterol LDL ("malo")	Menos de 100 mg/dl
Colesterol Total	Menos de 200 mg/dl
Triglicéridos	Menos de 150 mg/dl

Grasas que usted come

Las dietas que son altas en grasa saturada se han encontrado que elevan los niveles de colesterol en la sangre. Esto puede causar aumentar su riesgo de enfermedades cardíacas y de los vasos sanguíneos.

La mayoría de la grasa en su dieta debe ser en la forma de grasa monoinsaturada y poliinsaturada. Estas grasas aumentan el colesterol HDL y reducen el colesterol LDL. Ellas provienen de plantas e incluyen aceites que son líquidos a temperatura ambiente, por ejemplo, margarina y aceites de frutos secos, semillas, canola, semilla de algodón, girasol, soja, oliva y cacahuate. Escoja margarina que tenga un aceite líquido, tal como aceite de oliva o de soja, como su primer ingrediente en lugar de un aceite parcialmente hidrogendado o una grasa trans.

La grasa saturada aumenta el colesterol en la sangre (el colesterol total y el LDL), sin embargo su cuerpo crea una gran parte del colesterol que se halla en la sangre. Las grasas saturadas se encuentran en grasas animales, carnes, mantecas sólidas, algunos aceites vegetales (aceites de palma y coco, mantequilla de cacao), productos lácteos de leche entera (queso y mantequilla). Si sus grasas en la sangre están muy altas, su médico puede recetarle un medicamento que le ayudará a reducirlas, pero aún así usted querrá seguir su plan de comida.

Las grasas trans se producen cuando el aceite líquido se convierte en una grasa sólida mediante un proceso llamado hidrogenación. Las grasas trans actúan como las grasas saturadas y pueden aumentar sus niveles de colesterol. Desde el 2006 las grasas trans tienen que estar listadas en las etiquetas de nutrición y en las listas de ingredientes. Muchos alimentos de bocadillos, como las galletas, las papas "chips" y los productos horneados procesados, tienen grasas trans al igual que artículos de comida rápida como las papas fritas.

Guías para Ayudarle a Reducir la Cantidad de Grasa y Colesterol en Su Plan de Comida

- Utilice pescado, pollo, pavo y ternera en la mayoría de sus comidas que contienen carne para la semana. Busque nombres como lomo, cuarto trasero ("round"), magra, de primera o selecto.
- Quite toda la grasa visible de las carnes y la piel de las aves antes de cocinarlas.
- Evite freír por inmersión en aceite. Cocine con métodos que remuevan la grasa (como hornear, asar, barbacoa, etc.).

- Seleccione productos sin grasa o de grasa reducida cuando compre carnes frías, productos horneados, aderezos de ensaladas y productos lácteos.
- Evite el jugo de la carne, salsas y platos como cacerolas cremosas.
- Limite las yemas de huevo a cuatro por semana, incluyendo las que use para cocinar.
- Utilice un rociador antiadherente para cocinar en los sartenes y utensilios.
- Verifique las etiquetas de las galletas y postres "sin azúcar". Éstos pueden ser sin azúcar pero más del 60 por ciento de sus calorías pueden venir de las grasas.
- Verifique las opciones de Carne o de Sustitutos de carnes listados (carne magra y muy magra) en las páginas 58–62 para opciones de carne que son más bajas en grasa.

FIBRA EN SU DIETA

¿Qué es la fibra? No es una vitamina o un mineral, no contiene calorías y es una parte importante de su dieta.

Hay diferentes tipos de fibra que hacen diferentes cosas a su cuerpo. Algunas retienen agua; otras afectan la absorción de nutrientes. Cuando la fibra retiene agua está actuando como una esponja en su cuerpo, absorbiendo agua y haciendo que los contenidos del intestino (heces) tengan mayor volumen. Cuando usted come fibra, ésta suaviza sus deposiciones y pueden pasar con menos esfuerzo.

La fibra es buena para tratar o prevenir problemas estomacales e intestinales, incluyendo cáncer del colon. Una cantidad grande de fibras ayuda a mantener baja la grasa en la sangre (colesterol y triglicéridos).

El consumo de fibra para personas con diabetes debe ser el mismo que para aquellos sin diabetes.

> La cantidad diaria de consumo de fibra debe ser de 20 a 35 gramos por día de una selección grande de alimentos. Buenas fuentes deben incluir frutas, vegetales, granos enteros, semillas, frutos secos y legumbres (frijoles). Nosotros sugerimos que incluya alimentos altos en fibra en su plan de comida cada día.

Cómo Comer Más Fibra

1. Busque cereales que contengan "granos enteros" y al menos 3 gramos de fibra dietética por porción.

2. Compre galletas que contengan 2 gramos de fibra dietética por porción.

3. Trate de incluir en sus comidas alimentos altos en fibra como los frutos secos, trigo integral o germen de trigo. Mézclelos con cazuelas, carne al horno, relleno y ensaladas.

4. Escoja pasta de trigo integral, arroz integral y cualquier versión de trigo integral de otros alimentos que usted come.

5. Añada cualquier tipo de frijoles, maíz o guisantes a su plan de comida para sus opciones de almidón.

Contar la Fibra

Cuando hay suficiente fibra, ésta cambiará cómo usted cuenta los carbohidratos totales en sus comidas. Cuando un alimento de almidón tiene más que 5 gramos de fibra, usted resta la mitad de la fibra de la cantidad total de carbohidratos.

EJEMPLO:

40	gramos de Carbohidratos Totales
−5	gramos de Fibra
35	gramos de Carbohidratos Netos

25	gramos de Carbohidratos Totales
−3½	gramos de Fibra
21½	gramos de Carbohidratos Netos

Información Nutricional

Tamaño por Porción: 1 cup (55 g)
Porciones Por Envase: alrededor 7

Cantidad Por Porción

	Cereal	Cereal + 125 ml de leche sin grasa
Calorías	190	230
Calorías de grasa	20	25

	% Valor Diario*	
Grasa Total 2.5g	4%	4%
Grasa Saturada 0g	0%	0%
Trasa Trans 0g		
Colesterol 0 mg	0%	0%
Sodio 200 mg	8%	11%
Carbohidratos Totales 40g	13%	15%
Fibra Dietética 10g	40%	40%
Azúcares 16g		
Proteína 8g		2%
Vitamina A	0%	4%
Vitamina C	2%	2%
Calcio	25%	40%
Hierro	15%	15%
Ácido Fólico	100%	100%
Vitamina b-12	110%	110%

Total Fat	Calorías:	2,500	2,500
Grasa Total	Menos de	65g	80g
Grasa Saturada	Menos de	20g	25g
Colesterol	Menos de	300mg	300mg
Sodio	Menos de	2,400mg	2,400mg
Carbohidratos Totales		300g	375g
Fibra Dietética		25g	30g

Calorías por gramo:
Grasa 9 • Carbohidratos 4 • Proteína 4

Información Nutricional

Tamaño por Porción: 1 Bagel 2 oz. (57g)
Porciones Por Envase: 5

Cantidad Por Porción

Calorías 110	Calorías de Grasa 0

	% Valor Diario*
Grasa Total 0g	0%
Grasa Saturada 0 g	0%
Grasa Trans 0 g	
Colesterol 0 mg	0%
Sodio 210 mg	9%
Carbohidratos Totales 25 g	8%
Fibra Dietética 7g	
Azúcares 0g	
Proteína 6g	

Vitamina A 0%	•	Vitamina C 0%
Calcio 15%	•	Hierro 8%

*Los porcentajes de Valor Diario están basados en una dieta de 2,000 calorías. Sus Valores Diarios pueden ser más altos o bajos dependiendo de sus necesidades caloricas.

	Calorías	2,000	2,500
Grasa Total	Menos de	65g	80g
Grasa Saturada	Menos de	20g	25g
Colesterol	Menos de	300mg	300mg
Sodio	Menos de	2,400mg	2,400mg
Carbohidratos Totales		300g	375g
Fibra Dietética		25g	30g

Calorías por gramo:
Grasa 9 • Carbohidratos 4 • Proteína 4

Las siguientes listas le darán algunas ideas de cómo añadir alimentos altos en fribra a su plan de comida.

Frutas		
Fuentes Buenas		**Fuentes Pobres**
albaricoques (secos)	compota de manzana	jugo de manzana
manzanas (con cáscara)	albaricoques (frescos/enlatados)	jugo de uva
zarzamora	bananas	jugo de naranja
arándano azul	cerezas	jugo de piña
arándano agrio	toronja	
higos (secos)	mango	
papayas	ciruela pequeña	
parchas	nectarina	
peras	naranjas	
granadas	melocotón	
ciruelas	piña	
mandarina pequeña	sandía	
frambuesas	kiwi	
fresas		

Vegetales		
Fuentes Buenas		**Fuentes Pobres**
alcachofa común	espárragos	jugo de tomate
repollo	remolacha	
pepino	zanahorias	
brécol	coliflor	
col de Bruselas	apio	
chucrut		

Vegetales (cont.)

Fuentes Buenas		*Fuentes Pobres*
berenjena	lechuga	
soja	tomates	
judía verde	espinaca	
chirivía	calabacín	
hojas de nabo		

Almidones, Granos y Legumbres

Fuentes Buenas		*Fuentes Pobres*
galletas de centeno	trigo integral	pan, blanco
frijoles cocidos (alu-,	trigo desmenuzado	fideos
bias, pintos, negros,	arroz salvaje	galletas saladas
blancos)	maíz, cocido	Rice Krispies
guisantes, congelados,	palomitas de maíz	arroz soplado
hervidos	tortillas (maíz, trigo)	galletas de
habas	papas (blancas con	animales
frijoles, guisantes, len-	cáscaras)	pretzels
tejas secas	batatas	arroz blanco
calabaza (de invierno,	Triscuits, de grasa	
de bellota, sidra)	reducida	
cereal de salvado	germen de trigo,	
(All Bran, Bran Buds,	tostado	
Fiber One)	pasta de granos	
cereales con más	múltiples	
de 5 gramos de	garbanzos	
fibra	maíz	
caupí (chícaro salvaje)		

Frutos Secos, Semillas y Otros	
Fuentes Buenas	*Fuentes Pobres*
semillas de girasol	coco
semillas de calabaza	frutos secos (anacardo,
semillas de ajonjolí	almendras, pecana
	avellanas, cacahuates)

Plan de Comida de Ejemplo para una Dieta Alta en Fibra

Desayuno	*Almuerzo*	*Cena*
arándanos	sándwich de atún en	carne de res asada
hojuelas de salvado	pan de trigo integral	
huevo escalfado	sopa de vegetales	arroz integral
pan de trigo integral	palitos de apio	ensalada
margarina	fresas	brécol
leche libre de grasa		manzana fresca con cáscara
		pan de trigo integral
		margarina

Bocadillo de la Noche
galletas de centeno
mantequilla de cacahuate

RECURSOS PARA PLANEAR LAS COMIDAS

Cuando usted tiene diabetes, su dieta no puede ser a corto plazo sólo para perder peso o para controlar su azúcar en la sangre. Usted debe aprender un estilo completamente nuevo de comer que pueda seguir por el resto de su vida. Piense en esto como un cambio de sus hábitos viejos de comer por unos nuevos. Esto no es cosa fácil de hacer. Toma tiempo y práctica para formar los nuevos hábitos. Una buena fuente de ayuda es un dietista registrado (D.R.), un experto en dieta y nutrición.

Para encontrar un dietista registrado en su área, diríjase a http:www.eatright.org y haga un clic en "Find a Nutrition Professional" (Encuentre a un Profesional de la Nutrición). Ingrese su código postal (zip code) o su estado y seleccione "diabetes" como tópico. Para obtener información acerca de alimentos y nutrición, o si tiene preguntas acerca de las listas de reemplazo de alimentos, llame a la American Diabetes Association, 1 800 342-2383 o diríjase a www.diabetes.org, seleccione "Información en Español"; puede enviar un correo electrónico con sus preguntas a preguntas@ diabetes.org. Para información en inglés, seleccione "Nutrition" (Nutrición) y haga un clic en "Questions?" (¿Preguntas?). Chat con nosotros.

Le animamos a utilizar estos libros y libros de cocina incluidos en la lista de abajo para su ayuda e ideas.

Referencias

Todas las referencias o libros de cocina son de la Asociación Americana de la Diabetes. Llame al 1-800-342-2383 o vaya a http://store.diabetes.org

The Diabetes Carbohydrate and Fat Gram Guide, 3ra. edición, por Lea Ann Holzmeister, R.D., C.D.E., publicado por la Asociación Americana de la Diabetes, 2005.

■ Enseña cómo contar gramos de carbohidratos y grasa.

Complete Guide to Carb Counting, 2da edición, por Hope Warshaw, MMSc, R.D., C.D.E., Karmeen, MS, R.D., C.D.E., publicado por la Asociación Americana de la Diabetes, 2001.

■ Incluye conteos básicos y avanzados de carbohidratos en las comidas y usando las etiquetas. Contiene planes de menú para una semana.

Journal of the American Dietetic Association, Carbohydrate Issues: Type and Amount, Madelyn L. Wheeler, F. Xavier Pi-Sunyer, Abril 2008: páginas 534–539.

Guide to Healthy Restaurant Eating, por Hope Warshaw, R.D., C.D.E., publicado por la Asociación Americana de la Diabetes, 2002.

■ Incluye datos acerca de cómo comer fuera y escoger sus comidas sabiamente.

What to Eat When You Get Diabetes, por Carolyn Leontos, R.D., C.D.E., publicado por Wiley, John and Sons, 2000.

■ Maneras fáciles y apetitosas de hacer cambios saludables en sus comidas.

Nutrition in the Fast Lane, por Eli Lilly y Compañía, publicado por Franklin Publishing, Indianapolis, Indiana, 2004. 1-800-634-1993.

■ Una guía para los valores de Nutrición e Intercambio Dietéticos para las comidas rápidas.

Exchange Lists for Meal Planning, publicado por la Asociación Americana de la Diabetes, 2003.

The Calorie King, Fat and Carbohydrate Counter, por Allan Borushek, Family Health Publications, Costa Mesa, Calif. 2006. www.CalorieKing.com.

■ Libro fácil de llevar, tamaño bolsillo. Incluye 200 restaurantes de comida rápida.

Libros de Cocina

Magic Menus for People with Diabetes, 2da. edición, publicado por la Asociación Americana de la Diabetes, 2003.

- Contiene 200 recetas
- Las grasas, los carbohidratos, las calorías y los intercambios han sido calculados para usted.
- Fácil de regresar atrás a cualquier combinación de opciones de desayuno, almuerzo y cena.

Mr. Food Diabetic Dinners in a Dash, publicado por la Asociación Americana de la Diabetes, 2005.

- Contiene 150 recetas
- Cocina fácil y rápida

Betty Crocker's Diabetes Cookbook: Everyday Meals, Easy as 1-2-3, Editores Betty Crocker, Wiley, John and Sons, 2003.

- 140 recetas
- Usa información nutricional y de comidas actualizada.

Diabetes Cookbook for Dummies, 2da. edición, Alan Rubin, M.D., Chef Denise Sharf, Alison Acerra, R.D., Wiley, John and Sons, 2005.

- Consejos de cómo estar bien en los restaurantes o lugares de comidas rápidas
- Información nutricional e intercambios diabéticos para cada receta
- Una guía "visual" de los tamaños de porciones.
- Una guía de restaurantes para viajes.

Diabetes and Heart Healthy Cookbook, publicado por la Asociación Americana de la Diabetes, 2005

- Incluye platos bajos en grasa y de menos carbohidratos.

The Diabetes Holiday Cookbook: Year Round Cooking for People with Diabetes, por Carolyn Leontos, Debra Mitchell, Kenneth Weicker, Wiley, John and Sons, 2002.

- Más de 100 recetas para los días festivos.
- Opciones de ingredientes alternativos para dietas bajas en sodio o sin alcohol.
- Menús para 21 celebraciones de días festivos.

The Diabetes Menu Cookbook: Delicious Special Ocassion Recipes for Family and Friends, por Kalia Doner, Barbara Scott-Goodman, Wiley, John and Sons, 2006.

- 130 recetas para sus invitados y ocasiones especiales.
- Incluye aperitivos y bebidas, sopas y ensaladas, sándwiches, hamburguesas, envueltos, platos principales y postres.

Month of Meals: All-American Fare, 3ra. edición, publicado por la Asociación Americana de la Diabetes, 2002.

- Hay siete Meses de Comidas para planificar menús. Cada uno incluye 28 días de sabrosas selecciones de desayunos, almuerzos y cenas. Usted puede mezclar y combinar entre los planificadores de menús. Una sección de "ocasiones especiales" ofrece consejos para desayunos-almuerzos, días festivos, fiestas y restaurantes.

Month of Meals: Meals in Minutes, 3ra. edición, publicado por la Asociación Americana de la Diabetes, 2002.

Month of Meals: Classic Cooking, 3ra. edición, publicado por la Asociación Americana de la Diabetes, 2002.

Month of Meals: Vegetarian Pleasures, 3ra. edición, publicado por la Asociación Americana de la Diabetes, 2002.

Month of Meals: Soul Food, 1ra. edición, publicado por la Asociación Americana de la Diabetes, 2002.

Month of Meals: Old-Time Favorites, 3ra. edición, publicado por la Asociación Americana de la Diabetes, 2002.

Month of Meals: Festive Latin Flavors (español), publicado por la Asociación Americana de la Diabetes, 2002.

Healthy Calendar Diabetic Cooking, publicado por la Asociación Americana de la Diabetes, 2006.

- 340 recetas
- Contiene planes de comida y recetas mes a mes, semana a semana y día a día.
- Los menús vienen con listas de compras semanales.

CAPÍTULO 6

Análisis Casero para Azúcar en la Sangre

Los análisis caseros para azúcar en la sangre se han vuelto una de las herramientas más útiles en el cuidado de la diabetes. Al contrario de los análisis de azúcar en la orina, el azúcar en la sangre es una medida directa de su nivel de azúcar en la sangre—ésta proporciona información "al momento". Usted sabe inmediatamente si su azúcar en la sangre es muy alto, muy bajo o en el rango aceptable (el rango que usted acordó con su doctor).

El poder analizar su azúcar en la sangre en el hogar, trabajo o escuela, mientras hace ejercicio, juega, viaja o está enfermo, le da una vista más realista del patrón de azúcar en la sangre durante 24 horas, y también a través de varios días. Estudiando este patrón, usted y su doctor pueden tomar mejores decisiones acerca de su control del azúcar en la sangre y hacer los ajustes necesarios en sus medicamentos, ejercicio y plan de comidas. A través de estos ajustes usted puede mantener un control bueno o "ajustado" del azúcar en la sangre, lo que ayuda a prevenir o disminuir las complicaciones de la diabetes (vea las páginas 181–186). (Control "ajustado" significa que la mayoría de los azúcares en su sangre están en su rango normal o están cerca de su rango normal la mayoría del tiempo).

¿Cuál es su rango aceptable de azúcar en la sangre?

Si usted no sabe, vea la página 28 o discútalo con su doctor o enfermera de diabetes.

Los análisis caseros de azúcar en la sangre pueden ser realizados por cualquiera con diabetes. No importa si usa insulina, medicamento oral o si está controlando su diabetes con dieta solamente.

Los medidores de glucosa (o glucómetros) son máquinas pequeñas operadas por baterías que varían en tamaño, desde tan pequeñas como un bolígrafo hasta tan grandes como una calculadora y pesan unas pocas onzas. Cuando se prepara una tira especial con una gota de sangre, un número aparece en el medidor de glucosa indicando el nivel de azúcar en la sangre. La mayoría de los medidores leen el azúcar en la sangre desde 0–10 mg/dl hasta 600 mg/dl. Si el azúcar en la sangre está por debajo de los 10 mg/dl, el medidor le indicará que está bajo; si está por encima de los 600 mg/dl, el medidor le indicará que está alto. Los medidores de glucosa también le indican la condición de las baterías que los operan y ellos se apagan solos después de cierto período de tiempo.

Cualquier medidor de glucosa le proveerá lecturas precisas del azúcar en la sangre si sigue las instrucciones EXACTAS CUIDADOSAMENTE.

Para analizar su azúcar en la sangre usted necesita una gota de sangre, la cual puede obtener clavándose el dedo con una lanceta pequeña.

Debajo de la cubierta redonda hay una pequeña aguja puntiaguda.

Hay varios tipos de aparatos de lanceta que le facilitan a usted el clavar su dedo. Una lanceta es insertada en un aparato de lanceta, y un resorte provee la acción rápida para clavar el dedo. Éste también controla cuán profundo la aguja clava su dedo.

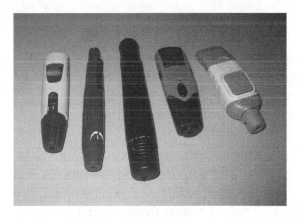

Las lancetas usadas son "objetos punzantes" y deben ser desechadas en forma segura. Como resultado de una nueva ley del año 2008, usted no puede tirarlas a la basura normal. Por favor vea la página 139 (en el capítulo acerca de insulina y jeringuillas) y siga el mismo procedimiento para desechar sus lancetas usadas.

Aquí hay algunos consejos útiles para recordar cuando se analiza el azúcar en la sangre:

1. Lave sus manos cuidadosa y completamente con agua tibia y jabón. Si usted usa alcohol,[1] esté seguro de que se ha secado completamente antes de clavarse el dedo.

2. Su mano debe estar caliente para aumentar el flujo de sangre hacia los dedos. Si su mano está fría, caliéntela lavándola en agua tibia, frotando sus manos o enrollando su mano con una toalla mojada tibia por unos cuantos minutos.

3. Clave el lado de su dedo o la yema del dedo entre la primera articulación de su dedo y la punta.

   No clave su dedo detrás de la uña—es muy sensitivo y doloroso. Algunas personas prefieren usar siempre un área y crear callos en ésta. Los callos no le causarán ningún problema, siempre y cuando sea posible sacar una gota de sangre.

4. Para obtener una gota de sangre apropiada, apriete el dedo completo desde donde el dedo se une a la mano hasta la punta, haciendo presión uniforme y constante.

5. Asegúrese que su medidor esté codificado correctamente para el código numérico en la botella de tiras que está utilizando.

---

[1] Si utiliza alcohol, analice la segunda gota de sangre, no la primera.

6. Verifique la fecha de expiración de las tiras. NUNCA use tiras expiradas. Cuando abra tiras nuevas, anote la fecha en la botella. Una vez abiertas, usted debería acabar la botella de tiras dentro de 90 días.

7. Alamacene su medidor de glucosa y las tiras en un lugar fresco y seco. No las guarde en baños o cocinas o en autos calientes. Éstos necesitan mantenerse a menos de 90°F.

8. Llame al número telefónico 800 en la parte de atrás de su medidor si tiene preguntas o problemas con el medidor. Hay alguien que lo podrá ayudar 24 horas al día.

9. **¡ESCRIBA TODAS SUS LECTURAS DE AZÚCAR EN LA SANGRE!**

   Mantener registros le permitirá ver **PATRONES** en su azúcar en la sangre. Los números le enseñarán cómo su azúcar en la sangre responde a los alimentos, enfermedades, medicamentos, estrés, etc. Éstos le ayudarán a tomar mejores decisiones en sus opciones de comida y a su médico a tomar mejores decisiones para los medicamentos de la diabetes. Lleve su registro de azúcar en la sangre consigo a cada visita al médico.

10. Discuta las veces que usted debería analizar su azúcar en la sangre con su médico o educador de la diabetes. La prueba más útil que usted puede hacer es unos minutos antes y 2 horas después de comenzar sus diferentes comidas.

Si todos los resultados de su azúcar en la sangre caen en su rango aceptable, entonces usted sabe que sus medicamentos, actividades y alimentos están balanceados. Si los resultados están fuera de su rango aceptable, entonces puede determinar si hay un patrón para los tiempos en los cuales está muy alto o bajo. Puede que haya un patrón en los cambios de su azúcar en la sangre de acuerdo a los días de la semana o a las horas del día. Por ejemplo, usted puede que tenga diferente azúcar en la sangre durante la semana que en los fines de semana, o su azúcar en la sangre puede que siempre esté alto en las tardes. Viendo estos patrones, usted y su doctor o educador de diabetes pueden hacer los cambios necesarios en las comidas, medicamentos y/o actividades para llevar su azúcar en la sangre a rangos aceptables tan frecuentemente como sea posible.

Hay muchas maneras para registrar su azúcar en la sangre. Use el diario que viene con su medidor, llame al número telefónico 800 en la parte de atrás de su medidor o haga uno usted mismo. Use la tabla de la página 114 como ejemplo. La columna de Comentarios es para registrar bajo azúcar en la sangre, enfermedad, comidas retrasadas, ejercicio, estrés emocional o cualquier cosa que esté afectando su azúcar en la sangre (vea las páginas 26–28).

---

11. Cuando su azúcar en la sangre está constantemente cayendo dentro de su rango aceptable, usted no necesita analizarse tan frecuentemente como cuando está fuera de su rango aceptable. Durante enfermedad o períodos de estrés, usted debe verificar su azúcar en la sangre más frecuentemente, y alrededor de 3 a 4 días antes de visitar al doctor, empiece a analizarse más frecuentemente para que tenga varios análisis para reportarle.

Mientras más se analice, mejor control logrará sobre su azúcar en la sangre.

YO ANALIZARÉ MI AZÚCAR EN LA
SANGRE:_____

YO DEBO LLAMAR A MI DOCTOR CUANDO MI
AZÚCAR ES:_____

Las personas con diabetes hoy en día tienen una ventaja tremenda sobre aquellos de solamente unos años atrás. Los análisis caseros de azúcar en la sangre (auto-monitoreo) han mejorado grandemente el control de la azúcar en la sangre. Ahora es posible que usted haga los ajustes en medicamentos dependiendo de los resultados de sus análisis de azúcar en la sangre. Su doctor le deberá dar consejos de cuándo y cómo hacer esos ajustes.

Recuerde que un control bueno, o "ajustado", puede prevenir, desacelerar o disminuir complicaciones a largo plazo de la diabetes, como también ayudarle a sentirse de lo mejor. Un control bueno puede ser alcanzado analizando su azúcar en la sangre y actuando de acuerdo a la información—

¡ASÍ
QUE HAGA
USO
DE ÉSTA!

Fecha	Desayuno		Med	Almuerzo		Med	Cena		Med	Hora de Dormir	Comentarios
	Antes	Después		Antes	Después		Antes	Después			

Cetonas y Cetoacidosis

Si usted tiene diabetes Tipo 1, necesitará analizar su orina para acetona o cetonas. Cuando no hay suficiente glucosa en la sangre (durante la reacción a la insulina) o cuando no hay suficiente insulina para permitir que la glucosa entre a las células, el cuerpo busca otra fuente de energía que la glucosa—la otra fuente son las grasas. Mientras las grasas son deshechas, se produce energía, pero usted tiene un producto de desecho llamado acetona o cetonas.

Las cetonas viajan a través de la sangre y son sacadas del cuerpo en la orina. Las cetonas en su orina son un aviso de que su cuerpo no está trabajando correctamente. Su azúcar en la sangre estará alto y su azúcar en la orina será 1 a 2% cuando sus cetonas son positivas. Si esto no es corregido rápidamente puede conducir a CETOACIDOSIS DIABÉTICA, lo cual es muy serio.

Durante la reacción a la insulina, no hay suficiente azúcar para quemar y obtener energía, así que su cuerpo va a descomponer de nuevo grasa. Durante este tiempo, su azúcar en la sangre será bajo y su azúcar en la orina negativo, pero las cetonas pueden ser positivas.

¿CUÁNDO HACER ANÁLISIS PARA CETONAS?[1]

- su azúcar en la sangre está por encima de 250 mg/dl

- su azúcar en la sangre ha aumentado en las últimas 12 a 24 horas

- si está enfermo

- si piensa que puede haber tenido una reacción a la insulina pero su azúcar en la sangre no es muy bajo (un análisis positivo para cetonas puede significar una reacción)

- el azúcar en la orina es 2% o mayor

LLAME A SU DOCTOR cuando

- su azúcar en la sangre es más alto de 250 mg/dl y las cetonas son positivas

- su azúcar en la sangre ha aumentado en las últimas 12 horas y las cetonas son positivas

- tiene náuseas o vómitos

PREGÚNTELE A SU MÉDICO O EDUCADOR DE LA DIABETES ACERCA DEL AÑADIR INSULINA DE ACCIÓN RÁPIDA CUANDO LAS CETONAS SON POSITIVAS.

---

[1] Éstas son guías, así que por favor pídale a su doctor o educador de diabetes instrucciones específicas.

Esto puede significar CETOACIDOSIS—¡UNA EMERGEN-CIA DIABÉTICA!

Las tabletas Acetest®, Ketostix® y Chemstrip K® son productos para análisis de cetonas en la orina que pueden ser compradas en cualquier farmacia sin receta. Hay un glucómetro (medidor de glucosa) llamado Precision Xtr el cual analiza cetonas en su sangre. Contacte a su doctor o educador de diabetes para información con respecto a este glucómetro y las tiras de cetonas.

Consejos Útiles para Análisis de Cetonas en la Orina

- Esté seguro que su tiempo es exacto—siga las instrucciones del envase.

- Mantenga las tabletas o tiras en un lugar fresco y seco—fuera de la luz del sol. No las deje en el carro caliente.

- Compre una botella a la vez—recuerde verificar la fecha de expiración.

- Cuando compare los colores de las tabletas o tiras con la tabla, sujételas cerca de la tabla de colores.

- Una buena luz es esencial para obtener resultados exactos.

- No guarde las tabletas o tiras en el baño—éstas pueden arruinarse con la humedad.

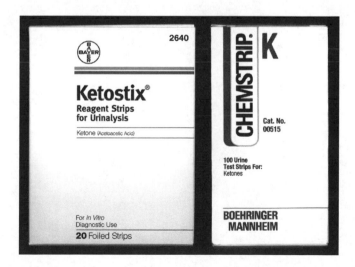

Medicamentos para Tratar la Diabetes

Hay varios medicamentos diferentes usados para tratar la diabetes. Cada grupo de medicamentos trabaja de una manera distinta. Puede que usted tome 1 ó más de estos medicamentos para controlar su azúcar en la sangre.

El seguir su plan de comidas y su programa de ejercicio es muy importante para ayudarle a estos medicamentos a funcionar.

Lleve consigo una lista de todos sus medicamentos, incluyendo cualquier otra receta, medicamentos sin receta, vitaminas, minerales y suplementos. Escriba sus nombres, dosis (por ejemplo, número de miligramos, unidades, etc.) y cuándo toma los medicamentos. Revise esta lista con su médico en cada visita.

MEDICAMENTOS ORALES

| | Sulfonilureas | | |
Nombre	Tamaño de la Tableta (mg)	Duración de la Acción (hr)	Dosis Máxima (mg)
Dymelor/ Acetohexamide[a]	250 500	12–14	1,500
Diabinese/ Chlorpropamide[a]	100 250	36+	750
Tolinase/ Tolazamide[a]	100 250 500	12–24	1,000
Orinase/ Tolbutamide[a]	250 500	6–12	3,000
Micronase/Diabeta/ Glyburide[b,c]	1.25 2.5 5	24	20
Glucotrol/ Glipizide[d]	5 10	24	40
Glucotrol XL[e]/ Glipizide	2.5 5 10	24	20
Glynase/ Micronized Glyburide[f]	1.5 3 6	24	12
Amaryl/ Glimepiride[g]	1 2 4	24	8

[a]De Diabetes Mellitus, 8va. edición, Lilly Research Laboratories, Indianapolis, IN, 1980.
[b]De Upjohn Therapeutic Profile of Micronase, mayo 1984.
[c]De Hoechst-Roussel, Somerville, NJ, 1984.
[d]De Roerig-Pfizer, Glucotrol, New York, NY, abril 1994.
[e]De Pfizer-Pratt, Glucotrol XL, New York, NY, abril 1994.
[f]De Upjohn, Glynase Prestabs, Kalamazoo, MI, marzo 1992.
[g]De Hoechst-Roussel, Somerville, NJ, diciembre 1995.

■ Las sulfonilureas le ayudan a su páncreas a crear insulina.

■ Estos medicamentos están relacionados a otras drogas sulfa y pueden producir reacciones alérgicas a la sulfa, pero pueden usarse con cuidado aún cuando se conoce que existe una alergia a la sulfa.

- Pueden tomarse una o más veces al día.

- Los efectos secundarios normalmente son mínimos. Éstos incluyen falta de apetito, náuseas, vómitos, erupción de la piel, dolor de cabeza o hipoglucemia.

- Para evitar baja azúcar en la sangre (hipoglucemia) cuando esté tomando estos medicamentos, tome solamente la cantidad de medicamento recetado y si las comidas están separadas por más de 4 ó 5 horas, añada un bocadillo. Revise las páginas 15–20 para tratamiento y prevención de hipoglucemia.

- *Precaución:* Si usted ingiere alcohol mientras toma uno de estos medicamentos (particularmente Diabinese/Chlorpropamide), usted podría tener una reacción que involucra síntomas como rubor; calor, hormigueo y sensación de quemazón en la cara y cuello; y mareos.

- El glucotrol o glipizide deben tomarse con el estómago vacío ($^1/_2$ hora antes de su comida). Cualquiera de los otros medicamentos pueden tomarse justo antes de comer.

- Si olvida tomar una píldora, tome su dosis normal la próxima vez que deba tomar una. NO doble la dosis o trate de "ponerse al día" por la dosis omitida.

- Cuando tenga que *ayunar* para un estudio o un procedimiento, no tome su píldora para la diabetes hasta que haya comido.

Meglitinidas			
Nombre	Tamaño de la Tableta (mg)	Duración de la Acción (hr)	Dosis Máxima (mg)
Prandin/ Repaglinide[a]	0.5 1 2	1.4	16
Starlix/ Nateglinide[b]	60 120	1.5	360

[a]De Novo Nordisk Pharmaceuticals, Inc, Princeton, NJ, 1997.
[b]De Novartis Pharmaceuticals Corporation, East Hanover, NJ, febrero 2001.

- Cuando el azúcar en la sangre sube (después de una comida), estas píldoras le ayudan a controlar el aumento causando que el páncreas libere más insulina. A medida que el azúcar en la sangre baja, el efecto de los medicamentos disminuye.

- Éstos deben tomarse antes de las comidas (0–30 minutos). Si usted deja pasar una comida, no tome los medicamentos.

- Los efectos secundarios usualmente son mínimos. Éstos pueden incluir hipoglucemia, náuseas, dolor de cabeza, malestar estomacal o diarrea.

- Si olvida tomar su píldora, tome su dosis normal la próxima vez que deba tomarla. NO doble la dosis o trate de "ponerse al día" por la dosis omitida.

Biguanidas			
Nombre	Tamaño de la Tableta (mg)	Duración de la Acción (hr)	Dosis Máxima (mg)
Glucophage/ Metformin[a]	500 850 1,000	6	2,000
Glucophage XR/ Metformin ER[b]	500 750	6	2,000
Riomet/Metformin Líquido[c]	500mg/5mL	6	2,000
Fortamet/Metformin[d] (de liberación prolongada)	500 1000	6	2,000
Glumetza/Metformin[e] (de liberación prolongada)	500 1000	6	2,000

[a]De Bristol-Myers-Squibb, Princeton, NJ, febrero 1995.
[b]De Bristol-Myers-Squibb, Princeton, NJ, octubre 2000.
[c]De Ranbaxy Laboratories, Princeton, NJ, 2005.
[d]De Sciele Pharma Inc., Atlanta, GA, 2007.
[e]De Depomed, Inc., Menlo Park, CA, 2008.

- Glucophage baja los niveles de azúcar en la sangre mayormente actuando en el hígado. También ayuda a la glucosa a entrar en las células de grasa y musculares.

- Cuando se utiliza solo, Glucophage no causa azúcar en la sangre bajo (hipoglucemia).

- Este medicamento baja los triglicéridos, colesterol total y colesterol LDL (malo) y aumenta el colesterol HDL (bueno).

- Puede ayudar con la pérdida de peso.

- Los efectos secundarios pueden incluir aumento de gas, náuseas, retortijones, sensación de llenura (hinchazón), diarrea y sabor metálico en la boca. Estos síntomas usualmente desaparecerán si se empieza el Glucophage lentamente, con comida, y la dosis se aumenta gradualmente.

- Glucophage XR o Metformin ER se da una vez al día y debería tomarse con la comida de la tarde.

- Glucophage debe dejarse antes de ser admitido al hospital o antes de recibir rayos-X o un procedimiento que involucre tinte. Discuta esto con su doctor.

- Glucophage no es para todos—sólo aquellos que tienen el hígado y riñón funcionando bien pueden tomarlo.

- Usted no debe tomar alcohol cuando está tomando Glucophage.

- Si olvida tomar una píldora, tome su dosis normal la próxima vez que deba tomarla. NO doble la dosis o trate de "ponerse al día" por la dosis omitida.

Tiazolidinadiones		
Nombre	Tamaño de la Tableta (mg)	Dosis Máxima (mg)
Avandia/Rosiglitazone[a]	2 4 8	8
Actos/Pioglitazone[b]	15 30 45	45

[a]De Smithkline Beecham Pharmaceuticals, Philadelphia, PA, mayo 1999.
[b]De Takeda Pharmaceuticals America, Inc., Lincolnshire, IL, julio 1999.

- Estos medicamentos bajan el azúcar en la sangre ayudando a la glucosa e insulina a entrar a las células de los músculos.

- Éstos deben tomarse *con* la primera comida del día. Si usted se olvida, tómelo con la próxima comida. No doble la dosis o trate de "ponerse al día" por la dosis omitida.

- Cuando se usan solos, éstos no causan azúcar en la sangre bajo (hipoglucemia).

- Si usted está tomando insulina u otras píldoras para la diabetes, su dosis puede que necesite bajarse. Analice su azúcar en la sangre y su doctor le aconsejará.

- Estos medicamentos pueden interferir con algunas píldoras para el control de la natalidad—discuta esto con su doctor.

- Por la manera en que estos medicamentos trabajan, puede tardar de uno a tres meses para ver qué tan bien éstos funcionan para usted.

	Inhibidores de las Alfa-Glucosidasas		
Nombre	*Tamaño de la Tableta (mg)*	*Duración de la Acción (hr)*	*Dosis Máxima (mg)*
Precose/ Acarbose[a]	25 50 100	2	300
Glyset/ Miglitol[b]	25 50 100	2	300

[a]De Bayer Pharmaceuticals Division, Wayne, NJ, 1997.
[b]De Pharmacia y Upjohn Company, NY, NY, 1999.

- Estos medicamentos bajan el azúcar en la sangre reduciendo la absorción de los carbohidratos (almidones o azúcares) después de la comida.

- Éstos *tienen* que tomarse con el primer bocado de una comida, y la comida debe incluir alimentos del grupo almidón (pan, arroz, pasta, papas, cereal, frijoles, etc.).

- Los efectos secundarios más comunes son diarrea y aumento de gas. El empezar con una dosis baja y aumentar la dosis lentamente puede ayudarle a limitar estos efectos secundarios.

■ Cuando son usados solos, éstos no causan azúcar en la sangre bajo (hipoglucemia).

■ Azúcar en la sangre bajo (hipoglucemia) puede ocurrir si estos medicamentos se usan con uno de los medicamentos sulfonilureas (vea las páginas 120–121) o insulina. Debido a la manera que éstos trabajan, los jugos normales, soda, dulce y leche usados para tratar el azúcar en la sangre bajo no subirán el azúcar en la sangre—usted *tiene* que usar pastillas o gels de glucosa.

Inhibidor de DPP-4			
Nombre	*Tamaño de la Tableta (mg)*		
Januvia/Sitagliptin[a]	25	50	100
Onglyza/Saxagliptin[b]	2.5	5	

[a]De Merck & Co., Inc., Whitehouse Station, NJ, 2006.
[b]De Bristol-Myers Squibb, Princeton, NJ, 2009.

■ Estos medicamentos tienen varias acciones:
1. reducen el azúcar en la sangre, especialmente después de y entre las comidas;
2. mejoran la cantidad de insulina producida por su páncreas;
3. reducen la cantidad de azúcar producida por el hígado, especialmente a la hora de la comida.

■ Estos medicamentos no son usados para tratar la diabetes Tipo I.

■ Los posibles efectos secundarios son: congestión o goteo nasal, dolor de garganta, resfriado, dolor de cabeza, dolor de estómago o diarrea.

■ Pueden tomarse con o sin comida.

Combinación de Medicamentos

Nombre	Tamaño de la Tableta (mg)	Duración de la Acción	Dosis Máxima (mg)
Glucovance[a]	1.25/250		10/2000
Glyburide y	2.5/500	24 horas	ó
Metformin	5/500		20/2000
Metaglip[b]	2.5/250		
Metformin y	2.5/250		
Glipizide	5/500	24 horas	20/2000
Avandamet[c]	1/500		
Avandia y	2/500	24 horas	8/2000
Metformin	4/500		
	2/1000		
	4/1000		
Actos plus Met[d]	15/500	24 horas	45/2550
Actos y	15/850		
Metformin			
Avandaryl[e]	4/1	24 horas	8/8
Avandia y	4/2		
Glimepiride	4/4		
Janumet[f]	50/500	24 horas	100/2000
Januvia y	50/1000		
Metformin			
Prandimet[g]	1/500	1.4–6 horas	10/2500 en 24 horas
Prandin y	2/500		ó
Metformin			4/1000 por comida
Kombiglyze XR[h]	5/500	24 horas	5/2000 en 24 horas
Saxagliptin and	5/1000		
Metaformin	2.5/1000		

[a]De Bristol-Myers Squibb Company, Princeton, NJ, agosto 2000.
[b]De Bristol-Myers Squibb Company, Princeton, NJ, octubre 2002.
[c]De GlaxoSmithKline, Research Triangle Park, NC, octubre 2002.
[d]De Takeda Pharmaceuticals, North America, Inc., 2005.
[e]De GlaxoSmithKline, Research Triangle Park, NC, diciembre 2005.
[f]De Merck & Co., Whitehouse Station, NJ, 2007.
[g]De Novo Nordisk, Princeton, NJ 2008.
[h]De Bristol-Myers Squibb Co., Princeton, NJ, noviembre 2010.

■ Las píldoras listadas arriba son todas combinaciones de medicamentos discutidos anteriormente en esta sección. Vea las páginas 120–121 para información acerca de Glyburide, Glipzide y Glimepiride, las páginas 122–123 para Metformin,

las páginas 123–124 para Avandia y Actos, las páginas
121–122 para Prandin, y la página 125 para Januvia.

Hay otros medicamentos que pueden afectar los medicamentos orales, así que es muy importante que verifique con su doctor antes de tomar cualquier otro medicamento y que tome sólo lo que su doctor le recete.

Mimético de Incretina			
Nombre	Dosis		
Byetta/Exenatide[a]	5 mcg		10 mcg
Victoza/Liraglutide[b]	0.6 mg	1.2 mg	1.8 mg

[a]De Amylin Pharmaceuticals, Inc., San Diego, CA, y Eli Lilly and Company, Indianapolis, IN, 2005.
[b]De Novo-Nordisk, Inc., Princeton, NJ, 2010.

■ Estos medicamentos tienen varias acciones: 1) ayuda con la producción de insulina en el páncreas inmediatamente después de una comida; 2) detiene la producción excesiva de azúcar en el hígado cuando ésta no es necesaria; 3) retrasa la velocidad con la que la comida sale del estómago; 4) ayuda con la pérdida de peso.

■ Ellos funcionan actuando sobre el aumento de azúcar en la sangre que ocurre después de las comidas.

■ Se administran por inyección (similar a la insulina) con una jeringuilla tipo bolígrafo precargada. Byetta se administra de 5–60 minutos antes del desayuno y de la cena. Victoza se administra una vez al día.

■ No se usan en la diabetes Tipo I.

■ Posibles efectos secundarios incluyen náuseas, vómitos, diarrea, nerviosismo, mareos, dolor de cabeza, malestar estomacal y baja azucar en la sangre.

■ Medicamentos como las pastillas anticonceptivas y los antibióticos deberían tomarse 1 hora antes de la Byetta y de Victoza.

■ Si usted se salta una dosis, espere a la próxima ocasión en que le toque administrárselas.

Mimético de Amilina	
Nombre	*Dosis*
Symlin[a]	30 mcg
Acetato de Pramlintide	60 mcg
	90 mcg
	120 mcg

[a]De Amylin Pharmaceuticals, Inc., San Diego, CA, 2005.

■ La amilina se usa con insulina en la diabetes Tipo I y Tipo II.

■ Ésta se administra por inyección de la misma manera que se administra la insulina.

■ Se toma a la hora de la comida junto a la dosis normal de insulina. Ésta no puede mezclarse con insulina.

■ Symlin tiene varias acciones: 1) retrasa la velocidad con que la comida sale del estómago; 2) reduce la secreción de glucagón (una hormona que aumenta el azúcar en la sangre); 3) reduce el azúcar en la sangre después de las comidas; 4) ayuda a perder peso.

■ El almacenamiento de Symlin es el mismo que para la insulina. Vea las páginas 131–132.

■ Los efectos secundarios pueden incluir hipoglucemia, náuseas, pérdida de apetito, vómitos o diarrea.

INSULINA

Usted puede que necesite insulina para mantener su azúcar en la sangre en su rango aceptable. Las personas con diabetes Tipo 1 *deben* usar insulina todos los días. Las personas con diabetes Tipo 2 puede que necesiten insulina durante tiempos de estrés como enfermedad, trauma emocional, embarazo, infección o cuando su propia insulina no puede trabajar suficientemente. Una vez que el evento de estrés se acaba, puede que sea posible parar de usar insulina y controlar su azúcar en la sangre con dieta o con dieta y medicamento oral.

Si usted es una persona que pesa demasiado, usa insulina y tiene diabetes Tipo 2, la pérdida de peso (especialmente con ejercicio) bajará su azúcar en la sangre, y posiblemente le permitirá suspender la insulina.

Sin importar la razón por la cual usted tiene que usar insulina, esta sección explica todo lo que necesita saber y algunos "trucos del oficio" para hacerlo más fácil.

De las tablas en las páginas 129–130, escoja su insulina(s) por el tipo, especie y compañía que la fabrica.

Insulina Lilly				
Tipo	*Especie*	*Inicio* (Hrs.)	*Nivel max.* (Hrs.)	*Duración* (Hrs.)
I. A. Humalog[a]				
Acción rápida	Humano	$1/4$	1–2	3–4
II. A. Humulin R				
Acción corta	Humano	$1/2$	2–4	6–8
III. A. Humulin N				
Acción intermedia	Humano	1–2	6–12	18–24
IV. Mezclas				
A. Humulin 70/30	Humano	$1/2$	6–12	18–24
B. Mezcla Humalog 75/25[b]	Humano	$1/4$	2–12	22
C. Mezcla Humalog 50/50[c]	Humano	$1/4$	2–12	22

[a]De *Humalog*®, Eli Lilly and Company, Indianapolis, IN, 1996.
[b]De Eli Lilly and Company, Indianapolis, IN, 2000.
[c]De Eli Lilly and Company, Indianapolis, IN, 2006.
Fuente: Insulin from Lilly, Eli Lilly and Company, Indianapolis, IN, 1994 y 1997.

Novo-Nordisk

Tipo	Especie	Inicio (Hrs.)	Nivel max. (Hrs.)	Duración (Hrs.)
I. A. Novolog		10–20		
Acción rápida	Humano	minutos	1–3	3–5
II. B. Novolin R				
Acción corta	Humano	$^1/_2$	$2^1/_2$–5	8
III. A. Novolin N				
Acción intermedia	Humano	$1^1/_2$	4–12	24
IV. A. Levemir[a]				
Larga acción	Humano	5.7	Sin nivel max.	24
IV. Mezclas				
A. Novolin				
70/30	Humano	$^1/_2$	4–12	24
A. NovologMix				
70/30[b]	Humano	$^1/_4$	1–4	24

[a,b]Novo-Nordisk Pharmaceuticals, Inc. Princeton, NJ, 2005.
Fuente: Novo-Nordisk Pharmaceuticals, Princeton, NJ, 2004.

Aventis

Tipo	Especie	Inicio (Hrs.)	Nivel max. (Hrs.)	Duración (Hrs.)
I. A. Apidra[b]				
Acción rápida	Humano	$^1/_4$	1–2	2–3
I. A. Lantus[a]				
Larga acción	Humano		Sin nivel max.	24

Fuente: [a]Aventis Pharmaceuticals, Inc., Kansas City, MO, 2000.
[b]Aventis Pharmaceuticals, Inc., Kansas City, MO, 2004.

Respecto a su insulina, es MUY IMPORTANTE para usted el recordar

- el nombre o tipo
- la especie (humano)
- la compañía que la produce
- la concentración (U-100)
- la dosis (número de unidades)
- verificar la fecha de expiración

INFORMACIÓN DE SU INSULINA PARA RECORDAR:

Nombre_____

Especie_____

Compañía _____

Concentración _____

Dosis _____

Fecha de expiración _____

Horario de Inyección

Cuándo usted se inyecta su insulina depende del tipo de insulina que utiliza. Algunas insulinas se inyectan a la hora de la comida y otras pueden tomarse a la hora de dormir. Pregúntele a su doctor o educador de la diabetes cuándo debería tomar su insulina.

Almacenamiento de Insulina

La insulina viene en botellas (llamadas viales) o en inyectores tipo bolígrafo. El mejor lugar para almacenar su insulina es en la puerta de su refrigerador (no importa si la botella está abierta o no). Una vez que el vial de insulina o el bolígrafo esté abierto para usarse, éste puede almacenarse a temperatura ambiente (40°–86°F) por 14(bolígrafo)–28(vial) días. Verifique las instrucciones que vienen con la caja de insulina para el número exacto de días. Anote la fecha en el vial de insulina o en el bolígrafo cuando lo abra.

Proteja la insulina de la luz del sol y no la deje congelar. No la almacene en lugares tales como autos, baños o cocinas. Aún si se almacena en el refrigerador, usted debería tirar a la basura cualquier vial/bolígrafo de insulina que ha estado abierto por más de 14 días para los bolígrafos y 28 días para los viales. La insulina comienza a perder su habilidad de funcionar correctamente.

Consejo: Si usted se inyecta insulina a temperatura ambiente en vez de insulina fría, usted puede evitar cualquier sensación de picadura y obtener una mejor absorción en sus tejidos.

JERINGUILLA PARA LA INSULINA

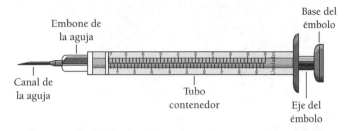

Las únicas partes de la jeringuilla que usted debe tocar son las partes que no entran en su cuerpo ni entran en contacto con la insulina. Usted puede tocar

■ el embone de la aguja

■ el tubo contenedor

■ la base del émbolo

Si usted toca las partes de la jeringuilla que entran en su cuerpo durante la inyección, usted puede ensuciar su jeringuilla y correr el riesgo de darse usted mismo una infección. Usted nunca debe tocar

■ el canal de la aguja

■ el interior del tubo

Reutilización de las Jeringuillas de Insulina

Muchas personas reutilizan sus jeringuillas de insulina, y los investigadores han reportado que esta práctica está bien para la mayoría de los diabéticos. (El uso sugerido es de 1–2 veces por jeringuilla). Usted debe ser muy cuidadoso cuando prepara su insulina y cuando se pone la inyección para mantener la jeringuilla y aguja muy limpias. Consulte con su doctor o educador de diabetes para ver si usted debe o no volver a usar sus jeringuillas de insulina.

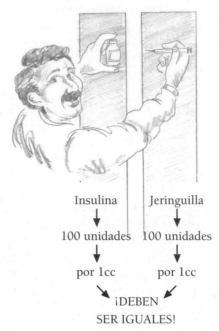

Insulina   Jeringuilla

100 unidades   100 unidades

por 1cc   por 1cc

¡DEBEN
SER IGUALES!

¡Esté seguro de comprar la jeringuilla apropiada para la concentración de insulina que usted está usando! Si usted tiene la jeringuilla incorrecta, puede que no se esté inyectando la cantidad correcta de insulina. Usted probablemente está usando insulina U-100, porque ésta es la insulina más común hecha en los Estados Unidos. (Las insulinas U-40 y U-80 ya no se producen más en los Estados Unidos). "U-100" significa que hay 100 unidades de insulina en 1 cc.

TÉCNICA PARA INYECTAR

Utilizar un tipo de insulina

Abajo están enumerados los pasos para guiarlo en la preparación de su insulina para inyección.

1. Lave sus manos.
2. Reúna su equipo: insulina, jeringuilla y alcohol.

3. RUEDE (20 veces) la botella de insulina entre sus manos—esté seguro que la insulina está bien mezclada.

4. Limpie la parte superior de la botella de insulina con alcohol y déjelo secar.

5. Ponga la aguja en la botella de insulina. Manteniendo la aguja en la botella, vírela completamente boca abajo. Tire del émbolo para llenar la jeringuilla con más insulina de la que usted necesita (alrededor de 10 unidades más de las que necesita).

6. Empújelo todo haciendo que vuelva a entrar en la botella y repita el paso 5.

7. Ahora mida la cantidad de insulina que usted necesita tirando del émbolo hasta la marca correcta.

8. Verifique que no hayan burbujas de aire en la jeringuilla, porque éstas toman el lugar de la insulina en la jeringuilla y le prevendrán tomar la cantidad correcta. Si ve alguna burbuja, repita los pasos 6 y 7.

9. Una vez a la semana, remueva el émbolo de la jeringuilla y ponga la aguja en la botella por dos o tres segundos. Esto mantendrá la presión de aire dentro de la botella de insulina igual a la presión fuera de ésta.

Al preparar la insulina y ponerse la inyección, sea muy cuidadoso de no tocar la aguja o dejarla caer. Si usted ensucia la aguja, bote la jeringuilla y empiece de nuevo con una nueva.

Una versión más corta de preparar una sola insulina:

1. Ruede la botella de insulina (20 veces), limpie la parte superior.

2. Ponga la aguja en la botella de insulina.

3. Vire la botella boca abajo.

4. Tire el émbolo hacia abajo rápidamente—más de lo que necesita.

5. Empuje toda la insulina de vuelta en la botella.

6. Tire hacia abajo el émbolo rápidamente de nuevo—más de lo que necesita.

7. Mida la cantidad exacta de insulina que necesita.

8. Verifique que no hayan burbujas de aire.

Utilizar dos tipos de insulina

Enumerados abajo están los pasos para guiarlo a mezclar dos tipos de insulina en una jeringuilla para inyección. (*Insulina turbia* se refiere a insulina NPH, e *insulina clara* se refiere a Regular, Novolog, Humalog o Apidra).

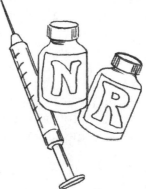

1. Lave sus manos.

2. Reúna su equipo: insulinas, jeringuilla y alcohol.

3. RUEDE (20 veces) las botellas de insulina entre sus manos—esté seguro que la insulina está bien mezclada.

4. Limpie los topes de las botellas de insulina con alcohol y déjelas secar.

5. Ponga la aguja en la botella de insulina clara y vírela completa-

mente boca abajo. Tire del émbolo para llenar la jeringuilla con más insulina de la que usted necesita (alrededor de 10 unidades más).

6. Empújelo todo en la botella y repita el último paso.

7. Ahora mida la cantidad exacta de insulina clara que usted necesita.

8. Verifique que jeringuilla no tenga burbujas de aire, porque éstas toman el lugar de la insulina en la jeringuilla y le impedirán tomar la cantidad correcta. Si ve alguna burbuja, repita los pasos 6 y 7.

9. Ahora ponga su aguja en la botella de la insulina turbia y SUAVEMENTE saque la cantidad de insulina turbia que usted necesite. Recuerde que usted ya tiene insulina clara en su jeringuilla, así que la cantidad total de insulina en su jeringuilla debe ser igual al TOTAL de ambas, la insulina clara y la turbia.

Al preparar la insulina y ponerse la inyección, sea muy cuidadoso de no tocar la aguja o dejarla caer. Si usted ensucia la aguja, bote la jeringuilla y empiece de nuevo con una nueva.

Una versión más corta de preparar dos insulinas:

1. Ruede las botellas de insulina (20 veces), limpie las partes superiores.

2. Ponga la aguja en la botella de insulina clara—mantenga la aguja en la botella y vírela boca abajo. Tire el émbolo hacia abajo rápidamente—más de lo que necesita.

3. Devuelva toda la insulina a la botella.

4. Nuevamente, tire el émbolo hacia abajo rápidamente— más de lo que necesita.

5. Mida la cantidad exacta de insulina clara que necesita.

6. Verifique que no hayan burbujas de aire.

7. Ponga la aguja en la insulina turbia y tire el émbolo hacia abajo SUAVEMENTE hasta obtener la cantidad TOTAL de insulina que usted necesita.

_____ unidades de insulina clara (Regular, Novolg, Humalog o Apidra)

_____ unidades de insulina turbia (NPH)

_____ Cantidad TOTAL de insulina para inyectar

Cómo Usar un Lápiz de Insulina

A continuación se encuentran los pasos para guiarlo cuando prepare su lápiz de insulina para inyectarlo.

1. Lávese las manos.

2. Reúna su equipo: lápiz de insulina y la aguja.

3. Si la insulina es turbia, ruede y gire el lápiz varias veces para lograr una mezcla uniforme de la insulina en el lápiz.

4. Coloque la aguja en el lápiz y remueva las tapas (hay dos).

5. Mida 1–2 unidades de insulina y presione el lápiz para empujar la insulina hacia la aguja. Asegúrese de que hay una gota de insulina en la punta de la aguja. Las instrucciones del lápiz de insulina llaman a este paso un "air-shot" o "safety shot".

6. Ahora mida la dosis de insulina que usted necesita.

Cómo Ponerse Su Inyección

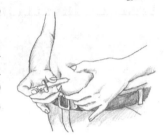

Ahora usted está listo para ponerse su inyección. Estos pasos están resumidos para guiarlo.

1. Escoja el área para su inyección—si es necesario, límpiela con agua y jabón. Si utiliza alcohol, deje la piel secar antes de inyectar la insulina.

2. Pellizque la piel entre su dedo pulgar y sus otros dedos.

3. Rápidamente inserte la jeringa o el lápiz de insulina en la piel, con un ángulo ya sea de 90 grados o de 60 grados. Su educador de diabetes lo guiará en el ángulo que debe usar.

4. Inyecte la insulina.

5. Cuente 2 segundos si está usando una jeringa o 5–10 segundos si está usando un lápiz de insulina y luego retire la aguja.

NO DESECHE LAS JERINGAS/LÁPICES DE INSULINA SIN TOMAR LAS PRECAUCIONES NECESARIAS. Antes de pasar a la próxima sección, nos gustaría explicar cómo desechar las agujas de sus jeringas/lápices de insulina, llamadas "objetos punzantes".

Como resultado de una nueva ley del 2008, usted ya no puede botar las agujas de sus jeringas/lápices de insulina a la basura. Pregunte en la oficina correspondiente de su ciudad o a la compañia local de recolección de basura para obtener instrucciones acerca de cómo deshacerse de estos "objetos punzantes". La mayoría de las ciudades/compañias de recolección de basura están estableciendo programas especiales.

Deshágase de sus objetos punzantes en forma segura, siguiendo las siguientes directrices:

- obtenga un contenedor aprobado para objetos punzantes (de color rojo) a través de su ciudad, compañia de recolección de basura o farmacia local

- llénelo sólo hasta alrededor de 3/4 de su capacidad —no lo llene completamente

- mantenga su contenedor para objectos punzantes en un área que sea segura para niños y animales.

- revise cuáles son los días de recolección de desechos peligrosos en su ciudad o pregunte al departamento local de bomberos, para deshacerse de sus contenedores para objectos punzantes.

Áreas de Inyección

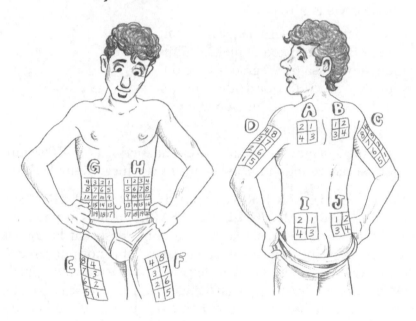

Los dibujos de arriba le muestran áreas de su cuerpo que son mejores para las inyecciones de insulina porque están lejos de articulaciones, nervios y vasos sanguíneos grandes.

Hay tres maneras de rotar sus lugares de inyección. Una manera es utilizar todos los lugares de inyección en un área (por ejemplo 1–8 en la áreas C y D) antes de moverse a la siguiente área. La segunda manera es utilizar solamente el abdomen y hacer uso de todos los lugares que usted tiene en esa área. La tercera manera es escoger áreas específicas para ciertos tipos de insulina u horas del día. Pregunte a su doctor o educador de diabetes para que le aconsejen.

Usted puede necesitar cambiar su patrón cuando planifique hacer ejercicio. La insulina inyectada cerca de un músculo que va a ser usado en ejercicio se absorberá más rápidamente por el aumento del flujo de sangre. Esto le da un riesgo mayor de tener hipoglucemia, así que, en ocasiones, usted podrá necesitar cambiar su patrón de inyección y usar un área lejos de los músculos que planifica usar durante los ejercicios.

> Es importante que ROTE SUS LUGARES para que no desarrolle abscesos, infecciones o se endurezca el área del lugar de inyección. Póngase sus inyecciones a $^1/_2$ pulgada de distancia (el ancho de su dedo). Las insulinas U-100 son más puras que insulinas más viejas y es menos probable que causen problemas en la piel por un uso a largo plazo.

Nosotros fuertemente recomendamos que un miembro de la familia o un amigo cercano sepa como ponerle sus inyecciones de insulina. Pueden haber momentos cuando usted esté demasiado enfermo para ponerse su inyección o puede que usted quiera un día libre de vez en cuando. A lo mejor otros pueden alcanzar lugares que usted no puede alcanzar. Su brazo es el lugar más difícil para ponerse una inyección correctamente, así que deje que otros usen este lugar. Para niños, los lugares localizados en las nalgas y los hombros son los mejores lugares que pueden usar los padres y otros.

Bombas de Insulina

Otra manera de recibir insulina es mediante una bomba de insulina. Las bombas operan con baterías, son del tamaño de un buscapersonas ("pager") y pesan unas cuantas onzas. Suministran insulina de acción rápida al cuerpo a través de un tubo plástico delgado con una aguja insertada debajo de la piel en el abdomen (la aguja necesita ser cambiada cada 2 días). Una cantidad fija de insulina (llamada insulina básica) es dada continuamente y luego dosis adicionales de insulina (llamadas bolos) son dadas a las horas de las comidas. El azúcar en la sangre es analizado frecuentemente a través del día, y la bomba es ajustada para dar la cantidad de insulina que el cuerpo necesita.

El usar una bomba de insulina puede proveer mejor control del azúcar en la sangre debido a la infusión constante de insulina, el monitoreo cuidadoso del azúcar en la sangre y el ajuste frecuente de las dosis de insulina.

Si usted desea más información acerca de las bombas de insulina, por favor hable con su doctor, educador de diabetes o vaya a estos sitios web:

medtronicminimed.com

Animascorp.com

DexCom.com

Accu-Chek.com

Myomnipod.com

RECUERDE: Todos estos medicamentos ayudan a controlar el azúcar en su sangre, pero no pueden hacerlo solos ni tampoco pueden curar la diabetes. Los MEDICAMENTOS necesitan SU AYUDA para funcionar.

Siga su plan   Haga ejercicios   Mida el nivel de
de comidas   azúcar en su sangre

Análisis de Laboratorio

AZÚCAR EN LA SANGRE EN AYUNO

Este análisis mide la cantidad de azúcar en su sangre después de haber ayunado por 8–12 horas. Un resultado normal de azúcar en la sangre en ayuno es por debajo de los 100 miligramos. Vea la página 28 para rangos aceptables para aquellos que tienen diabetes.

Cuando usted vaya a tener un análisis de azúcar en la sangre en ayuno, no coma o beba después de media noche la noche anterior hasta que la muestra de sangre sea sacada en la mañana (pequeños sorbos de agua son permitidos).

Si usted tiene diabetes, no tome su medicamento para la diabetes hasta que su sangre sea sacada *y usted esté listo para comer.*

AZÚCAR EN LA SANGRE DESPUÉS DE COMER

Este análisis mide la cantidad de azúcar en su sangre dos horas después de que usted haya comido una comida normal. Cuando su doctor ordene este análisis, usted debe

1. Tomar su medicamento para la diabetes como de costumbre.
2. Comer su comida normal en su horario normal.

3. Medir el azúcar en su sangre dos horas más tarde—2 horas después de comenzar la comida.

Si su azúcar en la sangre es muy alto, puede significar que necesita cambios en su plan de comida, insulina o medicamento oral. Si su azúcar en la sangre está bien controlada, los resultados deben estar en el rango aceptable (menos de 160).

RECUERDE: Un análisis de una sola vez de azúcar en la sangre en ayuno o después de comer puede no reflejar su control TOTAL—estos análisis son usados solamente como guías para usted y su doctor.

PROMEDIO ESTIMADO DE GLUCOSA (eAG)

(anteriormente conocido como Hemoglobina A1c)

El azúcar se une a la hemoglobina (glóbulos rojos de la sangre) y permanece ahí por la vida de estos, que es 120 días.

El resultado de este examen de sangre, llamado Hemoglobina A1c, le dice a usted y a su médico cuán bien se han controlado los niveles de azúcar en su sangre en los 2 ó 3 últimos meses. Piense que es un promedio de todos los niveles de azúcar en su sangre para cada momento en todos los días por ese período de tiempo.

A continuación se encuentra una tabla que le ayudará a entender los resultados de la Hemoglobina A1c (como un porcentaje) y qué significan acerca de su nivel promedio de glucosa en su sangre.

Hemoglobin A1c Resultado en %	*Promedio Estimado de Glucosa eAG en mg/dl*	
5	97	Normal
5.5	111	Normal
6	126	Normal
6.5	140	OBJECTIVO
7	154	OBJECTIVO
7.5	169	Demasiado alta
8	183	Demasiado alta
8.5	197	Demasiado alta
9	212	Demasiado alta
9.5	226	Demasiado alta
10	240	Demasiado alta
10.5	255	Demasiado alta
11	269	Demasiado alta
11.5	283	Demasiado alta
12	298	Demasiado alta
12.5	312	Demasiado alta
13	326	Demasiado alta

El examen de Hemoglobina A1c debe ser hecho cada 3 a 6 meses de forma que usted tenga un resultado del laboratorio indicándole su Promedio Estimado de Glucosa (eAG, por sus siglas en inglés) para compararlo con su nivel promedio de azúcar sanguíneo obtenido con su medidor de glucemia (o glucómetro).

Si usted mide su glucemia antes de comer y 2 horas después de comer, usted debería encontrar los resultados de su glucómetro cercanos al resultado del laboratorio del Promedio estimado de Azúcar (eAG). Usted va a estar midiendo su glucemia cuando ésta es menor, como antes de las comidas, y cuando ésta es más elevada, como después de las comidas.

Si usted mide su nivel de azúcar sanguíneo sólo en la mañana o antes de las comidas, usted puede encontrar que los resultados que obtiene de su glucómetro son más bajos que los resultados del Promedio estimado de Glucosa (eAG) provenientes del laboratorio. Esto se debe a que usted está midiendo su glucemia cuando los niveles de azúcar sanguíneo tienden a ser menores y no cuando estos niveles aumentan luego de una comida.

Un nivel normal de Hemoglobina A1c es menos de 6%.

El Promedio estimado de Glucosa (eAG) normal es menos de 126.

Cuando usted tiene diabetes or prediabetes, su OBJETIVO es:

Un Promedio estimado de . . . . .   menor que 154
  Glucosa (eAG)   (Preferiblemente bajo 140)

Hemoglobina A1c . . . .   menor que 7%
    (Preferiblemente menos
    de 6.5%)

Ejercicio

Ha sido comprobado que el ejercicio es EXTREMADAMENTE importante en el control del azúcar en la sangre. De hecho, para la mayoría de las personas con diabetes Tipo 2, ejercicio en combinación con pérdida de peso es todo lo que se necesita para controlar su azúcar en la sangre.

Durante el ejercicio, las células del cuerpo son mucho más sensibles a la insulina y glucosa, permitiéndole al cuerpo quemar la glucosa para obtener energía y requerir menores cantidades de insulina—ayudando a disminuir la "resistencia a la insulina" (vea la página 3).

LOS BENEFICIOS

Son muchos los beneficios del ejercicio:

Le ayuda a perder peso.

Es útil para mantener su peso.

Es útil para reducir la cantidad de medicamentos (insulina y medicamento oral) que usted debe tomar.

Puede reducir su azúcar en la sangre.

Reduce su presión sanguínea.

Reduce su pulso en reposo.

Fortalece su corazón.

Aumenta su colesterol HDL (bueno).

Aumenta la circulación de la sangre.

Aumenta su energía.

Reduce los efectos del estrés en su cuerpo.

Ayuda a sus pulmones a trabajar mejor, haciendo el respirar más fácil.

Le hace sentirse mejor acerca de usted mismo.

Todos estos beneficios por el ejercicio se traducen en un cuerpo en "condición física", esto es, un cuerpo en el que su corazón, pulmones y músculos pueden trabajar mejor con menos esfuerzo.

LOS TIPOS

Hay diferentes tipos de ejercicios que hacen diferentes cosas por su cuerpo. Veamos cuáles son.

Los EJERCICIOS ISOMÉTRICOS contraen los músculos sin producir movimiento. En otras palabras, éstos tensan los músculos contra otros músculos u objetos que no se mueven. Algunos músculos son fortalecidos, pero estos ejercicios producen tensión dentro de los músculos, causando un aumento en la presión sanguínea. Por esta razón, personas con presión sanguínea alta, problemas del corazón o retinopatía diabética (vea la página 183) deben evitar estos ejercicios.

Los EJERCICIOS ISOTÓNICOS tonifican los músculos y queman calorías. Éstos son usualmente actividades de parar-y-empezar como calistenias, trabajo de la casa y jardín, jugar bolos y golf. Debido a que no son actividades continuas, éstas solas no pueden ponerlo en buena condición física. Éstas (las calistenias particularmente) son buenas actividades para formar *parte* de su programa completo de ejercicios.

Los EJERCICIOS ANAERÓBICOS son ejercicios que involucran mucho movimiento de los músculos pero nunca duran lo suficiente para afectar su condición física. Algunos ejemplos incluyen caminar cinco pisos de escaleras, una carrera rápida al bus, una carrera de 100 yardas y nataciones rápidas. El hacer esto ocasionalmente no lo ayudará a desarrollar una condición física.

Los EJERCICIOS AERÓBICOS son actividades continuas que usan grupos de músculos principales y duran lo suficiente para utilizar oxígeno y subir el pulso a niveles que desarrollan y mantienen la condición física. Algunos ejemplos son caminar, correr, nadar, montar en bicicleta, bicicletas estacionarias, ejercicios en ruedas de andar o máquinas de remar y brincar cuerda. Éste es el tipo de ejercicio que usted debe hacer para alcanzar todos los beneficios enumerados en las páginas 147–148 y tener su cuerpo en condición física.

El mejor programa de ejercicio combina ejercicios isotónicos y aeróbicos. Cuando planifique la parte aeróbica, usted debe escoger más de una actividad. Un día usted puede disfrutar caminar y el próximo puede nadar. El cambiar las actividades le ayuda a usar los diferentes músculos.

LAS PARTES DE UN PROGRAMA DE EJERCICIO

Un programa completo de ejercicio incluye 4 partes:

1. Calentamiento   3. Entrenamiento o ejercicio aeróbico

2. Estiramiento   4. Enfriamiento

Calentamiento La sesión de calentamiento es 5 minutos de caminar o una versión suave de la actividad aeróbica que planifica hacer. Esto permite aumentar su pulso lentamente y que la sangre fluya a sus músculos.

Estiramiento Permita de 5–10 minutos para ejercicios de estiramiento para soltar sus músculos y coyunturas y prevenir dolores en los músculos y lesiones.

Estire todos los músculos de su cuerpo— cuello, hombros, espalda, brazos, abdomen, caderas, piernas, tobillos y pies. Tenga cuidado de no brincar durante su estiramiento o de estirar hasta el punto de sentir dolor.

Entrenamiento o ejercicio aeróbico Ésta es la parte principal de su programa de ejercicio, donde usted fortalece su corazón y pulmones y mueve su cuerpo hacia una mejor condición física. Al comienzo le será posible hacer la actividad que escoja por 1–5 minutos, pero usted debe aumentar *gradualmente* su ejercicio hasta 20–30 minutos de actividad continua.

Enfriamiento La sesión de enfriamiento es realmente una combinación de los períodos de calentamiento y estiramiento. Haga su actividad aeróbica a un paso lento por cerca de 5 minutos y después haga los ejercicios de estiramiento por otros 5 minutos. Esto le permite bajar su pulso y circulación.

¿Qué actividad aeróbica planea hacer usted?

QUÉ TAN FUERTE EJERCITARSE

Su pulso es la medida de qué tan fuerte su corazón está trabajando. Para obtener el mayor beneficio de su ejercicio, su pulso debe alcanzar y mantener (por 20–30 minutos) un cierto número de latidos por minuto durante el entrenamiento o ejercicio aeróbico. Esto es conocido como su PULSO IDEAL.

¿Cómo determina su pulso ideal? Siga los siguientes pasos:

1. Reste su edad de 220 para determinar su pulso máximo.

2. Cuando primero comience un programa de ejercicio, es mejor mantener su pulso entre 60 y 75% de su pulso máximo. Multiplique su pulso máximo por 0.6 (60%) y luego por 0.75 (75%), esto le da el rango de su pulso ideal.

3. Después de haber estado ejercitándose por un tiempo, usted querrá mantener su pulso entre 75 y 85% de su pulso máximo. Multiplique su pulso máximo por 0.75 (75%) y después por 0.85 (85%) para obtener el rango de su pulso ideal.

Una manera fácil de medir su pulso es contando el número de latidos en 6 segundos y luego añadirle un cero. Esto le da una estimación de su pulso por minuto.

Ejemplo #1 Juan tiene 55 años de edad y quiere estar seguro de que está alcanzando y manteniendo su pulso ideal durante su entrenamiento o la parte de ejercicio aeróbico. Para calcular su pulso ideal, tome

220
−55 (Edad de Juan)
= 165 (Pulso máximo para Juan)

$0.6 \times 165 = 99$ (60% del pulso máximo para Juan)

$0.75 \times 165 = 124$ (75% del pulso máximo para Juan)

Debido a que Juan está recién comenzando su programa de ejercicio, lo mejor es mantener su pulso entre 99 y 124 (60–75% de su pulso máximo).

Ejemplo #2 Juanita tiene 65 años de edad y por los pasados 12 meses ha estado caminando para ejercicio. Ella quiere estar segura de que está alcanzando y manteniendo su pulso ideal durante el ejercicio. Para calcular el pulso ideal para Juanita, tome

220
−65 (Edad de Juanita)
= 155 (Pulso máximo para Juanita)

$0.75 \times 155 = 116$ (75% del pulso máximo para Juanita)

$0.85 \times 155 = 132$ (85% del pulso máximo para Juanita)

Debido a que Juanita se ha estado ejercitando por un tiempo, ella debe mantener su pulso entre 116 y 132 (75–85% de su pulso máximo).

Calcule su propio pulso ideal, o use esta tabla como guía.

Edad	Latidos por Minuto		
	60%	75%	85%
20	120	150	170
25	117	146	166
30	114	142	161
35	111	138	157
40	108	135	153
45	105	131	148
50	102	127	144
55	99	123	140
60	96	120	136
65	93	116	131
70	90	112	127
75	87	108	123
80	84	105	119

Para los 3 niveles, mis pulsos ideales son

60%_____

75%_____

85%_____

CUIDADO: DISCUTA SU PULSO IDEAL CON SU DOCTOR. Puede que algunos de ustedes estén tomando medicamentos que no permiten que su pulso aumente durante el ejercicio y por lo tanto esta información no funcionará para ustedes. Usted necesitará instrucciones especiales.

Durante el entrenamiento o parte de ejercicio aeróbico tome su pulso para determinar si se está ejercitando a su pulso ideal. Verifique su pulso cerca de los 3 minutos de haber comenzado el ejercicio, después tome su pulso nuevamente un poco más allá de la mitad.

Si su pulso está dentro de su rango ideal	→	usted está trabajando su corazón y pulmones correctamente.
Si su pulso está por encima de su pulso ideal	→	usted está trabajando muy duro, así que baje la intensidad un poco.
Si su pulso está por debajo de su pulso ideal	→	usted no está trabajando suficiente, así que acelere un poco.

Cómo Tomar Su Pulso

Cuando tome su pulso va a necesitar un reloj con una manecilla de segundos.

1. Tome los primeros dos dedos de una mano y póngalos en el hueso de la muñeca en el lado del dedo pulgar de la otra mano.

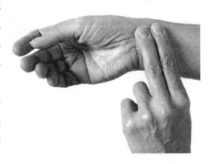

2. Mueva sus dedos aproximadamente un cuarto de pulgada hacia la parte de abajo de su muñeca.

3. Cuando sienta el latido (su pulso), cuente el número de latidos por 6 segundos.

4. Añádale un cero a este número. Éste es su pulso por minuto.

Si usted no desea medir su pulso, una manera simple de juzgar su ejercicio es:

No está esforzándose lo suficiente	→	puede cantar mientras hace ejercicio
Está esforzándose lo suficiente	→	puede hablar, pero un poco sin aliento
Se está esforzando demasiado	→	tan corto de aliento que no puede hablar

CUÁN A MENUDO HACER EJERCICIO

SEA CONSISTENTE y ejercítese un mínimo de cuatro a cinco veces por semana. Haga ejercicio por lo menos un día sí y uno no. No haga ejercicio por tres días corridos y luego pare por los próximos cuatro.

- Si usted está haciendo ejercicio para perder peso, debe hacer ejercicio de 5 a 6 veces por semana.
- El ejercitarse un día sí y uno no, le da tiempo a los músculos para que descansen.

¿Qué días planea hacer ejercicio usted?

CUÁNDO HACER EJERCICIO

Si no está seguro acerca de cuándo exactamente hacer ejercicio, discuta con su doctor, educador de diabetes o especialista de ejercicio cuál puede ser la mejor hora del día para usted.

- Haga ejercicio cuando su azúcar en la sangre tiende a estar más alto—de 1 a 2 horas después de una comida o en la mañana antes de tomar su medicamento para la diabetes y de comer su desayuno.

■ Si lo mejor para usted es hacer ejercicio justo antes de una comida, pregúntele a su doctor o educador de diabetes si necesita hacer algún ajuste a sus alimentos y/o medicamentos.

¿Qué hora del día es la mejor para hacer ejercicio?

CUÁNDO NO HACER EJERCICIO

■ Si usted tiene diabetes Tipo 1 y su azúcar en la sangre antes del ejercicio es sobre 250, salte la sesión de ejercicio—esto puede subir su azúcar en la sangre todavía más.

■ Si usted tiene diabetes Tipo 1, analice su orina para cetonas antes de hacer ejercicio. Si éstas son negativas (no hay cetonas en la orina), haga ejercicio. Si hay cetonas en la orina, no haga ejercicio.

■ No haga ejercicio si está enfermo.

SEÑALES DE ALERTA PARA DEJAR DE HACER EJERCICIO

Si usted siente cualquiera de estos síntomas durante el ejercicio, deténgase y descanse.

■ Dolor o presión en el pecho

■ Sentirse mareado o débil

■ Sentirse más cansado de lo normal

■ Ritmo cardiaco irregular

■ Sudor excesivo

■ Dificultad para respirar

Si los síntomas duran más de 5 minutos después de haber dejado de hacer ejercicio, busque atención médica inmediatamente.

GUÍAS PARA HACER EJERCICIO

■ Escoja una actividad que usted disfrute.

■ DISCUTA SUS PLANES PARA EJERCICIO CON SU DOCTOR O EDUCADOR DE DIABETES ANTES DE EMPEZAR SU PROGRAMA.
Esto es importante para aquellos que tienen diabetes, pero especialmente para aquellos que tienen cualquiera de las complicaciones de la diabetes (vea las páginas 181–188) o cualquier otro problema de salud.

■ Es sabio evitar actividades que requieren un grupo de personas, debido a que usted dependerá de muchas personas para hacer su ejercicio. También es sabio no hacer ejercicio solo. Escoja una persona para que sea su compañero de ejercicio, luego ustedes se pueden animar y apoyar uno al otro.

■ Cuando esté sólo comenzando, usted será capaz de hacer ejercicio al nivel de entrenamiento o aeróbico por sólo unos pocos minutos en forma seguida. Sea paciente y aumente su tiempo gradualmente hasta 20–30 minutos por sesión de ejercicio aeróbico.

■ Tenga un conocimiento profundo de hipoglucemia y también de cómo tratar o prevenir una reacción. ¡ESTÉ PREPARADO! *Siempre* lleve comidas rápidas de azúcar consigo.

■ Siempre tenga una identificación de diabetes consigo (vea las páginas 167–168).

■ Siga verificando su azúcar en la sangre—esto le dará información acerca de ajustes de alimentos o medicamentos que pueden ser necesarios, o si debe o no hacer ejercicio en un día en particular y cómo el ejercicio afecta su azúcar en la sangre.

■ Discuta con su doctor o educador de diabetes SUS NECESIDADES para ajustar la medicación y/o alimentos antes, durante o después de hacer ejercicio.

■ Espere 1 hora después de comer una comida antes de hacer ejercicio, para permitir que sus alimentos sean digeridos.

- Si usted usa insulina, inyéctela en un área que no va hacer utilizada durante el ejercicio (vea la página 140). Si la insulina es inyectada en un área que va a hacer ejercitada, va a ser absorbida más rápidamente y posiblemente cause azúcar en la sangre bajo. Por ejemplo, si usted va a caminar o correr, debe inyectar la insulina en su brazo o abdomen y no en un lugar en su pierna.

- Beba suficientes fluidos antes, durante y después de ejercitarse.

- Preste atención a sus pies—use zapatos que le acomoden bien y sean cómodos. Verifique sus pies diariamente para detectar dolores, ampollas y callos.

RECUERDE: EL EJERCICIO ES TRATAMIENTO. Mientras más ejercicio haga menos medicamentos necesitará.

FUENTES DE INFORMACIÓN PARA EJERCICIO

Aerobics for Women, por Mildred Cooper y Kenneth Cooper, M.D., M.P.H. Bantam Books, New York, 1972.

The Aerobics Program for Total Well-Being: Exercise, Diet & Emotional Balance, por Kenneth Cooper, M.D., M.P.H. Bantam Books, New York, 1982.

Armchair Fitness: Aerobics, un video con tres rutinas de 20 minutos para movimientos de estiramiento y fortalecimiento con música para todo aquel que le sea posible sentarse en una silla. Disponible a través de Joslin Diabetes Center, Boston.

Videos de Bailes con Sillas, por Jodi Stolove. Disponible a través de Chair Dancing Internacional, Inc., 2658 Del Mar Heights Road, Del Mar, CA 92014. Llame al (800)551-4FUN o al Fax (858)793-0747 o www.chairdancing.com.

Diabetes Sport and Exercise Book, por Claudia Graham, Ph.D., C.D.E.; Barbara Toohey y June Biermann. Lowell House, Los Angeles, 1995.

Diabetes: Your Complete Exercise Guide, por Neil F. Gordon, M.D., Ph.D. Human Kinetics Publishers, Champaign, IL, 1993.

The Fitness Book for People with Diabetes, por W. Guyton Hornsby, Jr., Ph.D., C.D.E., 1994. Susan H. Lau, American Diabetes Association, Alexandria, VA.

The Ultimate Fit or Fat, por Covert Bailey, Houghton Mifflin Co., New York, 1999.

Diabetes Exercise and Sports Association, 8001 Montcastle Dr. Nashville, TN 37221 o (800) 898-4322 o www.diabetes-exercise.org. La membresía incluye el boletín informativo "The DESA Challenge".

The Diabetic Athlete, por Sheri Colberg, Ph.D. 2001.

Días de Enfermedad

Resfriados, influenza, infecciones, lesiones, cirugía y momentos estresantes pueden subir sus niveles de azúcar en la sangre y aumentar su necesidad de insulina. Cuando su azúcar en la sangre aumenta, es hora de poner en acción su plan para día de enfermedad. ANTES de que surja la necesidad, ¡prepare SU plan para un día de enfermedad con su doctor o educador de diabetes para que ESTÉ PREPARADO!

Si usted no tiene todavía un plan para un día de enfermedad, siga las siguientes sugerencias:

- NUNCA omita su dosis diaria de insulina o medicamento oral. Use su dosis normal.
- Analice su azúcar en la sangre al menos 2–4 veces al día (antes de cada comida y a la hora de dormir)—en algunas ocasiones usted necesitará analizarse cada 2 horas.
- Si usted tiene diabetes Tipo I, analice su orina para cetonas por lo menos 4 veces al día.
- Llame a su doctor para ayuda

    Si su azúcar en la sangre es difícil de controlar o es mayor de 300 mg

Si está vomitando o tiene diarreas fuertes o fiebre

Si la enfermedad dura más de 72 horas sin ninguna mejoría

Si sus análisis de orina son positivos para cetonas

- Conserve su energía—¡DESCANSE!

- Beba grandes cantidades de agua y líquidos sin azúcar. Algunos ejemplos son Propel, té descafeinado, gaseosa sin azúcar, jugos sin azúcar, Snapple sin azúcar y aguas carbonatadas sin azúcar. Si no le es posible comer sus comidas normales, trate de comer las partes de carbohidratos en su dieta en líquidos o semi-líquidos—gaseosas regulares[1], caldos (use aquellos libre de sodio si tiene una restricción), frutas, jugos de frutas, Jell-O y cosas así. Usted debe ingerir cerca de 10–20 gramos de carbohidratos cada 1–2 horas mientras esté despierto. Verifique sus listas de opciones para leche, pan y fruta para alimentos, cantidad y contenido de carbohidratos.

Fruta: 1 porción = 15 gramos de carbohidratos

Leche: 1 porción = 12 gramos de carbohidratos

Pan: 1 porción = 15 gramos de carbohidratos

- Vuelva a su patrón normal de comer tan pronto como sea posible.

Cuando usted está enfermo usted puede desear tomar medicamentos para ayudar a aliviar sus síntomas. Hay muchos medicamentos sin receta para ayudarlo, pero sea cuidadoso cuando los escoja. Verifique los ingredientes del medicamento—

---

[1]Si sus análisis para sangre están altos para azúcar, use bebidas sin azúcar en vez de bebidas con azúcar.

azúcar, alcohol, dextrosa, etc. Algunos medicamentos afectan su azúcar en la sangre o presión sanguínea, así que pregúntele a su farmacéutico para que le ayude a conseguir el correcto.

Contenido de Carbohidratos en Alimentos Comunes

Cantidad	Alimento	Gramos de Carbohidratos
$1/2$ taza	gaseosas regulares(7-Up, cola, gaseosa de jengibre), *no de dieta*	10
$1/3$ taza	Jell-O regular	15
$1/2$ taza	jugo de manzana o piña	15
$1/3$ taza	jugo de uva o ciruela	15
$1/2$ taza	jugo de naranja o toronja	15
$1/2$ taza	helado de vainilla	15
$1/4$ taza	sorbete	15
$1/2$ taza	yogur congelado	15
1 rebanada	tostada	15
6	galletas saladas	15
7	galletas Ritz	15
3 cuadrados de $2^1/2$ pulgadas	galletas de trigo entero (graham)	15
$1/2$ de uno doble	Popsicle regular	10
$3/4$ taza	Gatorade regular	15
$1/2$ taza	cereal cocido	15
$1/2$ taza	natillas o pudín regular	15
$1/3$ taza	tapioca	15
2 tazas	sopas a base de caldo, mezclado con agua	15
1 taza	sopa cremosa	15

Contenido de Carbohidratos en Alimentos Comunes (cont)

Cantidad	Alimento	Gramos de Carbohidratos
1 taza	yogur natural o sin azúcar	12
1 cucharada	almíbar de Coke	10
$^{1}/_{2}$ taza	pudín sin azúcar	15

MI PLAN PARA UN DÍA DE ENFERMEDAD:

¿Cuán frecuentemente tengo que analizar mi azúcar en la sangre cuando estoy enfermo?

_____

¿Necesito analizar mi orina para cetonas?

_____

Si la respuesta es sí, ¿qué tan frecuente?

_____

¿Cuándo debo llamar a mi doctor?

_____

¿Quién me ayudará a controlar mi azúcar en la sangre cuando esté enfermo?

_____

¿Quién me ayudará a administrar mis medicamentos cuando esté enfermo?

_____

¿Quién me ayudará a administrar mis alimentos y líquidos cuando esté enfermo?

_____

Plan de medicamentos (cómo ajustar mi insulina o medicamento oral) para enfermedad:

_____

_____

_____

La Higiene Personal

Su piel es la primera línea de defensa del cuerpo contra las infecciones. Es muy importante mantenerla limpia, como también protegerla de grietas, cortaduras, llagas, etc. debido a que las infecciones pueden crear un caos en su habilidad para controlar su azúcar en la sangre.

Cuando el azúcar en la sangre es controlado pobremente, la diabetes puede causar la disminución del suministro de sangre a las piernas y los pies, llevando a una mala cicatrización. Si usted fuma, la nicotina de los cigarrillos puede dañar los vasos sanguíneos, también causando una disminución del flujo de sangre a las piernas y los pies.

El azúcar en la sangre que no se controla bien puede dañar los nervios, resultando en la pérdida de sensación. Cuando las piernas y los pies están dormidos, no es posible que usted sienta dolor cuando sus pies están lesionados. Un suministro pobre de sangre y falta de sensación hace bastante fácil que un problema pequeño se vuelva en un problema serio rápidamente.

El primer paso para prevenir los problemas en los pies es tener un buen control sobre su nivel de azúcar en la sangre. El segundo paso es tener buenos hábitos del cuidado de los pies para prevenir lesiones a sus pies. Finalmente, BUSQUE AYUDA MÉDICA INMEDIATAMENTE para cualquier problema como cortaduras o ampollas que no se estén sanando o callos.

EL CUIDADO DE LA PIEL

Las bacterias, levaduras y hongos se encuentran en la piel de todas las personas. Éstos tienden a instalarse y formar infecciones de la piel en áreas del cuerpo que son oscuras, húmedas y cálidas. Éstas incluyen el área vaginal e ingle, la axila y el pliegue de los senos.

Notifique a su doctor si usted

- Tiene un picor inusual
- Se da cuenta de una pestilencia o descarga
- Se da cuenta de una erupción
- Se da cuenta de una cortadura o hematoma que no sana

Recuerde, las infecciones de la piel pueden ser fastidiosas y peligrosas. Si las encuentra temprano, éstas pueden ser tratadas fácilmente y usted las puede prevenir con un buen control de su azúcar en la sangre.

Nuevamente, NO UTILICE remedios caseros.

EL CUIDADO DE LOS PIES

Aquí tiene una lista de algunos de los SI y NO para el cuidado de los pies:

SI (COSAS QUE SE DEBEN HACER)

- **MIRE TODAS LAS ÁREAS** de sus pies y piernas diariamente. Use un espejo si es necesario para ver todas las áreas de sus pies.

- Séquelas completamente, especialmente entre los dedos, con una toalla suave.

- Aplique una loción para suavizar su piel—pero no entre sus dedos.

- Lávese los pies en agua tibia con jabón suave.

- Corte sus uñas derechas en línea recta y lime las esquinas de manera que no hayan partes puntiagudas.

- Use zapatos todo el tiempo para proteger sus pies. Las zapatillas para la casa no deben ser usadas todo el día.

- Esté seguro que sus zapatos son cómodos y que le acomodan bien.

- Cambie sus calcetines y medias de nilón (nailon) diariamente.

- Empiece con zapatos nuevos lentamente—úselos por sólo 30 minutos el primer día y aumente su tiempo de uso media hora cada día.

- Las uñas encarnadas, callos, callosidades, etc. deben ser tratados por su doctor o podólogo (un especialista de pies).

- El polvo para los pies (use poca cantidad) puede ayudar a reducir la humedad causada por el sudor de los pies.

- Regla de las 24 a 48 horas—Si cualquier herida en sus pies no está sanando bien dentro de 24–48 horas, busque ayuda médica. No se demore en obtener tratamiento rápido y apropiado para cualquier cosa anormal en sus pies.

NO (COSAS QUE SE DEBEN EVITAR)

- Nunca camine descalzo.

- Evite los calcetines y las medias de nilón (nailon) que puedan causar ampollas.

- Evite el frío o calor extremo—no use botellas de agua caliente, paquetes de hielo o almohadillas de calor en sus pies. No pruebe la temperatura del agua con su pie—use su codo.

- No intente remedios caseros para callos, callosidades u otras llagas. Vea a su doctor o un podólogo.

- Evite las ligas u otras telas restrictivas en sus pies y piernas.

- Evite el cruzar sus piernas.

- No remoje sus pies rutinariamente a menos que sea aprobado por su doctor o podólogo.

- No fume—esto reduce el flujo de sangre a sus piernas y pies.

RECUERDE: EVITE LOS REMEDIOS CASEROS—vea a su doctor inmediatamente para tratamiento.

Identificación Médica

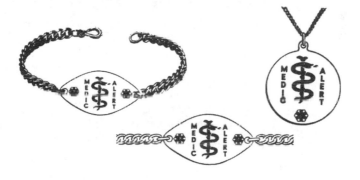

Es de máxima importancia que usted tenga algún tipo de identificación de diabetes EN SU PERSONA todo el tiempo.

Hay varias maneras de obtener tal identificación. Usted puede obtener una a través de su capítulo local de la Asociación Americana de Diabetes (American Diabetes Association; su número de teléfono lo puede encontrar en la guía telefónica). Muchas farmacias y joyerías tienen varias formas de identificación médica como pulseras y collares. A través de la Fundación de Alerta Médica (Medic Alert Foundation) usted puede obtener una identificación que incluya alergias o problemas médicos en adición a la diabetes.

Su dirección y número de teléfono son 2323 Colorado Avenue, Turlock, CA 95382, (888)633-4298 o el sitio web www. medicalert.org, fax (209)669-2450. Usted puede obtener una solicitud en la mayoría de las farmacias, hospitales y capítulos de la Asociación Americana de Diabetes o escribiendo directamente a la Fundación de Alerta Médica.

CAPÍTULO 14

El Estrés

El estrés afecta a todo el mundo. Puede ser físico (como dolor, deshidratación, fiebre, enfermedad, accidente o hipoglucemia) o emocional (como enojo, miedo o molestia).

Algo de estrés es normal, pero el estrés prolongado puede llevar a la hiperglucemia (niveles altos de azúcar en la sangre).

Durante situaciones estresantes se producen ciertas hormonas de "estrés" en el cuerpo de las personas. Estas hormonas son adrenalina, glucagón, hormona de crecimiento y cortisol. Éstas trabajan para subir el azúcar en la sangre en respuesta a la situación estresante. Esta glucosa adicional puede llevar a la hiperglucemia y, en algunas personas con diabetes Tipo 1, a la cetoacidosis.

Si usted no puede reducir o liberarse su estrés, usted necesita aprender a manejarlo. El primer paso es el reconocer algunos de los signos del estrés—fruncir el ceño, apretar los dientes, moverse nerviosamente, boca o quijada tiesa, tragar nerviosamente, respiración rápida y profunda, aguantar la respiración, hombros encorvados, tortícolis o cuello tieso, puños tiesos, cansancio continuo, problemas con el sueño, latidos del corazón rápidos y sudor.

Si su estrés es causado por una enfermedad, consulte a su médico para obtener ayuda y use su plan para días de enfermedad (página 162).

Evite el estrés de hipoglucemia (azúcar en la sangre bajo) comiendo las comidas y bocados a su hora; coma bocados cuando sea necesario antes, durante o después del ejercicio y use solamente la cantidad recetada de insulina o medicamento oral.

El EJERCICIO es uno de los mejores métodos para REDUCIR EL ESTRÉS. Éste relaja su cuerpo, aleja sus pensamientos del estrés, reduce el azúcar en la sangre al reducir las hormonas que causan el estrés, combate la depresión y provee una liberación de emociones reprimidas. La mayoría de los seguros médicos ofrecen ayuda con el estrés a través del Servicio de Salud del Comportamiento (llame al número de servicios para miembros). Busque en las bibliotecas, las iglesias y el Internet para obtener más recursos acerca del manejo del estrés. Vea el Capítulo 10 acerca del ejercicio.

Finalmente, si no le es posible reducir su estrés, usted puede hacer una diferencia en la manera que afecta a su cuerpo utilizando las técnicas de relajación. Algunos ejemplos de estas técnicas son biorretroalimentación, imágenes dirigidas, meditación, autohipnosis y relajación progresiva. Éstas requieren adiestramiento, así que pídale asistencia a su doctor o educador de diabetes. Para más información acerca de estas técnicas de relajación, vea *The Diabetic's Total Health and Happiness Book*, por June Biermann y Barbara Toohey (vea la página 198).

RECUERDE: El estrés hace una diferencia no sólo en su nivel de azúcar en la sangre pero también en la manera que uno se siente acerca de uno mismo. **¡Cúidese!**

Algunas fuentes adicionales de información sobre el estrés incluyen las siguientes

Stress without Distress, por Hans Seyle. New American Library, New York, 1975.

The Stress of Life, por Hans Seyle. McGraw, New York, 1970.

When I Say No, I Feel Guilty, por Manuel J. Smith, Ph.D. Bantam Books, New York, 1985.

Caring for the Diabetic Soul, American Diabetes Association, Alexandria, VA, 1997.

Diabetes Burnout: Preventing It, Surviving It, Finding Inner Peace, por William H. Polonsky, Ph.D., C.D.E., 1999.

101 Tips for Coping with Diabetes, por Richard Rubin, Ph.D., C.D.E.; Gary M. Arsham, M.D., Ph.D.; Catherine Feste, B.A.; David G. Marrero, Ph.D.; y Stefan H. Rubin.

Stress-Free Diabetes: Your Guide to Health and Happiness, por Joseph Napora, Ph.D., LCSW-C. American Diabetes Association.

Emociones— Son Parte de Nosotros

Cada vez que usted sufre una pérdida (como lo es perder a un ser querido, un trabajo o un amigo) o le dicen que tiene una enfermedad, todo tipo de sentimientos o emociones se estimulan—negación, ira, miedo, culpa, depresión. Estas emociones son bastante normales, y todo el mundo las siente de vez en cuando. Es muy importante que usted las entienda, que sepa cuando las tiene y que se permita tenerlas.

Los siguientes son ejemplos:

NEGACIÓN—No puedo creer que esto me está pasando a mí. Si no pienso acerca de esto, se irá con el tiempo.

IRA—¿Por qué a mí? Esto no es justo.

MIEDO—¿Qué va a pasar conmigo ahora? Yo no seré capaz de ir a ningún sitio.

CULPA—Si no hubiese comido tanto azúcar, esto nunca me hubiera pasado. ¿Qué he hecho para merecer este castigo?

DEPRESIÓN—Yo me siento muy solo. Nadie entiende.

Una vez que comprenda estas emociones usted alcanzará un mejor entendimiento de su pérdida o enfermedad. Esto es conocido como aceptación. A usted puede que no le guste, quiera o esté alegre acerca de tener diabetes, pero en este punto habrá escogido hacer los cambios necesarios para su propia buena salud y bienestar.

ACEPTACIÓN—Yo tengo diabetes ahora, así que voy a cambiar mis hábitos alimenticios, controlar mi azúcar en la sangre y perder el peso de más. Yo no soy aficionado de clavarme el dedo, pero si analizarme el azúcar en la sangre me ayuda a controlar mi diabetes, lo haré.

No hay un patrón específico o tiempo límite de cómo y cuándo estas emociones serán sentidas. Como personas sensitivas, lo que sentimos cambia todo el tiempo.

Las emociones pueden ser útiles a medida que usted crece y trabaja hacia un buen control de su diabetes, pero cada una puede volverse un problema y trastornar no sólo su control del azúcar en la sangre pero su vida también. ¿Cómo saber si cualquiera de estas emociones le puede estar causando un problema?

Aquí hay algunas pistas:

- ¿Cuánto dura la emoción?

  No hay tiempo límite para una emoción, pero cualquier tiempo extremo no es saludable. Por un corto período de tiempo después que le han dicho que tiene diabetes, es normal el negarse o no querer pensar acerca del problema. Sin embargo, si esa negación es extendida por años, no le será posible controlar su azúcar en la sangre, lo cual puede ser peligroso para su salud.

- ¿Cuán fuerte siente las emociones?

  Las emociones son sentidas en varios grados. Un día puede que se sienta deprimido y llore acerca de tener que ponerse una inyección de insulina; el próximo día se pone la inyección sin pensarlo. Es cuando la depresión es tan fuerte que no tiene la energía para preocuparse por usted mismo o no puede ponerse la inyección de insulina, que se vuelve enfermiza.

■ ¿Están sus emociones afectando su vida—las relaciones con los miembros de su familia, sus amigos, sus compañeros de trabajo, su trabajo o sus actividades?

Habrán ocasiones cuando sus sentimientos acerca de la diabetes afectarán estos aspectos de su vida, especialmente cuando su nivel de azúcar en la sangre está fuera de control o cuando recién lo han diagnosticado. Pero sea cauteloso—no use su diabetes como un chivo expiatorio. No todos los problemas en su vida estarán relacionados con tener diabetes y algunos podrían haber existido antes de la diabetes.

RECUERDE: ¡Es normal el sentir estas emociones—sólo no deje que interfieran con su cuidado PROPIO!

A medida que sienta estas emociones de negación, ira, miedo, culpa y depresión de vez en cuando, recuerde que son normales y saludables. Si usted o alguien especial para usted está luchando para superar cualquiera de, o todas, estas emociones, hay varias cosas que usted puede hacer para enfrentarlas mejor:

■ Tenga un buen entendimiento de cómo le hace sentir cada emoción.

■ Esté atento al momento en que usted y otros miembros de su familia, u otros seres queridos, comiencen a sentir estas emociones.

■ Utilice actividades como ejercicio, deportes y pasatiempos para enfrentar mejor estas emociones.

■ Escoja una o dos personas (fuera de la familia) que están dispuestos a escuchar cuando usted necesita hablar o quejarse. Los miembros de su equipo para el cuidado de su salud normalmente están dispuestos a ayudar.

■ Busque ayuda emocional en su familia, amigos, clero y equipo de cuidado para su salud. Grupos de apoyo formados por otros experimentando estas emociones y cambios pueden ser de mucha ayuda.

■ Si las emociones son suficientemente serias para interferir con su salud y bienestar, busque ayuda profesional de un consejero, trabajador social o psicólogo.

Los siguientes libros son excelentes recursos para obtener más información sobre emociones:

Caring for the Diabetic Soul. American Diabetes Association, Alexandria, VA, 1997.

Diabetes—Caring for Your Emotions as Well as Your Health, por Jerry Edelwich y Archie Brodsky. Addison-Wesley Publishing Co., Inc., Menlo Park, CA, 1986.

The Physician Within, por Catherine Feste. Henry Holt & Company, Inc., New York, 1995.

Psyching Out Your Diabetes, por June Biermann, Barbara Toohey y Richard Rubin, Ph.D. Lowell House, Los Angeles, 1992.

101 Tips for Coping with Diabetes, por Richard Rubin, Ph.D., C.D.E.; Gary M. Arsham, M.D., Ph.D.; Catherine Feste, B.A.; David G. Marrero, Ph.D.; y Stefan H. Rubin.

Behavioral Diabetes Institute (Instituto del Comportamiento de la Diabetes)—una organización que ayuda a las personas a superar los obstáculos emocionales y del comportamiento para vivir bien con diabetes. Su dirección es P.O. Box 501866, San Diego, CA 92150-1866. Su número telefónico es 858-336-8693. www.behavioraldiabetes institute.org.

Viajar con Diabetes

El tener diabetes no debería limitar sus planes de viaje. Una planificación cuidadosa y unas pocas precauciones especiales pueden asegurarle un viaje agradable y libre de problemas. Los siguientes son algunos consejos útiles para ayudarlo en su planificación.

- Tenga un chequeo médico general antes de irse.

- Si necesita vacunas, arregle el tenerlas temprano en caso de reacciones o efectos secundarios.

- Lleve alguna forma de identificación de diabetes—una pulsera o collar—en su persona.

- Pídale a su doctor que le recete medicamentos para prevenir náuseas y diarreas.

- Lleve de 2–3 veces el medicamento y equipo que usted necesitará—insulina, medicamentos orales, jeringuillas, materiales para análisis de sangre y/o orina, etc. LLEVE estos artículos CON USTED, no en el equipaje que se puede perder o almacenar a temperaturas extremas.

- Lleve una nota de su doctor indicando que usted tiene diabetes, especialmente si utiliza insulina y necesita llevar las jeringuillas para insulina.

- Lleve todos sus medicamentos en envases de la farmacia. Éstos mostrarán el nombre del medicamento y que le pertenecen a usted. Si necesita llevar jeringuillas, lleve la etiqueta de la receta de la caja de jeringuillas.

- Las guías para viajar con insulina pueden cambiar en cualquier momento. Verifique con su línea aérea o con la Administración de Seguridad en el Transporte (TSA, por sus siglas en inglés). Llame al 1-866-289-9673 o vaya a www.tsa.gov/public.

- Si va a viajar a un país extranjero, aprenda o tenga escritas frases útiles como "Soy diabético" y "Necesito un doctor".

- Para información en cuanto al cuidado de la diabetes o asociaciones para la diabetes en países extranjeros, escriba a

    The International Diabetes Federation
    Avenue Emile Demot 19
    1000 Brussels, Belgium
    www.idf.org/home/

- Si estará cruzando zonas de tiempo, planifique los ajustes al horario de insulina o medicamento con su doctor o educador de diabetes. También piense en el tipo de vacaciones que está planificando—excursión llevando mochila versus conducir, esquiar a campo travieso versus baños de sol. Verifique el Convertidor de Husos Horarios para información acerca de los husos horarios alrededor del mundo. www.timezoneconverter.com

- Cuando conduzca por períodos largos de tiempo, pare frecuentemente para estirar sus piernas y caminar.

- Lleve COMIDAS RÁPIDAS DE AZÚCAR todo el tiempo. También lleve un bocado que incluya una porción de los grupos de pan y carne como galletas y queso o sándwich de mantequilla de cacahuate.

- La línea aérea puede tener comidas especiales disponibles para diabéticos si usted llama al menos dos días antes de su vuelo.
- Donde sea que usted vaya, planifique el llegar en la tarde para que se pueda acomodar, dormir bien en la noche y empezar fresco en la mañana.
- Verifique los menús de los restaurantes antes de tiempo para que así conozca qué ofrecen. También evite las horas de apuro en las comidas.
- Preste atención especial al cuidado de sus pies, especialmente si esta haciendo turismo, haciendo caminatas a pie o esquiando.
- Si queda atrapado en una emergencia en el extranjero, llame a la embajada de su país.

> RECUERDE: ¡El cuidado de su diabetes puede requerir tiempo adicional y planificación, pero no deje que lo detenga de ir a cualquier sitio o hacer cualquier cosa que usted desee!

RECURSOS DE INFORMACIÓN ADICIONAL ÚTILES

The Peripatetic Diabetic, por June Biermann y Barbara Toohey. J.P. Tarcher, Inc., Los Angeles, 1984.

The Diabetic's Book: All Your Questions Answered, por June Biermann y Barbara Toohey. Sherbourn Press, Inc., Los Angeles, 1990.

The Joslin Guide to Diabetes, por Richard S. Beaser, M.D., con Joan C. Hill, R.D., C.D.E. The Joslin Center, Boston, 1995.

Directory of English-speaking Physicians throughout the World. International Association for Medical Assistance to Travelers, 417 Center Street, Lewiston, NY 14092, www.iamat.org/, (716)754-4883. Se requiere una pequeña donación.

International SOS Assistance, Inc. 8 Neshaminy Interplex, #207, Trevose, PA 19053-6956, www.InternationalSOS.com, (800)523-8662.

Los servicios incluyen médicos que hablan inglés en países extranjeros, cuidado médico y cuidado de emergencia internacional. Se requiere una membresía y un honorario.

The Diabetes Traveler, P.O. Box 8223 RW, Stamford, CT 06905, (203)327-5832. www.sath.org

Éste es un boletín informativo impreso cuatro veces al año para ayudar a las personas con diabetes a planificar un viaje seguro. Hay una cuota anual. Cada número discute lugares específicos como en España, Hawái, Vancouver o París; tipos de viajes como en tren, avión, vacaciones en condominio o en balnearios y otras sugerencias para viajar como nombres genéricos y en países extranjeros para medicamentos, maletas para viajar y llevar identificaciones médicas.

Centers for Disease Control and Prevention (Centro de Control y Prevención de Enfermedades): (800)311-3435. www.cdc.gov/ netinfo.htm

Travel Assistance International (Asistencia Internacional para Viajar): (800)821-2828. www.travelassistance.com

Traveler's Emergency Network (Red de Emergencia para Viajeros): (800)275-4836. www.tenweb.com/

Health Information for International Travel, por el Centro de Control y Prevención de Enfermedades (CDC). Publicado cada 2 años por el CDC como una referencia para los proveedores de cuidado médico pero puede ser útil para otros. Ordene de la Fundación Pública de Salud, (877)252-1200 o en http://bookstore.phf.org/cat24.htm

The Diabetes Travel Guide, por Davida Kruger, M.S.N., R.N., C.S., C.D.E.

CAPÍTULO 17

Complicaciones de la Diabetes

Un nivel de azúcar en la sangre alto, por largos períodos de tiempo, daña ciertos tejidos del cuerpo, causando complicaciones de la diabetes en los ojos, riñones, nervios, corazón y vasos sanguíneos. Las investigaciones han demostrado que un control estricto del azúcar en la sangre (dentro del rango normal la mayoría del tiempo y la Hemoglobina A1c por debajo de 7%—vea la página 28) puede retrasar el inicio y disminuye la gravedad de los daños a los tejidos.

Todos los miembros de su equipo de diabetes—doctor, enfermera de la diabetes, dietista, especialista de ejercicios y farmacéutico—recomiendan un control estricto del azúcar en la sangre como su arma en contra del desarrollo de complicaciones. No puede haber garantías, sin embargo; cualquiera con diabetes puede desarrollar una o más complicaciones y usted debe familiarizarse con ellas.

ENFERMEDADES DEL CORAZÓN Y VASOS SANGUÍNEOS

Cuando usted tiene diabetes, usted tiene mayor riesgo de enfermedades del corazón y de los vasos sanguíneos—lo cual puede conducir a un ataque del corazón, apoplejía y pérdida del suministro de sangre a las piernas y pies—especialmente si su azúcar en la sangre está fuera de control. La aterosclerosis (estrechamiento de las arterias) ocurre a una edad más temprana y progresa más rápidamente cuando el nivel de azúcar en la sangre y el colesterol están altos. Hay 4 tipos de colesterol que se miden en su sangre: el colesterol total, los triglicéridos, el colesterol HDL (bueno) y el colesterol LDL (malo). El historial familiar (genética) tiene mucho que ver con estas complicaciones. Hable con sus familiares para ver qué clase de problemas ellos han tenido. El control estricto del colesterol (vea la página 187, Conozca Sus Números) y del azúcar en la sangre es necesario para retrasar el comienzo y para disminuir la gravedad de estos problemas.

NERVIOS

Neuropatía significa cambio en los nervios del cuerpo. Las personas que han tenido diabetes por largo tiempo y han tenido pobre control del azúcar en la sangre pueden sentir cambios como calentura, hormigueo, adormecimiento, o pérdida de sensación en los

pies, piernas o manos; mareos, especialmente cuando se mueven de estar acostados a estar sentados o ponerse de pies; zumbidos en los oídos; incapacidad de digerir los alimentos correctamente; gas, diarrea o estreñimiento; impotencia en los hombres; disminución de la excitación sexual o resequedad vaginal en las mujeres e incapacidad de vaciar completamente la vejiga.

Se ha probado que el control estricto del azúcar en la sangre—mantener el azúcar en la sangre en el rango ideal la mayoría del tiempo y la hemoglobina A1c por debajo de 7%—previene o retrasa el comienzo de estos problemas.

LOS OJOS

La visión borrosa es muy común cuando su azúcar en la sangre está fuera de control—ya sea alto (hiperglucemia) o bajo (hipoglucemia). Se corregirá por sí misma cuando haya ganado nuevamente un buen control de su azúcar en la sangre.

Las cataratas y el glaucoma pueden ocurrir más frecuentemente en personas con diabetes.

La retinopatía es la ruptura y el sangrado de vasos sanguíneos muy pequeños en la retina, la cual está localizada en la parte trasera del ojo. Si esto ocurre muy frecuentemente y no es tratado, puede causar pérdida de la visión y ceguera. En las primeras etapas, usted no lo siente ni lo ve pasar, así que ¡EXÁMENES REGULARES DE

LA VISTA (incluyendo "dilatación") SON NECESARIOS CADA AÑO! Se ha probado que un control estricto del azúcar en la sangre—mantener el azúcar en la sangre en el rango ideal la mayoría del tiempo y la hemoglobina A1c por debajo de 7%—previene o retrasa el comienzo de estas complicaciones. Cuanto más temprano sea diagnosticado este problema, más exitoso será el tratamiento.

Si usted tiene una pérdida de visión, usted podría hallar los siguientes recursos útiles:

The Braille Institute (El Instituto Braille)
741 N. Vermont Ave.
Los Angeles, CA 90029
Teléfono: (323) 663-1111
www.brailleinstitute.com

National Federation of the Blind (Federación Nacional para los Ciegos)
1800 Johnson St.
Baltimore, MD 21230
Teléfono: (410) 659-9314
www.nfb.org

Diabetes Action Network—división de la Federación de Ciegos
3305 Stonebrook Circle NW
Huntsville, AL 35810
Teléfono: (256) 852-4143
www.nfb.org/voice.htm
La membresía incluye el boletín "Voice of the Diabetic" (La Voz del Diabético)

LOS RIÑONES

Las infecciones renales y de la vejiga son más que un problema cuando los azúcares de la sangre están fuera de control.

Después de muchos años de tener diabetes, especialmente si sus azúcares en la sangre han estado fuera de control, los riñones pueden mostrar cambios en los tejidos, lo que puede conducir a daños a los riñones. La alta presión sanguínea también puede llevar a daños en los riñones. Nuevamente, se ha probado que el control estricto de la presión sanguínea y el azúcar en la sangre—azúcares en la sangre en el rango ideal la mayoría del tiempo y la hemoglobina A1c por debajo de 7% y la presión sanguínea por debajo de 130/80 mm HG—previenen o retrasan el comienzo de estos problemas.

Chequeos regulares con su doctor son importantes. Un análisis de orina para microalbúmina puede ser realizado para ver si algún daño a los tejidos está ocurriendo en los riñones. Si es así, a usted le darán un medicamento para ayudarlo a proteger sus riñones. Es importante el encontrar estos cambios temprano.

LOS DIENTES Y LAS ENCÍAS

Si sus encías no están saludables, usted no solamente tendrá problemas con sus dientes, sino que además puede tener dificultades controlando el azúcar en su sangre. Tener diabetes aumenta su probabilidad de tener la enfermedad periodontal, especialmente cuando el azúcar en la sangre ha estado sin control por largos períodos de tiempo. La enfermedad periodontal es el enrojecimiento e hinchazón de las encías y puede incluir sangrado, encías sensibles, infección y pérdida de dientes. También eleva su riesgo de enfermedades del corazón, ataques cardíacos y apoplejía.

Cuide en forma especial sus dientes y encías, escobillando sus dientes y usando un hilo dental todos los días. Vea a su dentista o su higienista dental para que limpien y revisen regularmente sus dientes.

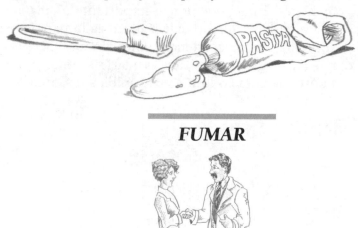

FUMAR

Si usted fuma, haga todo lo posible por parar. Ha sido probado que la nicotina en el tabaco daña las paredes de *todos* los vasos sanguíneos—los pequeños, como también los grandes. Este daño resulta en arterias reducidas o bloqueadas, reduciendo el flujo sanguíneo en todo el cuerpo. Por la reducción del flujo sanguíneo a los tejidos del cuerpo, usted aumentará sus oportunidades de tener una o más de estas complicaciones de la diabetes o empeorará cualquiera que ya tenga.

RECUERDE: Un buen control de sus azúcares en la sangre le prevendrá, retrasará o disminuirá la gravedad de las complicaciones de la diabetes.

Vea a su doctor regularmente y esté seguro de que usted tiene los siguientes análisis y chequeos:

- Promedio Estimado de Glucosa (eAG) (Hemoglobina A1c) cada 3–6 meses
- Colesterol, Triglicéridos, HDL y LDL cada año (pregunte a su doctor si éstos no están normales)
- Presión sanguínea examinada en cada visita
- Orina para microalbúmina cada año
- Chequeo de los ojos (con dilatación) cada año
- Chequeo dental/limpieza dos veces al año
- Chequeo de los pies por lo menos cada año

CONOZCA SUS NÚMEROS: Pídale a su doctor los resultados de sus pruebas y compárelos con los rangos meta para ver cuán bien usted está.

- Promedio Estimado de Glucosa (eAG)—Meta: bajo 154 (es preferible bajo 140)

  Hemoglobina A1c—Meta: debajo de 7% (preferible por debajo de 6.5%)

- Presión Sanguínea—Meta: debajo de 130/80 mmHg

- Colesterol—Meta: Colesterol total—menos de 200 mg/dl
  Triglicéridos—menos de 150 mg/dl
  HDL—más de 40 mg/dl en hombres
  más de 50 mg/dl en mujeres
  LDL—menos de 100 mg/dl (para algunas personas, menos de 70

Lo más importante que usted puede hacer es cuidarse a sí mismo—esto significa comer los alimentos correctos, tomar la cantidad correcta de medicamento, analizar su azúcar en la sangre y hacer ejercicio.

La Investigación Sobre la Diabetes

La diabetes mellitus es una enfermedad que ha sido conocida por el ser humano desde hace 3,000–4,000 años. Después de todo este tiempo, la causa de la diabetes mellitus sigue siendo un misterio, y todavía la medicina moderna no ha podido proveer una cura. Investigadores en todo el mundo están ocupados buscando la causa y cura para la diabetes, como también desarrollando equipos para ayudar a los diabéticos a mantener un mejor control de sus azúcares en la sangre.

Para la diabetes Tipo 1, la investigación se centra en

- Los trasplantes de páncreas (completo, parcial y células islote)
- El desarrollo de un páncreas artificial implantable (similar a los marcapasos) que pueda medir el azúcar en la sangre y proveer insulina de acuerdo a las necesidades del cuerpo
- Mejorar las bombas de insulina disponibles actualmente, (vea la página 141) para hacerlas más pequeñas, livianas y fáciles para operar

- Estudiar el sistema inmune del cuerpo humano (la habilidad del cuerpo para pelear contra tejidos extraños, bacterias, virus, etc.)

- Desarrollar una manera para prevenir el comienzo de la diabetes Tipo 1

- Desarrollar una bomba de insulina y sensor de glucosa (para medir el azúcar en la sangre) que puedan colocarse dentro del cuerpo

- Desarrollar medicamentos para prevenir que el cuerpo destruya las células del páncreas que producen la insulina

- Desarrollar otra manera para ponerse la insulina en vez de por inyección

Para la diabetes Tipo 2, la investigación se centra en

- Las causas de la obesidad

- Maneras seguras y efectivas para la reducción de peso— programas que incluyen modificaciones de comportamiento y grupos de apoyo como Weight Watchers y Over-Eaters Anonymous (comedores compulsivos anónimos)

- Maneras seguras y efectivas para controlar el apetito

- Desarrollar más medicamentos orales efectivos

- El por qué ciertos grupos de personas (Amerindios, Asiático-Americanos, Afro-Americanos y Hispano-Americanos) tienden a padecer más de diabetes Tipo 2

- Maneras para hacer las células de grasa y músculos más sensibles a la insulina

Tanto para la diabetes Tipo 1 como para la de Tipo 2, la investigación está enfocada en

- Estudiar el funcionamiento y mal funcionamiento del glucagón (otra hormona producida por el páncreas) que trabaja al contrario de la insulina

- Los efectos y beneficios del ejercicio

- La composición, combinación, desglose y absorción de varios alimentos y sus efectos en el azúcar en la sangre

- El estrés—sus efectos en el cuerpo y maneras para reducirlo utilizando modificaciones a la conducta y técnicas de relajación

- Encontrar maneras para hacer el embarazo seguro tanto para la madre como para el bebé

- Entender la causa de las complicaciones de la diabetes y mejores maneras para tratarlas

- Desarrollar otras maneras para dar insulina—oralmente, nasalmente y en gotas para los ojos

- Desarrollar maneras más fáciles para revisar el azúcar en la sangre

La investigación está cambiando muy rápidamente el cuidado y el manejo tanto de la diabetes Tipo 1 como de Tipo 2. La mejor manera de mantenerse al tanto con los nuevos cambios es leyendo *Diabetes Forecast*, *Diabetes Self-Management* y *Diabetes Health*. Vea la página 194 para información sobre estas revistas.

CAPÍTULO 19

Organizaciones y Recursos

Su capítulo local de la Asociación Americana de Diabetes (American Diabetes Association) participa activamente en muchos programas diferentes. Ésta fomenta la educación pública, ayuda a proveer fondos para investigar y patrocinar programas de educación a pacientes ambulatorios.

Si usted desea información adicional acerca de la diabetes, usted está bienvenido a contactar cualquiera de las oficinas de la Asociación Americana de la Diabetes. Llame o escriba a la oficina más cercana para usted:

Asociación Americana de la Diabetes
1701 N. Beauregard St.
Alexandria, VA 22311
(800)342-2383
www.diabetes.org

http://store.diabetes.org es el sitio web de la librería de la Asociación Americana de la Diabetes.

Juvenile Diabetes Research Foundation International
(Fundación Internacional para la Diabetes Juvenil)
120 Wall Street, 19th Floor
New York, NY 10005-4001
(800)JDF-CURE (533-2873)
www.jdrf.org

Taking Control of Your Diabetes
(Tomando Control de Su Diabetes)
1110 Camino Del Mar, Suite B
Del Mar, CA 92014
(800) 99TCOYD (800-998-2693)
www.tcoyd.org

Usted también podrá mantenerse al día de todas las nuevas ideas y
productos, como también actualizar su conocimiento al presente de la
diabetes leyendo cualquiera de las siguientes revistas:

Diabetes Forecast Magazine
American Diabetes Association, Inc.
1701 N. Beauregard St.
Alexandria, VA 22311
(800)806-7801
Esta obra también está disponible en español.

Diabetes Self-Management
P.O. Box 52890
Boulder, CO 80322-2890
(800)234-0943
www.diabetesselfmanagement.com

Diabetes Health
6 School St. #160
Fairfax, CA 94930
(800)234-1218 o (800)488-8468
www.diabeteshealth.com

DIRECCIONES DE PÁGINAS WEB

American Diabetes Association (Asociación Americana de la Diabetes): http://www.diabetes.org/

Canadian Diabetes Association (Asociación Canadiense de la Diabetes): http://www.diabetes.ca/

American Association of Diabetes Educators (Asociación Americana de los Educadores de la Diabetes): http://www.aadenet.org/

Diabetes Exercise and Sports Association (Asociación de Ejercicio y Deportes para Personas con Diabetes): http://www.diabetes-exercise.org

International Diabetes Federation (Federación Internacional de Diabetes): http://www.idf.org/

Juvenile Diabetes Research Foundation International (Fundación Internacional para la Diabetes Juvenil): http:jdrf.org

Children with Diabetes (Niños con diabetes): http://childrenwithdiabetes.com/

Diabetes Mall en Diabetes Net: http://www.diabetesnet.com

Eli Lilly's Managing Your Diabetes Patient Education Program (Programa de educación para el manejo de la diabetes de Eli Lilly): http://www.lilly.com/diabetes/

Diabetes Self-Management (Auto-manejo de la diabetes): http://www.diabetesselfmanagement.com

The American Dietetic Association (Asociación Dietética Americana): http://www.eatright.org/index.html

WebMD—información médica y servicios de calidad: http://www.webmd.com

About Health and Fitness (Acerca de Salud y Estado Físico): http://www.diabetes-about.com

Food and Nutrition Information Center (Centro de Información de Alimentos y Nutrición): http://www.nalusda.gov/fnic/

Joslin Diabetes Center (Centro Joslin para Diabetes):
http://www.joslin.org

The American Diabetes Association Bookstore(Librería de la
Asociación Americana de la Diabetes):
http://store.diabetes.org

The Diabetes Monitor (El monitor de la diabetes)
http://www.diabetesmonitor.com

The Merck Journey for Control Program (El Viaje de Merck
para el Programa de Control)
http://www.journeyforcontrol.com

National Diabetes Education Program (Programa Nacional
para la Educación de la Diabetes)
http://www.ndep.nih.gov

LIBROS DE REFERENCIA

Investigue en su librería local—si no puede encontrar los tí-
tulos mencionados a través de este libro, los siguientes son centros de recursos donde puede comprarlos.

The Joslin Diabetes Center
One Joslin Place
Boston, MA 02215
(800) 567-5461 o
(617) 732-2400
www.joslin.org/
Llame para obtener su catálogo.

The Diabetes Mall
1030 West Upas Street
San Diego, CA 92103
(800) 988-4772 o (619) 497-0900 teléfono o fax
diabetesnet.com

Librería de la Asociación Americana de la Diabetes
store.diabetes.org o (800) 342-2383

TELEVISIÓN

dLife TV es un programa de televisión acerca de todos los aspectos de la diabetes. Sintonícelo en:

Domingos, CNBC 7 P.M. ET
DirectTV 251 7:30 P.M. ET

Sábados, DishNetwork 9407 11:30 A M ET

También está disponible en el Internet: www.dlife.com

LIBROS

Diabetes—Caring for Your Emotions as Well as Your Health, por Jerry Edelwich y Archie Brodsky. Addison-Wesley. Menlo Park, CA, 1986.

Diabetes in the Family, American Diabetes Association, Inc. y Robert J. Brady Co., Prentice-Hall Publishing and Communications Co., Bowie, MD, 1987.

The Diabetes Sourcebook, por Diana Guthrie, R.N., Ph.D. y Richard Guthrie, M.D. Lowell House, Los Angeles, 2004.

The Diabetes Sport and Exercise Book, por Claudia Graham, C.D.E., Ph.D., M.P.H., June Biermann y Barbara Toohey. Lowell House, Los Angeles, 1995.

The Diabetic Man, por Peter Lodewick, M.D., June Biermann y Barbara Toohey. Lowell House, Los Angeles, 1999.

The Diabetic Woman, por Lois Jovanovic-Peterson, M.D., June Biermann y Barbara Toohey. J.P. Tarcher, Inc., Los Angeles, 2000.

The Diabetic's Book: All Your Questions Answered, por June Biermann y Barbara Toohey. Sherbourn Press, Inc., Los Angeles, 1998.

The Diabetic's Total Health and Happiness Book, por June Biermann y Barbara Toohey. J.P. Tarcher, Penguin, Los Angeles, 2003.

The Fitness Book for People with Diabetes, por W. Guyton Hornsby, Jr., Ph.D., C.D.E. Susan H. Lau, publisher. American Diabetes Association, Alexandria, VA, 1994.

The Joslin Guide to Diabetes, por Richard S. Beaser, M.D., con Joan V.C. Hill, R.N., C.D.E. Simon & Schuster, New York, 1995.

The Peripatetic Diabetic, por June Biermann y Barbara Toohey. J.P. Tarcher, Inc., Los Angeles, 1984.

The Physician Within—Taking Care of Your Well-Being, por Catherine Feste. Henry Holt and Company, Inc., New York, 1995.

Psyching Out Diabetes, por June Biermann, Barbara Toohey y Richard R. Rubin, Ph.D. Lowell House, Los Angeles, 1999.

Type II Diabetes and What to Do, por Virginia Valentine, R.N., M.S., C.D.E., June Biermann y Barbara Toohey. Lowell House, Los Angeles, 2000.

Women and Diabetes, por Laurinda M. Poirier, R.N., M.P.H., C.D.E. y Katharine M. Cohen, M.P.H. Bantam Books, New York, 1998.

Caring for Young Children Living with Diabetes: A Manual for Parents, por Margaret T. Lawlor, M.S., C.D.E., Lori M. Laffel, M.D., M.P.H., Barbara Anderson, Ph.D. y Anna Bertorelli, R.D., M.B.A., C.D.E. The Joslin Diabetes Center, Boston, 1996.

Everyone Likes to Eat, por Hugo J. Hollerorth, Ed.D. y Debra Kaplan, R.D., M.S. Chronimed Publishing, Minneapolis, 1993.

A Guide for Parents of Children and Youth with Diabetes, The Joslin Diabetes Center, Boston, 1994.

In Control, A Guide for Teens with Diabetes, por Jean Betschart, M.S.N., R.N., C.D.E. y Susan Thom, R.D., L.D., C.D.E. John Wiley & Sons, New York, 1995.

It's Time to Learn about Diabetes (A Workbook for Children), para niños de 8–10 años, por Jean Betschart, M.S.N., R.N., C.D.E. John Wiley & Sons, New York, 1995. También disponible en video a través de The Joslin Center.

A Magic Ride in Foozbah-Land, para niños 3–7 años, por Jean Betschart, M.S.N., R.N., C.D.E. Chronimed Publishing, Minneapolis, 1995.

Managing Your Child's Diabetes, por Robert Wood Johnson IV, Sale Johnson, Casey Johnson y Susan Kleinman. Master Media Ltd., New York, 1996.

Parenting a Diabetic Child, por Gloria Loring. Lowell House, Los Angeles, 1991.

Raising a Child with Diabetes: A Guide for Parents, por Linda M. Siminerio y Jean Betschart, M.S.N., R.N., C.D.E. American Diabetes Association, Alexandria, VA, 1995.

Sweet Kids, 2da edición, por Betty Brackenridge, M.S., R.D., C.D.E. y Richard R. Rubin, Ph.D., C.D.E. American Diabetes Association, Alexandria, VA, 2002.

When You're a Parent with Diabetes, por Kathryn Gregorio Palmer. Healthy Living Books. Hatherleigh Press, New York, 2006

The Power to Be Well, por Catherine Feste. Humedico, Inc., 2006.

Muchos de estos libros son actualizados con regularidad. Pregunte por la edición más nueva.

Respuestas a la Prueba de Hiperglucemia e Hipoglucemia

(página 24)

1. a. hiper	h. hiper	2. a
b. hipo	i. hiper	ⓑ
c. ambas	j. hipo	ⓒ
ch. hiper	k. hipo	ch
d. hiper	l. ambas (más	ⓓ
e. hiper	a menudo	ⓔ
f. hiper	hiper)	
g. hipo	ll. hipo	

Formularios para Planificar Comidas

En las siguientes páginas usted encontrará Formularios para Planificar Comidas en blanco. Haga tantas copias de éstos como desee. Úselos para planificar sus comidas. Llévelos con usted cuando vea a su dietista o educador de diabetes.

Plan de Comida Personalizado

Número de Calorías _____

Carbohidratos:_____ gramos Proteínas:_____ gramos

Grasa: _____ gramos

Hora del Desayuno: _____

_____ Opciones de Carbohidratos
   _____ almidón
   _____ fruta
   _____ leche
_____ Opciones de Carne
_____ Opciones de Grasa

Hora para el Bocado de la Mañana: _____

_____

Hora de Almuerzo: _____

_____ Opciones de Carbohidratos
   _____ almidón
   _____ fruta
   _____ leche
_____ Vegetales
_____ Opciones de Carne
_____ Opciones de Grasa

Hora para el Bocado de la Tarde: _____

_____

Hora de la Cena: _____

_____ Opciones de Carbohidratos
   _____ almidón
   _____ fruta
   _____ leche
_____ Vegetales
_____ Opciones de Carne
_____ Opciones de Grasa

Hora para el Bocado de la Noche: _____

_____

Plan de Comida Personalizado

Número de Calorías _____

Carbohidratos:_____ gramos Proteínas:_____ gramos

Grasa: _____ gramos

Hora del Desayuno: _____

_____ Opciones de Carbohidratos

_____ almidón

_____ fruta

_____ leche

_____ Opciones de Carne

_____ Opciones de Grasa

Hora para el Bocado de la Mañana: _____

_____

Hora de Almuerzo: _____

_____ Opciones de Carbohidratos

_____ almidón

_____ fruta

_____ leche

_____ Vegetales

_____ Opciones de Carne

_____ Opciones de Grasa

Hora para el Bocado de la Tarde: _____

_____

Hora de la Cena: _____

_____ Opciones de Carbohidratos

_____ almidón

_____ fruta

_____ leche

_____ Vegetales

_____ Opciones de Carne

_____ Opciones de Grasa

Hora para el Bocado de la Noche: _____

_____

Plan de Comida Personalizado

Número de Calorías _____
Carbohidratos:_____ gramos Proteínas:_____ gramos
Grasa: _____ gramos

Hora del Desayuno: _____

_____ Opciones de Carbohidratos
_____ almidón
_____ fruta
_____ leche
_____ Opciones de Carne
_____ Opciones de Grasa

Hora para el Bocado de la Mañana: _____

_____

Hora de Almuerzo: _____

_____ Opciones de Carbohidratos
_____ almidón
_____ fruta
_____ leche
_____ Vegetales
_____ Opciones de Carne
_____ Opciones de Grasa

Hora para el Bocado de la Tarde: _____

_____

Hora de la Cena: _____

_____ Opciones de Carbohidratos
_____ almidón
_____ fruta
_____ leche
_____ Vegetales
_____ Opciones de Carne
_____ Opciones de Grasa

Hora para el Bocado de la Noche: _____

_____

APÉNDICE C

Bibliografía

American Diabetes Association, *The Diabetes Food & Nutrition Bible*, American Diabetes Association, Alexandria, VA, 2003.

American Diabetes Association, *Footcare for the Diabetic*, folleto de la Asociación.

American Diabetes Association, *Complete Guide to Diabetes*, American Diabetes Association, Alexandria, VA, 2005.

American Diabetes Association, "Nutrition Recommendations and Principles for People with Diabetes Mellitus." *Diabetes Care* 21, suppl. 1, 1998.

American Diabetes Association/American Dietetic Association, *Exchange Lists for Meal Planning*. American Diabetes Association/American Dietetic Association, 2003.

Biermann, June y Barbara Toohey, *The Peripatetic Diabetic*. J.P. Tarcher, Los Angeles, 1984.

Biermann, June, Barbara Toohey y Claudia Graham, DCE, Ph.D., MPH, *The Diabetic's Sport and Exercise Book*. Lowell House, Los Angeles, 1995.

Binney, Ruth, ed., *The Complete Manual of Fitness and Well-Being*. Viking Penguin, New York, 1984.

Chaney, Patricia S., ed., *Managing Diabetics Properly*. Nursing 77 Skillbook Series, Intermed Communications, Horsham, PA, 1977.

Cooper, Kenneth, M.D., M.P.H., *Aerobics Program for Total Well-Being: Exercise, Diet, Emotional Balance.* M. Evans, New York, 1982.

Cooper, Kenneth, M.D., M.P.H., *The Aerobics Way.* Bantam Books, New York, 1977.

Davidson, Mayer B., *Diabetes Mellitus: Diagnosis and Treatment,* 4ta edición. W.B. Saunders, Philadelphia, 1998.

Edelwich, Jerry y Archie Brodsky, *Diabetes: Caring for Your Emotions as Well as Your Health.* Addison-Wesley, Menlo Park, CA, 1986.

Franz, M. J., et al., "Nutrition Principles for the Management of Diabetes and Related Complications." *Diabetes Care,* mayo 1994.

Gilmore, C. P., *Exercise for Fitness.* Time Life Books, Alexandria, VA, 1981.

Guthrie, Diane, RN, Ph.D. y Richard A. Guthrie, M.D., *The Diabetes Sourcebook.* Lowell House, Los Angeles, 1997.

Guyton, Arthur, C., M.D., *Function of the Human Body.* W.B. Saunders, Philadelphia, 1985.

Hodge, Robert H., Jr., M.D., et al., "Multiple Use of Disposable Insulin Syringe-Needle Units." *JAMA,* 244, no. 3, 1980.

Holler, H. J. y J. G. Pastors, eds., *Meal Planning Approaches for Diabetes Management.* American Dietetic Association, Chicago, 1994.

Holzmeister, Lea Ann, R.D., C.D.E., *The Diabetic Carbohydrate and Fat Gram Guide,* The American Diabetes Association, Alexandria, VA, 2005.

Jornsay, Donna L., R.N., BSN, CPNP, CDE y Daniel L. Lorber, M.D., "Diabetes and the Traveler." *Clinical Diabetes,* 6, no. 3, mayo/junio 1988, pp.52–55.

Kübler-Ross, Elizabeth, M.D., *On Death and Dying.* Macmillan, New York, 1969.

Lasker, Roz D., M.D., "The Effect of Intensive Treatment of Diabetes on the Development and Progression of Long-Term Complications in Insulin-Dependent Diabetes Mellitus." *New England Journal of Medicine,* 14, no. 329, sept. 30 1993, pp. 977–1036.

Leontos, Carolyn, M.S., R.D., C.D.E., Geil, Pattie, M.S., R.D., F.A.D.A., C.D.E., *Individualized Approaches to Diabetes Nutrition Therapy,* American Diabetes Association, Alexandria, VA. 2005.

Middleton, Katherine y May Abbott Hess, *The Art of Cooking for the Diabetic,* 3ra edición. Contemporary Books, Chicago, 1997.

Peragallo-Dittko, Virginia, RN, MA, CDE, ed., *A Core Curriculum for Diabetes Education,* 3ra edición. Publicado por American Association of Diabetes Educators, Chicago, 1998.

Rafkin-Mervis, Lisa E., M.S., R.D., "Carbohydrate Counting." *Diabetes Forecast,* feb. 1995, pp. 30–37.

Sutherland, David, M.D., PhD., et al., "Pancreas Transplantation—A Historical Overview and Its Current Status." *The Diabetes Educator,* 1, primavera 1982, pp.11–13.

"Syringe Reuse." *Diabetes Care,* 8, no. 1, enero-feb. 1985, pp. 97–99.

Torregiani, Seth, "Untangling the Net." *Diabetes Self-Management,* julio-agosto 1997, pp. 22–28.

"The United Kingdom Prospective Diabetes Study (UKPDS) for Type 2 Diabetes." *Lancet,* 352, 1998, pp. 837–852.

Vessby, B., "Dietary Carbohydrates and Diabetes." *American Journal of Clinical Nutrition,* marzo 1994.

Warshaw, Hope, R.D., C.D.E., *Diabetes Meal Planning Made Easy,* 2da edición, American Diabetes Association, Alexandria, VA, 2005.

"Standards of Care–Position Statement." *Diabetes Care,* volumen 26, suplemento 1, enero 2003, página 538.

"Clinical Practice Recomendations." *Diabetes Care,* volumen 29, suplemento 1, 2006.

"Translating the A1c Assay Into Estimated Average Glucose Values," *Diabetes Care*, Volumen 31, Número 8, agosto 2008, pp. 1–6.

ÍNDICE

Los numerales de páginas que aparecen en letra itálica señalan páginas donde se encuentran tablas y figuras.